FINDING
IRELAND

OTHER BOOKS BY RICHARD TILLINGHAST

Poetry

The New Life
Six Mile Mountain
Today in the Café Trieste
The Stonecutter's Hand
Our Flag Was Still There
Sewanee in Ruins
The Knife and Other Poems
Sleep Watch

Essays

Poetry and What Is Real
Robert Lowell's Life and Work: Damaged Grandeur

Translation

Dirty August: Poems by Edip Cansever
(with Julia Clare Tillinghast)

As Editor

A Visit to the Gallery
(poems about works of art)

Finding
IRELAND

A Poet's Explorations of
Irish Literature and Culture

RICHARD TILLINGHAST

University of Notre Dame Press

Notre Dame, Indiana

Manufactured in the United States of America

Library of Congress Cataloging-in-Publication Data

Tillinghast, Richard.
Finding Ireland : a poet's explorations of Irish literature
and culture / Richard Tillinghast.
p.   cm.
Includes index.
ISBN-13: 978-0-268-04232-5 (pbk. : alk. paper)
ISBN-10: 0-268-04232-2 (pbk. : alk. paper)
1. Literary landmarks—Ireland.   2. Authors, Irish—Homes
and haunts—Ireland.   3. English literature—Irish authors—
History and criticism.   4. Ireland—Intellectual life.
5. Tillinghast, Richard—Journeys—Ireland.   6. Ireland—
Description and travel.   I. Title.
PR8731.T55   2008
820.9'9415—dc22

                              2008028330

To Mary

CONTENTS

Contents

ACKNOWLEDGMENTS

The writing of this book has been interwoven with friendships with people in many parts of Ireland, some of whom I would like to acknowledge: Seona Mac Réamoinn, Terence Brown, and George O'Brien at the Trinity College Summer School in Dublin; Bob and Becky Tracy in Berkeley and Dublin; my friends from the Poets' House in Falcarragh, County Donegal, especially Janice, Ben, and Anna Simmons; Gordon and Esther-Mary D'Arcy near Ballindereen, Tom Kenny in Galway Town, and Helen and Roger Phillimore, Jeff and Áine O'Connell, and John and Primm ffrench in Kinvara, County Galway; Sabra Loomis on Achill Island; Dennis O'Driscoll and Seamus and Marie Heaney in Dublin; John Ennis in Waterford; Mark and Jane Roper near Piltown, County Kilkenny; Sliabh, Holly, and Grace Wells and all the neighbors in Glenaskeogh, County Tipperary. Thanks as ever to Thomas Lynch for his hospitality in Moveen West, County Clare.

Some old and dear friends have died during the years this book was being written, including George MacBeth, James Simmons, and Tom and Jean Flanagan. Their conversation, their support and loyalty, their songs and stories, their drollery, their laughter are greatly missed.

Acknowledgment and thanks go to the editors of the following journals, where some of the essays in this book appeared in earlier versions: the *Hudson Review, Ireland of the Welcomes, The New Criterion, The New York Times, and Poetry Ireland Review.* Many thanks to Barbara Hanrahan, Director, University of Notre Dame Press, for her enthusiasm about this book, as well as to Fred Marchant and William O'Rourke for their suggestions on the manuscript.

1

Finding Ireland

To visit a country whose authors we have read, to read books by writers from lands we have visited—these are two ways we learn about cultures beyond the one we were born into. The desire to visit places we first encountered in books must be among the commonest instincts of literate people. As readers we live through our imaginations; one reason we want to travel to the places we read about is to find out whether those places are as they appear in books. A recent book, *The Literary Tourist: Readers and Places in Romantic and Victorian Britain*, by Nicola J. Watson, examines this phenomenon disapprovingly. Her view is that literary tourism is "typically defined . . . by nostalgic belatedness and by a constitutive disappointment," and that "the power of fiction is actually confirmed by the tourist's disappointment." According to her, "the internal workings of an author's works . . . produce place, not the other way around." My view is somewhat different. More typically, an author produces fictional places not as pure products of the imagination, but by creatively modifying actual places. We learn a lot about how an author's imagination works by comparing the raw material with the fictional result. I have seldom been disappointed on my literary pilgrimages.

Samuel Johnson has written, "The use of traveling is to regulate imagination by reality, and instead of thinking how things may be, to see them as they are." Dr. Johnson gives pride of place here to "reality"; in her poem "Questions of Travel," Elizabeth Bishop wonders whether the traveler might not be deficient in imagination: *Is it lack of imagination that makes us come / to imagined places, not just stay at home?"* The book you hold in your hands, *Finding Ireland*, has emerged from my own explorations of Irish literature, which have been closely intertwined with my getting to know Ireland itself. I do not claim, however, to have found Dr. Johnson's "reality." My Ireland, even now that I live here, remains an imagined place.

No doubt many non-Irish readers of the current book are happy to stay at home, read novels and poems by Irish authors, see plays by Wilde, Synge, Friel, Tom Murphy, Connor McPherson, and other Irish playwrights, and be content to visit Irelands of the mind. I hope there is plenty in the present book for readers belonging to this school, who would agree with Emily Dickinson that "There is no frigate like a book / To take us lands away." In the chapters that follow, starting with the "letters" written in 1990, 1998, and 2005 for the *Hudson Review* and the *New Criterion*, my intent is to serve the non-Irish reader as a foreign correspondent, reporting back from Galway, Dublin, and other parts of this island. Throughout *Finding Ireland* I attempt to take the reader along with me on a virtual tour of the settings, actual and imagined, of the books I write about and even to a few of my favorite pubs. Irish literature, as much as any other in the world, is local and personal, rooted in particular places, glorying in strong and eccentric personalities. I hope that reading my book will be the same voyage of discovery for you that writing it has been for me.

As for Irish readers, I hope they will tolerate the brashness of an American expressing opinions about a culture that is his own only by adoption. I would even venture to hope that the insider-outsider vantage-point of an American who now makes his home in this country would bring a certain freshness to familiar topics. It must be said that not being American has never stopped Irish people from setting themselves up as experts on the United States. You can find a specialist on American life in every pub from Waterford to Donegal. And there is something oddly appropriate about this: Ireland is more closely intertwined with America than any other European country is. (I use the term "America" in this book as often as "United States," incidentally, in conformance with customary Irish parlance.)

While I am trying to define this book, it might be well to declare what it is not. It is certainly not comprehensive: there is nothing of substance here on writers whose work I love, such as Michael Longley, Michael Hartnett, Paul Durcan, Eavan Boland, Paula Meehan, Paul Muldoon, John McGahern, and Ciarán Carson. At some point I would like to write about two recent enthusiasms: George O'Brien's series of memoirs beginning with *The Village of Longing*; and Brian Lynch's poetry and especially his novel, *The Winner of Sorrow*. And how could I have left out Seumas O'Kelly's great story, "The Weaver's Grave," or Gerald Griffin's "The Brown Man," which sends chills down my spine every time I read it?

This is not on the other hand a miscellany, though my essays touch on more or less any aspect of Irish culture and history that has caught my attention. It is not a history book, either, though the conflicts of Irish history form the background for nearly all these essays. For me, an awareness of history is essential when one is exploring modes of expression ranging from high literary art to architecture, to gardening, to traditional Irish music. Likewise, this is neither a guidebook nor exactly a memoir, though I hope the fact that I am an American blow-in living in Ireland lends enthusiasm of perception to this book. In short, *Finding Ireland* is something of a hybrid: mostly literary criticism, but unequivocally more than just that. If the book succeeds, my curiosity is brought into play on behalf of the curiosity that I hope my readers will feel toward this singular culture, this history that is both tragic and yet strangely triumphant when viewed over the long curve of the centuries.

While my literary essays are largely concerned with books from the nineteenth and twentieth centuries, my "letters" deliver a picture of contemporary Irish life—a culture in transition. Ireland today is a country where the farmer takes his wife on skiing holidays in Switzerland and is proud of his wine cellar, where the parish priest shows up at the local meditation group, a country full of immigrants from Europe, Africa, and Asia. For Americans, for Irish Americans in particular, Ireland is a mythic land where time has stood still; and a good many stereotypes stand in the way of our seeing the country for what it really is—what it was historically as well as what it has become. My "letters" are meant to give a picture of the culture as it changes. Mine is, to use academic language that I hope on the whole to avoid, a "non-essentialist" take on Irish culture. Ireland and Irishness have never had the neat simplicity and immutability that nationalists from Eamon de Valera to Gerry Adams have promoted.

It is almost impossible to imagine a book about Ireland written by an American as recently as ten or twenty years ago that did not feel obligated to ring the changes on certain canonical themes: immigration, the Great Hunger, poverty, the role of the Catholic Church in Irish history, sectarian conflict, the Civil War, etc. At this point there seems to me little point in rehashing these admittedly important issues—at least not at length. They have been discussed, and discussed illuminatingly, elsewhere. From being a self-doubting culture plagued by the defensiveness and self-defeating stratagems typical of societies emerging from colonialism, Ireland has become confident, even cocky; some people worry about what is being lost in this brave new world. Dublin's chattering classes are having the time of their lives overturning old verities.

That the Irish are ethnically Celtic has been accepted as "fact" for generations. For example, we use a ruler in our house called the Irish History Ruler. On one side are the centimeters and millimeters of European measurement, on the other side a chronological table that lists the important historical dates in Irish history. The first item confidently records "Celtic Conquest, c. 500–150 B.C." In a piece titled "Our ancestors weren't Celts, they were copycats," Fintan O'Toole in his February 3, 2007, *Irish Times* column called "CultureShock" relishes the opportunity to *épater le bourgeois* by outing a subject that has been common knowledge among archaeologists for a dozen or so years now: the Celtic origins of the Irish people.

> There is a great secret in Irish culture. Like most Irish secrets, it is known to a lot of people. Most of them are archaeologists, and few of them like to utter it outside of their own circles. The reluctance is understandable—the secret undermines a thriving industrial conglomerate with branches in the arts, intellectual life, religion, sport, tourism, politics, popular entertainment and consumer marketing. The conglomerate's brand name is Celtic. From the Celtic Twilight to the Celtic Tiger, from Celtic spirituality to Celtic jewelry, from Glasgow Celtic to the Boston Celtics, from Celtic Woman to the Celtic Tenors, from Celtic Sheepskin (ugg boots a speciality) to Celtic castles (all built by the Normans), from Celtic Crest spring water to Celtic crosses, it covers a vast variety of images and products. . . .
>
> The secret of Celtic Ireland is that it is all bogus. There never was a Celtic invasion of Ireland or Britain. . . .

These words came as bitter medicine to a lifelong Boston Celtics fan like myself! O'Toole traces the myth of Celtic origins back to an early-eighteenth-century Welsh scholar, Edward Lhuyd, whose claims that Gaelic, Cornish, Breton, and Welsh were related to the languages spoken by the ancient Gauls, turn out to be as unsubstantial as they were attractive:

> With the rise of 19th-century cultural nationalism, this ready-made genealogy, with its neat racial distinction be-

tween Celts and Saxons, was far too useful to be refused. . . . The Celtic Twilight (or as that rare sceptic James Joyce called it, the Cultic Twalette) added a rich layer of modern cultural prestige. The bandwagon was rolling and new forces—New Age mysticism, the American search for roots, pan-European sentiment—keep giving it a push.

If the Iron Age tribes who lived all across Northern Europe, whom the Greeks and Romans called Celts, had invaded or migrated to Britain and Ireland, there would be an archaeological record—pots, dwelling places, burial sites, coins, etc.—which there is not. The presence of high-end items crafted in a style typical of the European Celts has a surprising explanation: the local chieftains, familiar with Continental fashions, became Celtic wannabes.

What did happen in the Iron Age is that an emergent aristocracy began to adopt the international style they knew from trade and other contacts. Local craft-workers produced their own versions of Celtic chic—a bit like us copying Gucci or Prada. It was a way for the nobs to distinguish themselves from the yobs. As the archaeologist Simon Jones puts it, " 'Celtic art' . . . is not a marker of ethnic identity but of status, wealth and power". If we are Celts today because our elites developed a taste for continental bling, then half the denizens of Foxrock and Montenotte [upscale suburbs] are Italians.

The redefinition of Irish culture I am speaking of is not limited to intellectuals. Croke Park, the venerable athletic stadium in Dublin, has for many years been home to the GAA, or Gaelic Athletic Association, whose mission is to foster indigenous Irish sports like Gaelic football, hurling, and camogie (the women's version of hurling). Games like soccer and rugby, which the nationalists termed "foreign sports"—just as they labeled the foxtrot and the waltz "foreign dances"—have always been banned from Croke Park. Even though in the United States we call baseball "the national pastime," it is almost impossible for Americans to fully appreciate the almost religious devotion with which the typical Irishman regards hurling or Gaelic football. Gaelic games have, since the birth of the nationalist movement, been the heart and soul of what many men feel it means to be an Irishman.

To appreciate the iconic status of Croke Park, American comparisons are not really very helpful. It's true that Yankee Stadium is The House That Ruth Built, that Fenway Park will always carry the aura of the 1941 season when Ted Williams hit .406, batting five-for-five in his last game—and the legendary 2004 season when the Red Sox finally won the World Series. But baseball's mystique is not inextricably tied up with the American Revolution or the Civil War. Croke Park, on the other hand, commemorates Bishop Croke, the nineteenth-century patron of Gaelic Games. Hill 16 in the Park was built with rubble carried from Sackville (now O'Connell) Street after the Easter Rising in 1916. Hogan Stand is sacred to the memory of Tipperary footballer Michael Hogan, who along with eleven other Irishmen was shot dead on the pitch by the notorious Black and Tans during the War of Independence.

So in 2007 when the GAA rescinded its rule against "foreign" sports (never mind that many Irish people play and follow rugby fanatically), the gesture was revolutionary. The *Guardian* in England editorialized: "That the vote went the way it did is a sign of changing times, a tribute to the welcome new mood of mutual respect in these islands, as well as to the money to be made from 82,000 rugby fans flocking to what is a truly historic venue." I might add that for an Englishman to use the term "these islands" rather than the old "British Isles" shows how much times have changed.

In the *Irish Times* a week after his column outing the Celts, Fintan O'Toole weighed in on what he called "the odd history of Irish sporting tribalism":

Big forces—media globalization, the death of the old rural Ireland, the transcending of nationalism, the waning of religion as a marker of national identity in the Republic—have all changed the nature of the game. Identity has become more complex, and though we still use sport to mark it, we use it in different ways. Instead of the old either/or sense of belonging, we have become a both/and people. . . . The truth is that nothing could be more distinctively Irish in the 21st century than rugby and soccer at Croke Park. . . .

Despite the presence outside the stadium of a hundred or so protestors from Republican Sinn Féin, a splinter group of what is usually referred to as "the political wing of the IRA," the match was played without incident, even to the display of the Union Jack and the strains of the Irish Army Band playing "God Save the Queen." What gave this "historic" event its crowning note of poetic justice was that the match was a walkover: the Irish clobbered the English, and everyone went home with a sense that justice had been done.

When I first came to this country in 1990, the time of my "Letter from Galway," Ireland was new to me, and it would be fair to say that my view of this country was a bit bright-eyed and naïve. Other first-time visitors would and do respond similarly. At the same time, I believe that, living for a year on Galway Bay in Kinvara, at that time a quiet fishing village, I caught glimpses of the traditional rural and small-town culture just at the point when it was starting to change forever. I consider myself lucky to have caught a whiff of the old Ireland just before the deluge. I shall never forget the feast of Corpus Christi in Kinvara that year, when the whole town brought their holy pictures out to have them blessed by the clergy, who processed solemnly through the town. My two subsequent letters from Dublin, now no longer the provincial backwater of Joyce's *Dubliners* but a major European capital city, chronicle the coming of the Celtic Tiger and its aftermath. Traditional Irish culture is now stretched thin, even in the remote countryside in Tipperary where I now live.

Everyone in these parts still turns out for a funeral, there is still a place by the fire and a cup of tea for the visitor in a farmhouse kitchen, conversation is still obligatory, lengthy, and redolent of weather and local news. But even in the nearby village of Grangemockler (proud home of the aforementioned Michael Hogan), mass is sparsely attended; whatever cultural unity the nation still has, comes more often from the television screen than from the pulpit.

I spent an hour or so recently in the local garage having new tires put on my car and couldn't help reflecting on how ethnically diverse Ireland had become, even out here, miles from nowhere. The young man who installed my tires had a Welsh father and a German mother. While this work was slowly proceeding, a young Polish man stopped in, rock 'n' roll blaring from his car speakers in Polish, to have a headlamp fixed. A Ukrainian farmworker bought petrol. I, of course, am an American. Except for Micheál, the garage owner, we were all blow-ins. Ten years ago only 1.5 percent of Irish residents were foreign born; now foreign-born residents represent 10 percent of the population. Rotimi Adebari, who arrived in Ireland seven years ago as an asylum seeker from his native Nigeria, was recently elected mayor of Portlaoise, County Laois.

To return to Galway and Dublin, both places are suffused with powerful myths largely fueled by the authors who have written about them. Galway is Yeats country, though Yeats was born in Dublin and had strong family ties to Sligo, where he spent much of his childhood. The tower he restored at Ballylee near Gort and made a symbol of his poetry, the semi-feudal life surrounding Coole Park, home of his patron and friend Lady Gregory, put Galway on the map for readers from London to New York, to Sydney to Tokyo and beyond. The city of Dublin "belongs" to James Joyce in the same way that County Galway "belongs" to W. B. Yeats. You will notice that this book contains no chapter on Joyce, while Yeats's poetry haunts the entire book; so perhaps this is the place to say something about the choices I have made in writing it. I have written more about Yeats than Joyce perhaps because I am by temperament and trade a poet rather than a fiction writer, perhaps because I am drawn more to the countryside than to the city.

In truth, I have written here about books that appeal to me—about authors who have engaged my imagination. But also, like any critic, I have chosen to write about books and authors where I feel I have things to say that haven't already been said. You'll find no essay here about James Joyce because I don't think I have anything genuinely new to add to the mountain of scholarship and criticism that has already been published. Seamus Heaney, certainly the best-known contemporary Irish poet, is a different case, however. I have watched him unfold his vision from his first book onwards. From early days I have been intrigued by a picture of the poet as mediator, assuager, balancer; and so in 1995 when he published *The Spirit-Level*, which contains in its very title an image of balance, I felt my intuition was confirmed. I have not seen this emphasis noted by other critics. With W. B. Yeats, one certainly might be justified in feeling there was no more to be said; but the publication of R. F. Foster's two-volume biography of the poet in 1997 and 2003 brought to light many things about the poet's life that were simply unavailable previously, making it possible for me to write my chapter "W. B. Yeats: The Labyrinth of Another's Being."

For Irish readers, as well as for readers from the United States and elsewhere who are familiar with Irish literature from a distance, my choices of authors such as Flann O'Brien and John Millington Synge will hardly seem novel. This book attempts to give thoughtful readings of O'Brien and Synge in addition to some other late-nineteenth-, twentieth-, and early-twenty-first-century classics, not particularly to introduce readers to new authors they might not have heard of. My aim is to offer the reader a solid though not comprehensive grounding in modern Irish literature and show how this literature is related to Irish culture. Synge is probably Ireland's greatest playwright after Oscar Wilde, just as Brian Friel has more recently established himself as a contemporary classic. Flann O'Brien is as essential a figure for the Irish as Aziz Nesin is for the Turks or Mark Twain for Americans. Much loved as a humorist whose cynical take on life and whose sense of the absurd are deeply Irish, he is also widely acknowledged by more sophisticated readers as a postmodernist *avant la lettre*.

My chapter "Flann O'Brien: No Laughing Matter" discusses an aspect of O'Brien's sensibility that can easily escape those of us who did not live through the years when de Valera ran the government and Archbishop McQuaid regulated public morals—the disillusionment many people felt when the reality of life in newly independent Ireland failed to live up to the high expectations that followed the war of national liberation, which overthrew the old order and set about establishing something new in its stead. I take this disillusionment as the key to O'Brien's cast of mind. A powerful visual image of the same attitude is Seán Keating's *An Allegory*, painted in 1922–23, which serves as the frontispiece of this book. In the background stands the ruin of a Palladian big house, symbol of the old ruling class. In the foreground is a grouping of significant figures. On the far right, two men are digging a grave; one wears the uniform of the Free State army, while the other, in civilian clothes, may be taken as representing the IRA. These opposing factions in the fratricidal Civil War are digging a grave to bury a coffin wrapped in the Irish tricolored flag. Perhaps they are burying the Irish nation, which, between the two of them, they have done to death.

On the far left a parish priest, decked out in clerical black, a shiny silk top hat set confidently on his head, has a tête-à-tête with a heavy-set man in overcoat, hat, and gloves, who is leaning on a cane and wearing spats. He is a man of power in the new state, perhaps a businessman. The sense of inflexibility about the priest is emphasized by the way he stands with his hands clasped in front of him. He is not a man to whom you would go in expectation of compassion. These two are power brokers in this brave new world, and their tight-lipped grimness suggests they are up to no good. They stand on the far side of a tree from the gravediggers—a tree whose lower limbs have been hacked off, perhaps for firewood. Slumped against the tree in an attitude of weariness is the enigmatic figure of a man. He may be a self-portrait of Keating, who earlier had painted heroic canvases portraying the struggle for Irish freedom, such as *Men of the West*. Beside this figure, seated in a chair and nursing a baby, is a young woman—thoughtful, with down-turned eyes. Her white skirt and the white baby blanket give notes of brightness to a grim scene. But there is no smile on the young mother's face, no happy expectation of the future. Perhaps she, like Mary in the Bible, "[keeps] all these things and ponder[s] them in her heart." It is a powerful image, not designed to comfort or to cheer.

Half a dozen of the authors I write about here are what is called Anglo-Irish. Synge, Elizabeth Bowen, George Moore, Violet Martin, and Edith Somerville sprang from the old landed gentry, W. B. Yeats and William Trevor from the commercial and professional middle classes. Derek Mahon is a modern cosmopolite who was born in Protestant Belfast, educated at Trinity College, and has lived in Dublin and London, where he wrote plays and was a producer for the BBC. Now in his sixties, he is ensconced in Kinsale, County Cork. Even given the distances that stretch between them in time, George Moore and Derek Mahon share little in terms of social background—Moore was a member of the landed gentry from the remote Mayo countryside, Mahon was born a middle-class Belfast boy. The Moores were Catholics, but George Moore himself became almost violently, tiresomely anti-Catholic in his maturity. Something Moore and Mahon do have in common is their ambivalence about Ireland and their having established careers for themselves in London.

Many of Ireland's greatest writers have, until recently, been Protestants, somewhat to the discomfiture of Catholic Irish, particularly Irish Americans. (It should be said that the words "Protestant" and "Catholic" in Ireland have more to do with cultural differences between segments of the population than they do with religion per se; Yeats and Joyce, for example, though "Protestant" and "Catholic" by background, could not accurately be said to be Christians.) Certainly Anglo-Irish or Protestant authors like Somerville and Ross and Elizabeth Bowen have tended to be slighted in Irish and Irish-American literary criticism, and there is a most peculiar tendency, particularly in Ireland, to condescend toward Yeats, Ireland's greatest writer. Seamus Heaney has been a notable exception to this critical trend. On this subject let me quote a paragraph from the late Thomas Flanagan, the historical novelist whose *Year of the French* became a best-seller, and author of the pioneering 1959 study, *The Irish Novelists, 1800–1850*:

> Some years ago, at a Christmas party in what were then the offices of the Irish Consulate in New York, a mildly intoxicated Irish-American asked me if I could identify the series of portraits which stretched along one wall. Yes, I told him, they are the great writers of the Irish Literary Renaissance, and I identified those closest at hand—Yeats, Synge, Lady Gregory, Douglas Hyde, Wilde, Sean O'Casey. "Well," he said, pleased and proud. "And yet you'll still find people who say that Catholics can't write." "In fact," I said, "those particular Irish writers were Protestants." "All of them?" he asked, looking a bit unnerved. "All of them," I said firmly, although O'Casey didn't really look Protestant. "Well, how about that?" he asked gamely. "Of course, I knew that James Joyce was a Protestant." After I had instructed him on that point, he headed off to the bar. I had not the

heart to call after him that the Guinesses and the Jamesons were also Protestants. All in all, it would seem "we" owe "them" quite a lot.

To suppose that Irish history has been a battleground between two groups, Irish and English, Celt and Saxon, is to engage in a simplified view of things that makes better sense in the pub-talk and ballad sessions of Camden Town and South Boston than it does in a serious discussion of history. In the first place, Ireland, like many parts of Europe, had little consciousness of itself as a nation before the nineteenth century. The Gaelic ethnic purity of the kind around which de Valera founded the modern Republic of Ireland has always been more mythic than real, even before the discovery that there was no Celtic conquest. Ireland was in medieval times an island inhabited by tribes ruled by petty kings—feudal land barons and warlords.

Then the Vikings came, establishing the first towns, most notably Dublin, the "Black Pool" at the mouth of the Liffey. (Red hair, which was associated with Irishness in the States when I was growing up, is said to be a genetic trait inherited from the Vikings.) The Anglo-Normans who seized the country in the twelfth century descended from the Northmen who had conquered northern France and gone on to overwhelm England before moving farther westward. Recent critical studies such as Declan Kiberd's *Inventing Ireland* have exploded the Republican myth of ethnic purity and its simplistic view of Irish history. There is a strong desire among many people in the country today to rediscover the diversity that was a part of what it meant to be Irish before the ethnic cleansing of Irish culture under the nationalists.

The Anglo-Irish were no more a cohesive social group than the "unhyphenated" Irish. The question that lurks behind Tom Flanagan's story about his encounter with the mildly intoxicated Irish-American gentleman at a Christmas party is, how did the Anglo-Irish manage to produce so many first-rate writers? An answer, though not a complete answer, must lie in these people's awareness—often humorous—of their difference, of the precariousness of their position in this country where they served as army officers, administrators, merchants, bankers, landlords, as well as small farmers, servants, clerks, et al., in the economy of empire that ran Ireland for hundreds of years.

The insecurity of their position was clear even as early as the 1170s to one Maurice Fitzgerald, a Norman baron who came to Ireland with Strongbow. Under siege in Dublin, he appraised the situation in these terms: "Such in truth is our lot that while we are English to the Irish, we are Irish to the English. For the one nation does not detest us more than the other." One might say that this difference, this precariousness, made the Anglo-Irish watchful and observant. The history of the Anglo-Irish position may be read in the tonal changes with which the team of Somerville and Ross and, later, Elizabeth Bowen and William Trevor make their observations about life on this island. Somerville and Ross, writing at the end of the nineteenth century and on into the years following the first World War, are full of the assurance of belonging. Bowen and Trevor, on the other hand, show how edgy and tentative the Anglo-Irish had become once the Irish became masters of their own fate. Trevor's generation has had to cope with the reality that, in the words I use as the title of my essay on him, "They were as good as we were."

Years ago, when I posted some letters and bought some stamps at a rural post office, the clerk informed that my total came to £10.14 (this was before the introduction of the euro). "Ten fourteen," he told me, then paused to reflect, and added: "Battle of Clontarf!" For Irish readers the nation's history is, or was until recently, seamlessly interwoven into both life and literature. Because Irish history has been so difficult, so contentious, it has insistently entered the literature of the country in a way that is not always so obvious in, say, English literature from the eighteenth century onwards, when times have been more settled and there was little threat of civil war, starvation, or foreign domination. In addition, though its culture is ancient, Ireland as a political entity is a very recent entry in the community of nations. Newer nations tend to be more self-conscious about themselves than do older ones.

I remember the experience of reading "The Dead" by James Joyce in college. While my professor gave us a convincing reading of the story in terms of Jungian archetypes and the epiphany Gabriel Conroy experiences at the end of the story, he had not a word to say about the story's political overtones. And yet for anyone familiar with Irish history and the political conflict in Ireland in the early years of this century, the story cries out to be read as a demonstration of how fatally implicated the Irish middle classes were in the culture of England rather than that of their own country, to the extent that in Joyce's view their life lacked authenticity. The fiendishly clever way Joyce packs significance into every nook and cranny of the story prepares one well for his later masterpiece, *Ulysses*.

When Gabriel looks at the pictures on the wall above the piano in his aunts' flat, the reader notes, even if Gabriel does not, how even the old ladies' choices in interior decoration point to a cultural milieu drawn from English literature and history: "A picture of the balcony scene in *Romeo and Juliet* hung there and beside it was a picture of the two murdered princes in the Tower which Aunt Julia had worked in red, blue, and brown wools when she was a girl." Likewise, the politically aware reader will not miss the significance of the statue of William of Orange in the comical story Gabriel tells after dinner at that same Christmas party. His grandfather Patrick Morkan, having made a modest fortune from his glue factory, decides to "drive out with the quality to a military review in the park." So he harnesses Johnny, the horse that was normally employed to walk round and round to drive the mill, and "put on his very best tall hat and his very best stock collar and drove out in the grand style":

"Out from the mansion of his forefathers," continued Gabriel, "he drove with Johnny. And everything went on beautifully until Johnny came in sight of King Billy's statue: and whether he fell in love with the horse King Billy sits on or whether he thought he was back again in the mill, anyhow he began to walk round the statue."

Patrick Morkan's social insecurities literally revolve around the stature of William of Orange, who secured English domination over Ireland by his victory over James II at the Battle of the Boyne in 1690. All this is of a piece with other indications in the story of an Irish nation that, even in 1914 when *Dubliners* finally saw publication, was, as far as Joyce was concerned, "dead" or else slumbering un-self-consciously—though it was just two years before the Easter Rising, when, in Yeats's words, everything would be "changed, changed utterly: A terrible beauty is born." As a historical footnote, May 2007 saw the Taoiseach, Bertie Ahern, and the First Minister of Northern Ireland, the Reverend Ian Paisley, meet amicably at the site of the battle for a groundbreaking ceremony at the new visitors' center there, celebrating, in their words, Ireland's "complex shared" history. The ceremony came a few weeks after Paisley's Democratic Unionist Party formed a power-sharing government in Northern Ireland with Sinn Féin's Martin McGuinness as Deputy First Minister.

Like the postal clerk who remembered that 1014 was the date of the Battle of Clontarf, when Brian Boru defeated the Vikings and is traditionally credited with driving them out of Ireland, Irish writers are extraordinarily attuned to the country's history and politics. It is woven into their work, and once we start to see this, our reading experience is made immensely richer. This is just as true in the case of Ascendancy writers like Somerville and Ross, whose class would stand to lose most from an end to British rule. The two cousins, who wrote as a team, lived in a time of relative calm between the agitations of the

Land Wars of the 1870s and the War of Independence and Civil War in the 1920s, but they were keenly aware of the recent unrest. In "The Waters of Strife" from *Some Experiences of an Irish R.M.*, the police inspector Murray recalls the days of the Land Wars:

> "I remember in the Land League time how a man came one Saturday night to my window and told me there were holes drilled in the chapel door to shoot a boycotted man through while he was at mass. The holes were there right enough, and you may be quite sure that chap found excellent reasons for having family prayers at home next day!"

In the chapters that follow, I take pains to sketch in the bits of Irish political and social history I think the reader needs to be aware of to read these authors knowledgeably.

In some cases and not in others, I also tell about the lives of the authors I write about. This practice seems to make more sense for prose writers than for poets, whose work perhaps forms a world of its own, where a different air from our ordinary oxygen is breathed. In the chapters that follow, I have taken a biographical approach to Flann O'Brien, Somerville and Ross, Elizabeth Bowen, W. B. Yeats, and George Moore.

Let me briefly discuss three of these authors here. The work for which George Moore is remembered is his bitchy three-volume memoir, *Hail and Farewell*, which sketches an indelible if unreliable picture of literary life in Dublin in the late nineteenth and early twentieth centuries, specializing in artful character assassination. One would want a little grounding in biography and social history from other sources in order to see Moore's views in perspective, and I attempt to supply those.

In the case of those two remarkable women who formed the writing team of Somerville and Ross, I quote at the beginning of my chapter on them from the letter Violet Martin (her nom de plume was Martin Ross) wrote to her cousin Edith Somerville in 1889 in the Carbery district of West Cork. Her remark neatly sums up the essence of their work as it begins in observed life and ends in fiction: "Let us take Carbery and grind its bones to make our bread, and we will serve it up to the spectator so that its mother wouldn't know it." Books like *The Real Charlotte* and *Some Experiences of an Irish R.M.* are a delight for the uninitiated, and an even richer delight for those who have gained a glimpse of their origins.

My view is that reading is about connecting imagination with experience. In my "Letter from Galway" I write about the mental picture of Yeats's tower I formed when I first read the tower poems as a young man, and how surprised I was when I first came to see Thoor Ballylee. Part of the alchemy of reading has to do with how we form our own images of characters and places, and how outraged we sometimes are when we see a film that has been made from one of our favorite books. "*That's not what Gabriel Conroy looks like!*" we might say when we see the late Donal McCann playing the lead in John Huston's adaptation of "The Dead"—as great an actor as the man was. The process works in reverse as well. When one reads about houses such as Danielstown in Elizabeth Bowen's book *The Last September*, one will be inclined to draw on big houses one has visited; the imagination presses into service, in other words, material from the lumber room of memory. Sometimes the imagined place or character takes pride of place, sometimes what we bring from experience becomes the standard by which we will judge the work of imagination.

I am particularly attracted to places where the word and the world intersect, and I enjoy visiting places like Edith Somerville's hometown of Castletownshend in West Cork as well as the site of Bowen's Court near Mallow. Since this country's greatest literature was produced in the late nineteenth and twentieth centuries, the period *Finding Ireland* concentrates on, those traces left by the men and women who created that literature—real people with lives much like our own—are still relatively fresh. I am sure I am not the only reader of *Ulysses* whose mouth waters as he passes Davey Byrnes's pub near the corner of Duke Street and Grafton Street in Dublin, remembering that Leopold Bloom lunched there on Gorgonzola and burgundy on June 16, 1904. Likewise when I turn the corner from Nassau onto Kildare Street and look at the comical limestone carvings of apes playing pool that grace the columns outside what used to be the Kildare Street Club, I think of George Moore and W. B. Yeats sitting by the fire there when it was the unofficial headquarters of the Anglo-Irish establishment.

The Shelbourne Hotel further down Kildare Street on St. Stephen's Green has been at the center of Dublin life since it opened in 1867. Young ladies and their chaperones stayed at the Shelbourne when they came to Dublin for the coming-out parties that George Moore satirized in *A Drama in Muslin*—parties where Moore, in his own self-description, cut a poor figure: "his lank yellow hair (often standing on end), his sloping shoulders, and female hands—a strange appearance which a certain vivacity of mind sometimes rendered engaging." In 1916 British troops fired from the roof of the hotel on the rebels, including soldiers in the detachment commanded by Countess Markiewicz, whom Yeats immortalized along with her sister in his elegy "In Memory of Eva Gore-Booth and Con Markiewicz": "Two girls in silk kimonos, both / Beautiful, one a gazelle." Elizabeth Bowen lived at the Shelbourne off and on during what de Valera called The Emergency (the rest of the world called it World War II); she even wrote a book about the place. In my own day I have seen Edna O'Brien sitting in the lobby looking beautiful and distant, once had my progress to the Horseshoe Bar there interrupted by a film crew directed by Anjelica Huston, and back in the 1990s, used to drink tall glasses of Ballygowan in the bar on the Kildare Street side with Derek Mahon.

As I have suggested, a lot goes into forming a rounded picture of Irish culture. If one hopes to have a still richer feel for this country's culture and history beyond what can be gleaned from books, I think one would naturally want to learn something about Irish architecture, art, music, and even garden design. That seems like a tall order. I am an amateur in those areas; to invoke the old-fashioned, etymological meaning of the term, I am a lover of architecture, art, music, and gardening, without having much formal training.

To begin with architecture, the Georgian buildings one sees in Dublin and in provincial Irish towns, those "grey eighteenth-century houses" Yeats writes about in "Easter 1916," are, in all their geometrical simplicity and austerity, among the glories of domestic architecture. By dint of not being bombed in World War II, Dublin retained some of its great Georgian squares. I write about these buildings here and there in this book, especially in my 1998 Letter from Dublin. They are important in their own right, but also because they are a legacy of the Anglo-Irish Ascendancy, and they form part of the aesthetic that Yeats defiantly championed in the new Ireland that was coming to birth after the War of Independence. Sadly, the new nation allowed ignorance and greed to destroy some of this great cultural heritage.

The Georgian squares, the Houses of Parliament on College Green (now the Bank of Ireland), and the great public buildings designed by James Gandon had their counterpart in the country houses of the gentry. Nothing on the scale of the great manor houses of England was possible, because Ireland has, until recently, lacked the wealth of its neighboring island. Still, Ireland has many jewels to boast of, even considering the two hundred or so houses that were burned during the Troubles of the 1920s. Elizabeth Bowen is the master of writing that celebrates these country houses, both in her fiction and in her chronicle named after the family seat, *Bowen's Court*. "After an era of greed, roughness and panic, after an era of camping in charred or desolate ruins (as my Cromwellian ancestors did certainly), these new settlers who had been imposed on Ireland," she writes in "The Big House," "began to wish to add something to life.

The security that they had, by the eighteenth century, however ignobly gained, they did not use quite ignobly. They began to feel, and exert, the European idea—to seek what was humanistic, classic and disciplined."

While Ireland now has as vibrant an art scene as any country in Europe, it did not, before the twentieth century, excel in the art of painting. Life was too rough and unsettled, and the aristocratic patronage that fosters achievements in portraiture was lacking. The raw material for Ireland's great art was language, a resource that war, military occupation, famine, and deprivation could not rob her of. Even when the native language was all but exterminated, the Irish genius adapted the language of the colonizer and used it to create a great literature. Still, significant painters did manage to flourish here in the early twentieth century—Sir John Lavery, William Orpen, Paul Henry, and Jack B. Yeats among the best. Since those days Louis le Brocquy, among others, has flourished, as well as the pioneer of Irish abstract art, Tony O'Malley, and his successors such as Anne Madden, Camille Souter, and Barrie Cooke. Orpen is one of my favorites, and my 2005 letter reviews a show of his work.

Irish traditional music had all but died out by the end of the 1950s, only to be revived in the 1960s by a group of young musicians including instrumentalists Frankie Gavin, Alec Finn, Jackie Daly, Charlie Piggott, and a remarkable group of singers that included Maura O'Connell, Dolores Keane, Frances and Mary Black, and my favorite, Niamh Parsons. This is far from "folk music" in the Peter, Paul, and Mary sense, but it is indeed folk music, with a long and deep history. You can hear some of the best of it in Milwaukee, San Francisco, New York, and Chicago; and you can hear some of the most banal of what calls itself traditional music in the pubs of Temple Bar in Dublin. At its best there is nothing like it. What a lucky thing it is that one of Ireland's best contemporary poets, Ciarán Carson, is also a traditional musician. Anyone with an interest in the music will want to read his classic, *Last Night's Fun*. My chapter, "Listening to Irish Traditional Music," will give you a leg up.

I have included a chapter on the remarkable gardens at Mount Stewart in County Down, since gardening is an art, too, a form of architecture achieved with living materials. Edith, the seventh Marchioness of Londonderry, who created the garden at Mount Stewart, was a remarkable woman whose story I hope you will enjoy reading. The book concludes with "From Venice to Tipperary," a meditation on Irish architecture and history. The two became intertwined with the poetry of the old Gaelic dispensation, as bards like Aogán O'Rahilly tried in vain to navigate the shifting waters of what even then was a new Ireland. Since the greater part of this book has to do with the nineteenth, twentieth, and twenty-first centuries, I wanted to conclude by going back to the time of the Irish kings, to the old order of things before invaders—first the Anglo-Normans, then the British—changed Ireland forever. Every act of writing is situated somewhere, and I write in a done-up garden shed in Tipperary, on the slopes of Sliabh na mBan. To me it makes sense to end my book where I sit typing these words.

Letter from Galway, 1990

Thirty-five years ago when I first came under the spell of poetry, Yeats was my introduction to Ireland. More truly, Yeats *was* my Ireland. It follows that my Ireland was a land of myth—austere, medieval, and aristocratic. I was enchanted by the opening of his poem "In Memory of Major Robert Gregory":

> Now that we're almost settled in our house
> I'll name the friends that cannot sup with us
> Beside a fire of turf in th' ancient tower,
> And having talked to some late hour
> Climb up the narrow winding stairs to bed . . .

This poem elegized a man who seemed larger than life. The place names in Yeats's poems memorialized places I, a boy in Tennessee reading books from the public library, had never heard of: Castle Taylor, Esserkelly, Mooneen, "cold Clare rock, Galway rock and thorn." Yeats handled place names with an authority that made me feel not only that these places were significant, but that everyone must know about them except me. In "An Irish Airman Foresees His Death," Yeats has Robert Gregory say, "My country is Kiltartan Cross, / My countrymen Kiltartan's poor." Surely these people in Kiltartan, poor though they may have been, were important people! Through such inspired myth-making Yeats put the West of Ireland on the map for me.

When the Amy Lowell travel grant from Harvard made it possible for me to take my family anywhere in the world to live for a year, I chose a village in the West of Ireland: Kinvara, in the southern part of County Galway, just over the line from County Clare, twelve miles from Yeats's Thoor Ballylee. Not that I was on a Yeatsian pilgrimage. But in a not easily definable way, Yeats's poetry has lodged somewhere near the center of my understanding of Ireland.

Standing on the quay at Kinvara facing north in the direction of Galway City, which is eighteen miles away, I look out toward the sixteenth-century Dun Guaire Castle. The more architecturally sophisticated refer to Dun Guaire not as a castle but as a "tower house," as Thoor Ballylee is, of the late-medieval type that can be seen in varying degrees of ruination throughout Ireland. Built for wealthy landowners, tower houses were fortified residences three to six stories high that provided a superior command of the surrounding countryside and—with their battlements, lancet windows, and machicolations from which one could shoot, drop or pour things on attackers—a strong defensive position in troubled times. Their presence is a reminder of Ireland's feudal past, and of the unsettled conditions that prevailed until much later here than in most other European countries. Yeats liked to imagine the Celtic and Anglo-Norman soldier-adventurers who built these towers: "Rough men-at-arms, cross-gartered to the knees / Or shod in iron, climbed the narrow stairs." Dun Guaire was restored by Yeats's friend, the novelist Oliver St. John Gogarty, with Yeats himself designing the restored archway through which one enters the castle courtyard.

Kinvara quay was built in the eighteenth century, an era when sea roads were faster and more reliable than those on land, which were dusty and muddy by season. According to Daniel Corkery's classic, *The Hidden Ireland*, "vast crowds of beggars, many of them blind, swarmed upon them," along with "pedlars, packmen, horses laden with goods, wagons, carriages, coaches— and occasionally highway men." Sturdy sailing ships called Galway Hookers tied up at the quay—enlarged, incidentally, in 1807 by the Gregorys of Coole—to unload turf from Connemara, which was burned for fuel. Then they turned around and sailed back to that stony, boggy country northwest of here, loaded with produce from the fertile farmland surrounding Kinvara. If I walk out the front door of the early-nineteenth-century house where we are living, with its tiny walled garden, and go a hundred yards up the Gort Road toward Coole Park, I can look down over the village and see how the bounty of the farms, the root crops, the meat and milk of the pastures, seem poised, economically and geographically, to be carted downhill to Kinvara quay. Things must have gone this way for centuries.

References to Kinvara reach back to the age of legend that predates the pages of recorded history. One chronicler tells us that the legendary general Finn Mac Cumhail "defeated the chieftain Uinche in a battle at Ceann Mara [Irish, "head of the sea"] now known as Kinvara, on the Bay of Galway." Rory O'Shaughnessy, who built Dun Guaire Castle in 1540, used stones from an earlier fortress that belonged to Guaire, King of Connacht, in the seventh century, traces of which remain on a promontory to the east of Dun Guaire. Reminders such as these of how ancient Celtic civilization is, put a strange spin on one's sense of time. While nineteenth-century buildings at home are "old," here they seem "new."

A vestige of Ireland's more recent past is Seamount, the convent school that looms over the village from its hill above the Galway Road, which is also Kinvara's main street, curving through the village south into Clare—the house's eminence bolstered by a stone retaining wall containing blocks of limestone so huge one wonders how they could have been lifted into place.

Letter from Galway, 1990

Until 1921, when it was willed to the Sisters of Mercy, Seamount was one of the "big houses," part of the social and economic structure of landowner and tenant that dominated Irish life right up to the twentieth century. At dawn and dusk one hears the raucous cawing of rooks that nest in the convent beeches, along with the high-pitched cries of seagulls that glide in off the Atlantic. These birds give the village its characteristic sound. Kinvara has its characteristic fragrances as well: briny sea-air, salt-stung and rain-washed, with at all hours a whiff of turf smoke, that peaty aroma evocative of single-malt whiskey and the boglands from which the turf is dug.

The village is defined architecturally by its two- and three-story limestone, semi-detached houses, erected in the eighteenth and nineteenth centuries, faced with plaster in most cases and painted sky blue, lemon, chartreuse, in accordance with a love of dramatic colors, which more recently have given way to sedate hues like eggshell, white, and oyster. Whatever their color, these buildings are a triumph of vernacular architecture and sound aesthetic values. Their reassuring bulks rise unhurriedly from strong foundations, which are "battered" (sloped outward slightly at the base) so as to support their weight, up to the dignified pitch of their slate roofs, topped with Dickensian chimney pots where crows nest, rivaling the rooks with their throaty chatter.

The merchants, corn factors, and publicans who built these splendid edifices may subconsciously have been making a statement about how the land confronts the unpredictability of the sea here. No force off the Atlantic, one feels, could threaten their angles or budge their masses. Their solidity, based on the security of agriculture and trade, asserts itself defiantly in the face of the ruins that are everywhere to be seen across the Irish countryside: skeletons of medieval churches and abbeys, castles and tower houses, farm cottages abandoned during the Famine or as recently as the past decade, when the owners migrated to London, Boston, or Sydney, the cottages' thatched roofs collapsing under the relentless Irish weather.

Immured in the heart of Kinvara, its existence unguessed-at by most visitors, invisible except for one ivy-covered gable that can be seen from a corner of the quay, is another example of how modern Ireland is built on the ruins, and in this case literally on the bones, of her past. Last week after a few pints of Guinness at John Griffin's pub, the Ould Plaid Shawl, the local historian and journalist Jeff O'Connell and I decided to have a look round St. Coman's Church and the graveyard that surrounds it. In one form or another a church has stood on this spot for approximately a millennium and a half. Two desperadoes, the O'Curry brothers, pillaged and burned St. Coman's in about A.D. 540. Guilt-stricken, they later rebuilt the church, which was then modified in the Hiberno-Romanesque style in the twelfth century, with some Gothic features added in the fifteenth and eighteenth centuries. Through famine and emigration Kinvara's population was cut in half during the twenty-year period leading up to 1870, and in that decade St. Coman's was abandoned in favor of a newer church. Houses were built around the churchyard, gradually cutting off access to it.

As recently as a hundred years ago Monsignor Fahey, historian of the diocese, wrote that "The ruined church . . . still flings its shadow on the 'dark blue tide' [a phrase from an old poem about Kinvara] from the lofty eminence within the town which it crowns." Some ten years ago when water mains were being repaired along the main street, workers dug up a huge quantity of bones, which were carted away and buried elsewhere. The street and the houses fronting it had been dug right into the side of the ancient burial ground. Jeff and I, guided by two of John Griffin's boys, Patrick and Noel, made our way through the old stables behind the pub, through bramble thickets and the indiscriminate piles of refuse that find their way into back yards, around the stone walls of the church, and into the ruins of the building through the Romanesque south doorway, a beautiful round arch piled two feet above ground level with earth and discarded building materials. A fine fifteenth-century window had been jammed with roofing paper and rubbish. We scraped the mud off two broken slabs to look at the medieval crosses chiseled into their surface. Who knows how many treasures like St. Coman's there are hidden away in forgotten corners of Ireland?

Kinvara's claim to fame as far as most people are concerned, however, is not its architectural history and antiquarian associations, but rather its pubs. A village population of roughly five hundred contrives, with stout contributions from the residents of outlying areas, to support a total of nine pubs including the Ould Plaid Shawl. Irish people don't seem to enjoy drinking at home. Drinking means drinking at the pub. And drinking at the pub involves conversation. Anyone not willing to slow down for a few minutes and pass the time of day is considered to be seriously lacking in common courtesy. You don't so much as buy a postage stamp in Ireland without prefacing the transaction with a few remarks about the weather. This is civilized behavior.

Well equipped as it is with pubs, Kinvara is a major center for traditional Irish music. It is a rare Saturday night when we are not in the pub at Winkle's Hotel, where some of the best-known musicians in Ireland perform. Traditional music largely means instrumental music. When a song is to be sung, the musicians and the pub owner call for silence, and the song is "given" unaccompanied. The faster tunes—and most of these tunes run fast—are categorized according to what sort of dance step they would accompany: reel, jig, and hornpipe predominate. The slow tunes are called airs. Instrumentation normally consists of fiddle, accordion, and sometimes concertina, wooden flute, tin whistle, guitar, or piano. Tight ensemble playing is the mark of this music at its best, and it swings. To the uninitiated ear the tunes can at first sound alike. As the ear becomes more finely tuned, the subtle variations, the emotional shadings, and the virtuosity of individual performers reveal themselves.

As with jazz, traditional music is enhanced by the setting in which one listens to it: a smoky, crowded pub where one arrives usually no earlier than ten o'clock, sits at the bar with a pint of porter or a glass of Bushmill's at the ready, and stays till the wee hours. Official pub closing times are eleven in winter, half past eleven in summer—and this is about when the session starts to get rolling. The peculiarity of Irish licensing laws means that though the pub closes its doors to newcomers at about 11:30, those patrons inside may continue to be served drinks for as long as the management pleases. This practice may not be strictly legal, but in Ireland a fine disregard for the petty details of the law is traditional—dating, one would suppose, from the days of British rule. Recently we found ourselves coming home from a session at Winkle's at six in the morning—the sun was rising and the music was still going. As Somerville and Ross remark in *The Big House of Inver*, "People get to bed late, and sleep late, in the listless Western villages."

Though, as I have said, the music moves along at a sprightly pace, it is often tinged with melancholy. Many people feel that this music, a genuine survival from the old Ireland, expresses the Irish people's endurance in the face of centuries of poverty, military occupation, eviction from the land, systematic attempts to eradicate the native religion, and finally, the sadness associated with the emigration that has been a feature of Irish life since the "Flight of the Earls" following their defeat by the English in the first decade of the seventeenth century. Perhaps the sadness one hears in traditional music based on dance tunes finds its counterpart in Yeats's "Lapis Lazuli," where survivors of tragedy endure it with the defiant insouciance displayed by these ancient Chinese sages:

> One asks for mournful melodies;
> Accomplished fingers begin to play.
> Their eyes mid many wrinkles, their eyes,
> Their ancient, glittering eyes, are gay.

From "Lapis Lazuli" and its ancient Chinese sages to the town of Gort, which according to Thackeray "looked as if it wondered how the deuce it got itself in the midst of such desolate country, and seemed to bore itself there considerably," might seem a great distance indeed. My oldest son goes to Our Lady's College in Gort, a gritty little market town on the main street of which may be seen Burke's welding shop. Burke's sports a tasteful plaque quoting Yeats's poem "To Be Carved on a Stone at Thoor Ballylee":

I, the poet William Yeats,
With old mill boards and sea-green slates,
And smithy work from the Gort forge,
Restored this tower for my wife George;
And may these characters remain
When all is ruin once again.

Burke's did the blacksmith work for the restoration at Thoor Ballylee. Thus does the building trade intersect the life of the imagination.

I trust no reader will contact the Garda Síochána when I confess that, following local custom, I poached my Christmas tree from the grounds of Coole Park. The woods at Coole are extensive. It is a great shame that Coole House, perhaps the most important locus for the Literary Revival except for Yeats's tower itself, was torn down in 1941 and the stones carted off by local farmers. According to tradition the Gregorys were good landlords who did not evict tenants, nor exact rents from those who could not afford to pay. Sir William Gregory's father is said to have died from a fever he contracted while nursing a sick tenant back to health. That some members of the Anglo-Irish gentry connived to alleviate the evils of a system whereby English settlers over the course of several centuries took the land away from the Irish and then in turn rented it back to them, may be laudable; Edmund Burke's comment, though, cuts to the heart of the matter: "Connivance is the relaxation of slavery, not the definition of liberty."

The other day Jeff O'Connell and I drove over to Gort to have a chat with Gerry Keane, an old gentleman who owns a grocery and dry goods emporium where the Yeatses used to buy their provisions. We had a drink in the pub that, following the pattern of old-fashioned Irish shops, is situated at the back of the establishment. Mr. Keane, a sprightly old man though practically blind, wearing a red bow tie, remembers Yeats and Lady Gregory well. She was a Persse, and the Persses had the reputation of being Protestant proselytizers. The gifts of tobacco she would take to the county workhouse, where she collected Irish folktales, were said to have been wrapped in religious tracts. The handsome mahogany desk in Mr. Keane's office had belonged to Lady Gregory. A pencil drawing by her son Robert hung on the wall, and three antique swords that had belonged to Sir William Gregory hung above the bar. The desk and the swords were magnificent, the drawing somewhat less so.

Mr. Keane remembers Yeats, wearing a wide-brimmed black hat, pince-nez, and the flowing bow tie familiar from pictures of the poet, waiting out in the chaise "dreaming" while his wife went in to do the shopping. He had little time, Mr. Keane said with a little smile, to spare on such folk as the local merchants, folk who "fumbled in a greasy till," he quoted. Yeats would also stand on the bridge in Gort on these expeditions into town, looking down at the water, which, the old man said, "was a living thing to him." When a local workman, irked because he could never get Yeats to speak to him, was hired to install a lock at Thoor Ballylee, the man deliberately installed the lock upside down. "Then," Mr. Keane said, "Yeats had plenty to say to him."

Leaving the shop, we drove north from Gort and took the turnoff past Kiltartan crossroads to the tower. Thoor Ballylee, built right on the edge of the stream that runs past it, at the far end of a stone bridge, gives an immediate impression of monolithic strength. It is compact and assertive, with none of the fanciful medievalism I had imagined when I first read Yeats's tower poems. A thatched cottage facing the road that crosses the bridge abuts the tower, sheltering beneath its massiveness. "My idea," Yeats wrote in a letter, "is to keep the contrast between the medieval castle and the peasant's cottage." Following his principle expressed in *A Vision* of "striking through the mask" and becoming one's opposite through action, it is easy to see why Yeats the dreamer "founded here," as he says in his poem "My House," where "A man-at-arms / Gathered a score of horse and spent his days."

Contemporary Irish literary opinion fidgets under the absoluteness of Yeats's achievements, and of all Irish sins, envy is the deadliest. The begrudgers have a point, though: for Yeats, myth substituted for history, and his notion of what it meant to be Irish did not provide a reliable foundation for the new national literature. But even his severest critics must grant that the old master brought together, both in his work and in this emblematic residence, a cluster of symbols exemplifying several of the most important strands of Irish culture. His emphasis on the tower's martial past honors the tumultuous and aristocratic Middle Ages, with perhaps a glance at the violence of the Civil War and a premonition of the troubles in Northern Ireland. The cottage acknowledges Ireland's folk traditions of craft, song, and talk. Yeats's own affinities with *Il Penseroso*'s Platonist (in his "Meditations in Time of Civil War"), who "toiled on / In some like chamber," call to mind the austere traditions of the monastic scholar-poets of the past. Yeats's vision of the country no longer defines Ireland—the real place is more complex and absorbing than any one man's vision of it could encompass—but it is hard to dispute that in Yeats "the indomitable Irishry" found its noblest spokesman.

Letter from Dublin, 1998:
The Celtic Tiger

What has drawn me to Dublin once or twice a year over the past decade has nothing to do with the Celtic Tiger. Dublin is an incomparable if constantly threatened gem of Georgian architecture, the contemplation of which freshens one's sense of pure form. Like the music of Mozart, Dublin's streets and squares and monumental public buildings are a Euclidean fragment of the eighteenth century cast adrift in the perilous waters of the present. Its literary world is as contentious, and even vicious, as anywhere on earth, yet this is a city where poetry thrives. The theatre here, though tiny by comparison with London's, is vital and innovative. Above all, Dublin is a stage where personality dominates and wit is savored through an ongoing network of conversations. Given the city's complex and tragic history, in which hardship and disappointment have been the norm, it is not surprising that the dominant mode is irony.

I can hardly recall a conversation in Dublin this summer when no one has mentioned the "Celtic Tiger," that irritating catchphrase commonly used to describe the runaway Irish economy. This boom or bubble is transforming the country, in particular the capital city—and not necessarily for the better. While prosperity is obviously welcome, it is happening too fast. Before winning her independence from Britain in the 1920s, this country, with its large landed estates, was practically a feudal society. A commonly expressed witticism asserts that Ireland has leapt straight from the nineteenth century to the twenty-first, bypassing the twentieth altogether. One might even enlarge on that exaggeration by asking whether the Romantic movement ever hit Ireland—in which case the leap forward began somewhere in the late eighteenth century.

One strenuous dissenter to the unironic brave new world of Italian suits, penne and arugula, air-kisses and mobile phones, is the poet Derek Mahon, who last year published *The Yellow Book*, a sequence of twenty poems, most of them in rhyming couplets. Its title and many of its references evoke the fin de siècle of a hundred years ago:

> My attic window under the shining slates
> where the maids slept in the days of Wilde and Yeats
> sees crane-light where McAlpine's fusiliers,
> site hats and brick-dust, ruin the work of years.
> The place a Georgian theme-park for the tourist,
> not much remains . . .
>
> ("Night Thoughts")

(McAlpine is a construction company; "site hats" are what are called "hard hats" in America.)

When one looks up to refresh one's eye with a view of the Georgian rooftops and chimney pots that make the vistas in this city such a delight, the view these days is all too likely to be intruded upon by a building crane wheeling across the sky like some genetically modified praying mantis. It is all about money, naturally. Mahon comments resignedly: "foreign investment conspires against old decency, / computer talks to computer, machine to answering machine."

Another poem from *The Yellow Book*, titled "'shiver in your tenement,'" contrasts our moment to the literary scene in Dublin "long ago in the demure '60s / before the country first discovered sex." Familiar figures from those days, sporting wide-brimmed black hats acquired from clerical supply shops, included the poets Patrick Kavanagh and Austin Clarke, the novelist and humorist Flann O'Brien, and the playwright Brendan Behan: "Those were the days before tourism and economic growth, / before deconstruction and the death of the author, / when pubs had as yet no pictures of Yeats and Joyce / since people could still recall their faces, their voices." The poem speculates about the relation between art and repression: "Nothing to lose but our chains, our chains gone / that bound with form the psycho-sexual turbulence, / together with those black hats and proper pubs." Mahon's irony is frequently tinged with bitterness; the poem's attack is provocative, reactionary, and uncompromising: "Those were the days; now patience, courage, artistry, / solitude things of the past, like the fear of God, / we nod to you from the pastiche paradise of the postmodern."

To return to the Celtic Tiger. Peter Somerville-Large, in his excellent chronicle *Dublin: The Fair City* (1979, revised edition 1996), to which I am indebted, quotes Jonathan Swift's animadversions in the 1730s on excessively rapid growth, as well as John Faulkner's complaints in 1757 in the *Dublin Journal* about the "rows of empty buildings, and our builders still proceed in their folly." Just as those grousings were being voiced, the city was entering a golden age, and the empty buildings of 1757 did after all find tenants. Eighteenth-century speculators were no doubt as surely driven by greed as their twentieth-century counterparts; the difference is that the buildings that went up during the Georgian period were uniformly handsome.

Letter from Dublin, 1998

The Georgian row house is as simple and perfect a design idea as the nail, the pencil, or the hammock. Two or three times taller than its width, it is a rectangular brick box whose plain verticality, topped by an unobtrusive gray-slated, hipped roof with a tidy little row of chimney pots, makes it one of man's most pleasing creations. In a typical townhouse, three windows wide—like 82 Merrion Square, which in the 1920s belonged to W. B. Yeats—the door is set off-center in the farthest right of the ground floor's bays. The columns or pilasters that flank the doorway, the modest flourishes of fancy brickwork above the windows, and the round-arched fanlight above the door are the house's chief ornaments. The classical elegance of this style of domestic architecture is complemented by the choice of building materials. The brick of which eighteenth-century Dublin was constructed has been mellowed by Ireland's cold, damp weather, as well as by the smoke from coal fires lit to combat the damp and cold, so that the houses glow russet, peachy, or amber in the thin northern sunlight.

It is sad that so much of this irreplaceable Georgian city has been destroyed. Many mansions became tenements in the bleak years that followed 1801, when Britain, alarmed by the rebellion of 1798, instated the Act of Union, dissolving the Irish Parliament in order to rule the country directly from Whitehall. Almost overnight Dublin lost its status. The Georgian townhouses filled up with those hundreds of thousands forced off the land by the Famine, and the city declined over the course of the nineteenth century into the backwater familiar to readers of Joyce's *Dubliners*. More damage was done in the 1960s, when it was easier for speculators to get their ugly business past the public because many people associated the old buildings with the centuries of English domination. Preservationists were caricatured as "a consortium of belted earls and their ladies and left-wing intellectuals."

The upwardly mobile citizens of the new nation were glad to see the old piles pulled down. One particularly infamous episode involved the condemnation, as "structurally unsound," of numbers 13 to 28 Lower Fitzwilliam Street by the Electricity Supply Board. The ESB enlisted the English architect Sir John Summerson, who, to his everlasting shame, described the block in question as "simply one damned house after another." This had been what Somerville-Large calls "the longest Georgian street in Europe." Its lines of perspective looked straight out past the rooftops of the city up toward the Dublin Mountains. And under the wrecker's ball these houses fell. All, naturally, in the name of progress and modernization. The lovely sequence of brick townhouses was replaced by a row of buildings that looks like a prefabricated savings and loan office in Sioux City, Iowa.

If much has been destroyed, much remains. Fitz-william and Merrion squares retain their unity of design. And set within Dublin's fabric of domestic structures are ten or a dozen public buildings—their grey stone counterpointing coolly the red brick row houses—that one never tires of looking at. The Bank of Ireland, formerly the seat of the Irish Parliament, with its semicircular colonnades curving around both sides of a central, pedimented portico, is one of the most beautiful and surprising buildings in the world. It achieves its effects on the horizontal plane and does so by presenting a curved façade. The result is a modesty often missing in classical structures, which can look cold and presumptuous. Inside, the intimate scale of the chambers built for parliamentary use gives it a charm that is characteristic of Irish Georgian architecture. In the introductory epistle to her 1806 novel, *The Wild Irish Girl*, Lady Morgan made an incisive comparison between the first and second cities of the British Empire: "This city is to London like a small temple of the Ionic order, whose proportions are delicate, whose character is elegance, compared to a vast palace whose Corinthian pillars at once denote strength and magnificence."

Letter from Dublin, 1998

Dublin stretches along the north and south banks of the river Liffey from its westernmost suburbs to where the river empties into the Irish Sea in the east. James Gandon was Dublin's greatest architect—and like many who have made major contributions to the cultural life of this island, he was English. His two finest buildings are both found on the north quay of the Liffey: to the west, Dublin's legal center, the Four Courts; to the east, the Custom House. With their oxidized copper domes showing prominently against both the grey sky and the colors of other buildings, they define the city's skyline. Or they did before the city fathers allowed the historic Liberty Hall, heavily bombarded by British gunboats during the Easter Rising in 1916 but fully restored later, to be pulled down and replaced by a multistory glass box totally out of scale with the rest of the city, where a four-story building looks tall. This abomination is topped by a wavy tin rooftop ornament resembling a cartoon toupee.

The architectural historian Maurice Craig characterizes Gandon as eclectic and mannerist. Certainly Gandon does something surprising with the domes of his two Dublin masterpieces. The Custom House, two ample stories lighted by tall windows, topped by a smaller course with windows half the size of those below, gives the impression of being long and low because it spreads out horizontally, sitting parallel to the Liffey. Atop this long, low block sits a Palladian dome that looks surprisingly small in relation to the horizontal expanse it surmounts. In the Four Courts, my favorite of the two, Gandon laid out, at the extended arms of an X, the four courts after which the building is called: King's Bench, Chancery, Exchequer, and Common Pleas. These four arms meet in a central, octagonal hall, over which the architect has floated a glorious dome upheld by a tall cylindrical ring of columns. Like the dome of Saint Paul's in London or of Haghia Sophia in Istanbul, the dome of the Four Courts is an assertion of majesty. The majesty of empire.

I have rooms for the summer at Trinity College, south of the Liffey. Like many residents of this part of town, I seldom venture to the northside except to go to the theatre at the Abbey or the Gate or to attend traditional Irish music sessions at Hughes', a pub up behind the Four Courts. One day, however, I crossed the Ha'Penny Bridge to the north quay and walked past the Four Courts to Collins Barracks, formerly the Royal Barracks, where many holdings from the National Museum in Kildare Street have been moved. One can see from the size of Collins Barracks how large a garrison the British maintained in Dublin. In his discussion of the Four Courts, Maurice Craig notes that its architect would have endeavored to soundproof it from the noise of military parades: "We know from Gandon's *Life* that anxiety was felt at the time lest the troops marching daily from their barracks to the castle, with fife and drum, with flam, drag, and paradiddle, might disturb the slumbers of the Bench."

The barracks, with its severe classicism, is the perfect architectural representation of order and power. The massive elevations, three granite stories over solid rusticated arcades, look out over dizzyingly vast parade grounds. It is ironic, and thus fitting, that the National Museum used this setting to mount an exhibit called "1798: Fellowship of Freedom," commemorating the unsuccessful rebellion that took place two hundred years ago. That the 1798 Rising was a failure is one of the tragedies of Irish history, not least because the leadership, the United Irishmen, represented Protestants, Catholics, and Freethinkers, with some of its strongest support in fact coming from the Presbyterians of Ulster.

When Ireland did eventually win her freedom in the War of Independence following the 1916 Easter Rising, the new nation, defining itself as Gaelic, Catholic, and nationalist, became anti-intellectual and inward-looking to a pathological degree. Thanks to the Church's control of intellectual life, few of the country's modern literary masterpieces could be bought in Ireland. John Charles McQuaid, archbishop of Dublin, had a horror of what he thought of as "obscene" books, and was directly involved, to name one example out of many, in having the novelist John Mc-Gahern fired from his job as a national school teacher and his books removed from the shelves of libraries and bookshops. Had the rising of 1798 succeeded, there was a chance that the new nation might have been founded on Enlightenment principles similar to those of the American Revolution, an important model for the rebellion's leaders such as Wolfe Tone and Lord Edward Fitzgerald. And incidentally, Dublin's architectural legacy might then have been seen as Ireland's national heritage, not the imposition of a colonial style, and could have been preserved rather than vandalized.

The most powerful drama I have seen this summer is *The Weir* by twenty-seven-year-old Connor McPherson. The play consists of a series of ghost stories told in a pub in rural Ireland and illustrates two points: that the new generation of Irish writers still has the strong narrative gift, and that the supernatural still holds a grip on the Irish imagination—and not only for those who live in thatched cottages. The pub's regulars, while retailing their stories absorbingly, distance themselves, dismissing the stories as a kind of local color, "an old cod." Ironically, the character whose experience of the paranormal is most heartfelt and disturbing is not one of the countrymen, with their colorful turns of phrase and old-fashioned ways, but a young woman down from Dublin, taking a break from her yuppie life to recover from a painful personal episode. *The Weir* is living proof that so-called "text-based" theatre has nothing to apologize for, and that like *Waiting for Godot*, a play based on talk can still hold an audience's attention.

At the Abbey Theatre, Conall Morrison has directed a new production of Dion Boucicault's 1860 melodrama, *The Colleen Bawn*. Dismissed as a theatrical hack by admirers of serious modern Irish drama, Boucicault has found a new appreciation among commentators here for his anticipation of the twentieth century's technological approach to entertainment.

In *The Colleen Bawn*, the poteen-swilling Myles-Na-Coppaleen dives into a Killarney lake to save the colleen from drowning after the villain charmingly played by Pat Kinevane pushes her in. In some nineteenth-century productions the lake was represented by a huge aquarium. In this production a smoke machine provided an illusion of mist-shrouded waters. At the preview I attended, the smoke machine went out of control and engulfed the first few rows of theatregoers, whose coughs and vigorous attempts to wave away the smoke made the rescue scene especially hilarious. An observer trying to gauge the national mood might draw the conclusion from this extravagant production that contemporary Ireland, as represented by its national theatre, is in a buoyant enough mood not to shy away from mounting a nineteenth-century parody of itself, stage-Irishness, poteen jug, drunken priest, and brogues all around.

Whether by happenstance or design, while the Abbey was presenting Boucicault's Myles-Na-Coppaleen upstairs, the Peacock Theatre downstairs—the Abbey's experimental wing—was mounting an adaptation of *At Swim-Two-Birds*, by Flann O'Brien, better known by the nom de plume Myles na Gopaleen (a variation of Boucicault's spelling), whose *Irish Times* column, "Cruiskeen Lawn," was the "Doonesbury" of its time. The column's title alludes to a song from *The Colleen Bawn*. The story was clearly baffling to the audience the night I went—some package tours had bought blocks of tickets for their clients—and indeed would not have made much sense to anyone who had not read the book. What were the punters to make of Mad Sweeny, half-naked and smeared with dirt and blood crouching up in a tree or on a chair during the novel's poker game, while the Fairy (a disembodied voice) raises and checks from her perch in the pocket of the Pooka MacPhellimey's overcoat? They did respond in a spirited fashion to a recitation of O'Brien's famous bit of inspired doggerel in praise of porter, one stanza of which I will give here:

> When money's tight and is hard to get
> And your horse has also ran,
> When all you have is a heap of debt—
> A PINT OF PLAIN IS YOUR ONLY MAN.

One Sunday evening, displaced from the lounge of the Shelbourne Hotel where I had gone for tea by a film crew, I retreated down Lower Baggot Street to Doheny & Nesbitt's public house. Having secured without competition the front snug of the pub, there amongst the honest plain wood and down-at-heels Edwardian décor, I read randomly O'Brien's novel *At Swim-Two-Birds*, hoping to clear my mind of tigerism and recover the feel of old Dublin's ironic anti-Romanticism. For such refreshment, Myles, like the "pint of plain" he espouses, is "your only man." Romanticism, as I suggested at the beginning of this letter, never found fertile soil in Ireland; irony, as I have also mentioned, is too pervasive here to support extravagant flights of fancy.

The last word in my letter goes to Flann O'Brien on Jean-Jacques Rousseau. His narrator and some friends are leaving the pub after an evening of drinking:

> a small man in black fell in with us and tapping me often about the chest, talked to me earnestly on the subject of Rousseau, a member of the French nation. He was animated, his pale features striking in the starlight and his voice going up and falling in the lilt of his argumentum.

I did not understand his talk and was personally unacquainted with him. But Kelly was taking in all he said, for he stood near him, his taller head inclined in an attitude of close attention. Kelly then made a low noise and opened his mouth and covered the small man from shoulder to knee with a coating of unpleasant buff-colored puke. Many other things happened on that night now imperfectly recorded in my memory but that incident is still very clear to me in my mind. Afterwards the small man was some distance from us in the lane, shaking his divested coat and rubbing it along the wall. He is a little man that the name of Rousseau will always recall to me.

I raise my glass to the hope that Dublin will never forget the wise and skeptical Myles na Gopaleen.

Letter from Dublin, 1998

Letter from Dublin, 2005: Wilde, Synge, and Orpen

Old Dublin is hard to locate these days—the city James Joyce, Seán O'Casey, Flann O'Brien, and Patrick Kavanagh wrote about, with its tobacco-brown pubs, drizzle, and the sound of the Angelus on the radio every day at noon and six p.m. The Angelus is still rung on RTÉ (Radio Telefís Éireann), but the old, serious, repressed Ireland has all but disappeared. Attendance at mass is down to about one percent in the urban centers. Ireland has become part of a prosperous, secular Europe; the Celtic Tiger has seen more than a decade of economic boom now, achieving for the Irish a per capita income above that of the United States. One has mixed feelings about many of the recent changes. A new, aggressively acquisitive attitude in a country that once saw itself as "the land of saints and scholars" can be distressing. I do like the smoking ban, which means that one can spend an evening in a pub without needing to have one's clothes washed the next day. And I like the wooden footpath that has been constructed along the north quay of the Liffey, a simple but bold civic-planning project that makes the river accessible to strollers, loungers, and lovers.

The other day I was sitting at the café on the footpath near O'Connell Street Bridge in the center of Dublin. French was being spoken to one side of me, some Eastern European language to the other—and for a moment I was seized with the delusion that I had fetched up in Paris. I don't mean simply that I was reminded of Paris, I mean that for a moment I thought I was *in Paris*. And it wasn't just the strong coffee, diesel fumes, and the sound of the languages other than Hiberno-English. This old city had suddenly become a grand place made summery by global warming, bisected by a great river, with notable bridges and a cosmopolitan population. Most of all one felt a sense of freedom, well-being, and a big, open sky.

Expansiveness is what many people seem to feel in Dublin these days. The future appears at last to have arrived. One very noticeable feature of the new Dublin is the presence of immigrants from all over the world. No longer a country that exports its best and brightest to London, New York, Boston, San Francisco, and Sydney, Ireland now welcomes or at least accepts immigrants from all over the world to serve as laborers, restaurant and hotel workers, and entrepreneurs. Many of the Internet cafés in Dublin seem to be run by Chinese. At least the taxi drivers are still Irishmen; unlike their counterparts in New York, they know their way around the city. With all the changes, however, a certain level of endearing parochialism still prevails. The following anecdote appeared recently on www.overheardindublin. com: "I was standing at a bus stop on O'Connell Street. There were two girls beside me talking in Irish to each other. Next thing you know, two local Dubliners walk by and hear the girls talking. One of the Dubliners looks at the two girls and says 'Hey, f★★k off back to yer own country'."

The question on many observers' minds is whether, with the disappearance of "dear dirty Dublin," the haunt of Leopold Bloom and Stephen Dedalus, with its pent-up intensity, its literary pubs whose louche, flamboyant talk was the flip side of Catholic Ireland's repressed self-consciousness and caution, the city has been permanently altered. I think the answer to that question is yes.

Letter from Dublin, 2005

U nlike other sectors of society, literary and theatrical Ireland has not cut its ties with its past. Dublin is still the place to see definitive performances of the Irish dramatic canon. This past summer theatregoers got the chance to see productions of two Oscar Wilde plays staged by Dublin's two leading companies. The Gate Theatre gave a stylish, straightforward rendition of the society drama, *Lady Windermere's Fan*. The Abbey Theatre performed the society farce, *The Importance of Being Earnest*, with an all-male cast.

When the curtain fell after the first two acts of *Lady Windermere*, I walked out for a breath of fresh air feeling rather restive and unimpressed; the play seemed altogether too conventional. After the interval, however, the final two acts brought the play to a powerful, deeply satisfying conclusion. One felt that Wilde as a wise, experienced commentator on human life had set us up in the first part of the play with something formulaic and then delivered the goods once he had us in the palm of his hand. In *The Importance of Being Earnest*, on the other hand, one went out at intermission into a lobby buzzing with the excitement of a vibrant, innovative theatrical experience. Conall Morrison's ploy of having the female characters played by male actors in drag seemed to pay off brilliantly—a gimmick, yes; but a gimmick that worked. The second half of the play, however, seemed repetitive; the gimmick had become tiresome.

The intricate plots of the nineteenth century, with their secrets, their characters' shadowy pasts, their sudden denouements, were as essential to popular melodrama, the novels of Dickens, and the operettas of Gilbert and Sullivan as they were to the plays of Wilde and his contemporaries. When we see one of Wilde's plays today we cannot fail to be aware that the man his contemporaries viewed as a social and literary celebrity was leading the double life that would ultimately ruin him. His plays, whether in the serious form of society dramas like *Lady Windermere's Fan* or the farcical carry-on of *The Importance of Being*

Earnest, now seem obsessed with a secret life that could only be hinted at. It is as though Wilde were, in a kind of dramatic irony enhanced by the passage of time, speaking about his life to those who would, in time to come, be aware of the full dimensions of his private drama. Clearly he feared and perhaps he had fore-knowledge that his double life would, in the rigid moral atmosphere of Victorian England that underlay the brilliance and decadence of the fin de siècle Nineties of his plays, eventually bring him down.

Wilde wrote all his best parts for women. Mrs. Erlynne in *Lady Windermere's Fan* is one of the greatest of his female characters, and it was a thrill to see the role played by the incomparable Ingrid Craigie. The director, Alan Stanford, and the costume designer, Peter O'Brien, had the good sense, for her first appearance onstage at Lady Windermere's evening party, to have her dressed in a black dress that distinguished her from all the other female characters in their conventional pastel ball gowns. She is set apart from the other characters in the play because she is, as Wilde would soon be, touched by scandal; she has passed beyond the pale of social acceptance. She has the deeper knowledge of human life never attained by people who live conventional lives. As she says to Lady Windermere in an impassioned speech:

> You don't know what it is to fall into the pit, to be despised, mocked, abandoned, sneered at—to be an outcast! To find the door shut against one, to have to creep in by hideous byways, afraid every moment lest the mask should be stripped from one's face, and all the while to hear the laughter, the horrible laughter of the world, a thing more tragic than all the tears the world has ever shed.

In the theatre, voice is everything. And Ingrid Craigie's voice was different from that of every other actor on stage at the Gate. It was the deep, throaty voice of a woman who has achieved the hard-won knowledge of the speech quoted above. In the all-male version of *The Importance of Being Earnest,* on the other hand, voice is exactly where the play failed.

The director chose to frame the play by presenting the audience with Oscar Wilde *in propria persona* sitting toward the end of his life in a Paris café, breakfasting on champagne and absinthe and musing over his glory days on the London stage. "With good-humoured mischief, he casts the play from the café's elegant male clientele," the program tells us. Alan Stanford (who directed *Lady Windermere's Fan* at the Gate) did a brilliant impression of Oscar Wilde in the opening scene and was really masterly as Lady Bracknell, both because he has a commanding stage presence and also because there is perhaps something inherently magisterial and masculine about high society *grandes dames.* But when it came to male actors playing the sweet young things Gwendolen and Cecily, one got tired of hearing men doing the camp thing of imitating women's voices. Having the whole play take place within the life and milieu of its author turned out in the end to be, for all its cleverness, a bit airless and claustrophobic. As much as he may have enjoyed the company of boys, I don't think Wilde would have wanted the beauty of young women and the freshness of their voices excluded from one of his plays.

The opposite of the Abbey's brilliant airlessness was DruidSynge, a marathon presentation of John Millington Synge's oeuvre staged at the Olympia by the Druid theatre company, based in Galway. The Olympia is a magnificently grand old theatre with crimson velvet and gilt woodwork, creaky underfoot and bearing the faint olfactory imprint of the thousands of audiences who have been entertained here since it opened. The primal quality of Synge's drama stood in marked contrast to this plush, raffish setting. Synge found the pagan wildness of Irish life in Connemara, that part of the country least touched by British colonization, and gave it a voice in English.

His story is well known to aficionados of the Irish Literary Revival. Born in 1871, twenty years later than Wilde, to an upper-middle-class Anglo-Irish family with an estate in Wexford and a line of Church of Ireland bishops in their family tree, in the 1890s Synge was living the bohemian life in Paris, rather directionless, writing imitation Symbolist poetry. Here he met Yeats, who took him under his wing and advised him to go to the West of Ireland and absorb himself in the Gaelic culture there, as his friend and patron Lady Gregory was already doing near Galway. Yeats memorializes Synge both in his *Autobiographies* and in his elegiac poem "In Memory of Major Robert Gregory":

> long travelling, he had come
> Towards nightfall upon certain set apart
> In a most desolate stony place,
> Towards nightfall upon a race
> Passionate and simple like his heart.

I saw *Riders to the Sea, Deirdre of the Sorrows, The Playboy of the Western World,* and *The Shadow of the Glen,* all directed by Druid's founder and guiding spirit, Garry Hynes. For all but *Deirdre,* a story from Irish mythology that came across less well than the vernacular plays, Druid used the same set, a stylized West-of-Ireland cottage with a turf fire burning and a door that could open when it needed to admit some visitor from the world outside. The sound of the relentless wind one hears during the long winter nights on this island set the stage for the action of the plays. Living in Galway as most of Druid's actors do, in touch with that portion of life in the West that retains its contact with the old ways, these repertory actors, except for the younger members of the cast, have voices that are equal to Synge's dialogue. Like Synge himself, they have heard it from the mouths of the people. Hearing the old troupers like Catherine Walsh,

Mick Lally, and Marie Mullen speak Synge's musical and eloquent lines reinforced my sense that theatre at its most essential is all about voice, and that Irish playwrights are the best in the world at making dialogue sing.

L ike the playwright Synge, whom he greatly admired, the painter William Orpen was Anglo-Irish and was born in the 1870s. Like Wilde and many another artist before him, he lived at a time when London was a magnet for Ireland's cultural elite; and he flourished there in the period before the first World War. He died of alcohol poisoning in 1931. Orpen has long been a favorite of mine, and I was thrilled by this summer's exhibition in Dublin, jointly sponsored by the National Gallery of Ireland and the Imperial War Museum in London. Like Whistler and Sargent, both of whom influenced him, Orpen became rich and celebrated as a portrait painter; he is perhaps undervalued by art historians for that reason. It is said that in his day queues of chauffeur-driven limousines formed outside his Chelsea studio.

A good portrait painter has to be adept at staging the scenes in his pictures, and Orpen was a master at making costume and stance count. His 1909 canvas of George Moore on one side of a table set for tea in some gentleman's club, clearly overawing with his presence five other men grouped on the other side of the table, including the painter Walter Sickert and the art patron Sir Hugh Lane, emphasizes by its placement of the figures Moore's force of personality. The late, unbuttoned portrait of the tenor John McCormack in a rumpled linen suit, his hair untidy, handsome features sagging, is a study in fatigue. The way Orpen poses the dim-wit Prince of Wales, later Duke of Windsor, in golfing togs, his features obscured by his golf cap, is a triumph of sly satire.

Orpen's work managed to be self-conscious and referential as early as 1899, in a way that is now called postmodern, while at the same time illuminating character and offering, in Matthew Arnold's phrase, "a criticism of life," impressing with its innovative eye for composition, crisp technique, and gorgeous painterly finish. He liked painting his friends and fellow artists and enjoyed alluding to other pictures. Augustus John was a favorite subject; Orpen's 1900 portrait of John quotes from Whistler's portrait of Thomas Carlyle—an allusion John didn't like, because when Whistler painted him, Carlyle was old and defeated, while John at the time of the portrait was at the height of his powers. In the painting of George Moore mentioned above, called *Homage to Manet*, a painting by the French master hangs on the wall above the tea table. There is a further play within a play here; Moore as a young man in Paris had been one of Manet's favorite sitters. It's no accident that his first painting to win notice, while he was still studying at the Slade, was a fanciful picture of an eighteenth-century audience watching the play scene from *Hamlet*. Augustus John embraces his fiancée to one side of the stage, Orpen's brother-in-law William Rothenstein explains to two ladies what is going on onstage, and Orpen himself crouches unnoticed among a group of spectators—all of them in period costume.

I can think of no painter other than Rembrandt who executed so many self-portraits. Orpen was short, and evidently thought he was ugly. He exaggerated such features as a protruding lower lip. In *The Dead Ptarmigan* he poses as a hunter, holding up the dead bird and staring defiantly out of the picture. In *The Jockey* he has painted himself in racing silks. In *Self-Portrait as Chardin* he stands before a half-finished canvas, brushes and easel in hand, wearing the buffoonish costume he wore to a fancy-dress party. Perhaps the strangest and most memorable of these works is the 1917 canvas, *To Start: Self-Portrait*, painted on the eve of his duties as an official war artist for the British government. We see Orpen staring out of the mirror with his searching eyes full of vulnerability, wearing the tin-pot helmet of World War I and a gorgeous fur waistcoat, standing against wallpaper of pink roses picked out against a background of army green. Out the window is a glimpse of houses that tells us we are in France, and in the foreground is an effortless grouping of books and liquor bottles. The mixture of frivolity and seriousness is both unsettling and captivating.

This is Orpen on the eve of his stint as a war artist, an experience that horrified him and taught him an admiration for the ordinary fighting man and a contempt for the diplomats and heads of state who, after tragically bungling the war, swanned into the negotiations at Versailles to patch together a peace treaty the results of which have bedeviled our world ever since. Abandoning the sumptuous finish of the society portraits he had done back in London, Orpen developed at the front a different palette, capable of capturing harsh sunlight on battlefield scenes or a strange, artificial green light where the landscape is illuminated by searchlights. According to Robert Upstone, this palette "of soft purples and mauves, white, and bright green . . . recalls the Post-Impressionist colouring and dry medium of painters like Spencer Gore and Harold Gilman."

These paintings and sketches show the desolation of the trenches, the dead and the wounded, the exhaustion of the Tommies, the ghoulish hilarity with which the armistice was celebrated in French towns. In *Changing Billets, Picardy*, dated 1918, searchlights probe an eerie sky above a horizon of half-destroyed houses and rubble, while in the foreground a helmeted Tommy in full battle dress embraces a young barefooted prostitute, as one of his comrades stretches out, exhausted, indifferent to the transaction.

Orpen is at his best in his paintings of women. The distance and irony with which he portrays men, including himself, disappear when a woman is his subject. Three paintings hanging side by side in this exhibit offer an exquisite contrast. Orpen's wife Grace, painted in 1907, is holding something of herself back; she is swathed in the elegant fabric of her dress, she is wearing long gloves, and her hat is topped by a veil. There is nothing intimate about the picture. *The Angler*, 1912, depicts the artist's friend and neighbor Vera Hone, arms crossed, holding a fly rod and wearing a blue hat with bird's wings, reminiscent of the helmet worn by the winged Apollo in Greek statuary. Orpen had learned Sargent's knack of showing the sitter both as herself and as the role she was playing in the painting. One senses a flirtatiousness between artist and model, and Vera Hone as she peers out from underneath the blue hat that is both silly and sublime seems to be indulging Orpen in his fantasy of her as a fisherman, while at the same time mockingly asking, "Why have you posed me in this silly way?"

The third of the three canvases, *Early Morning*, 1922, depicts Orpen's mistress, Yvonne Aubicq, gloriously in the nude, sitting up in bed. She is viewed from above, from a position of dominance, with a background of rumpled sheets, her golden hair undone, the morning coffee cup in her hand, a crumpled letter or two scattered about her. The white of the draped sheets and the coffee cup, the silver of the coffee pot and spoon, the gathered bits of black, yellow, and red bedclothes in the front right-hand corner of the canvas, all complement the sumptuousness of her flesh and hair. The theme of this show is "Politics, Sex and Death." Orpen addressed all three, and is an artist worthy of being much better known and acknowledged. Positioned between the attention-getting waves of Impressionism and Modernism, he suffers from the obscurity of that historical stage.

The poet Fred Johnston recently speculated in *The Irish Times* that, with all the current immigration, Ireland's next Nobel Prize winner might conceivably be born abroad. The country is struggling with changes that threaten its cultural identity. Recent reinterpretations of Irish tradition, such as Declan Kiberd's *Inventing Ireland*, have challenged the myth of Irish identity that has prevailed since Independence, the Civil

War, and the long domination by Eamon de Valera and his radical nationalist orthodoxy—the myth of a Catholic, Gaelic, essentialist Ireland where the country's multicultural roots were denied.

Even a glance at the country's Nobel Prize winners shows that the nationalist myth does not apply very well. Yeats, Shaw, and Beckett all came from Protestant, Anglo-Irish backgrounds. Yeats propounded the Anglo-Irish position eloquently and looked for Irish identity not through Catholicism but through the pagan Irish myths. Shaw, a socialist and freethinker, spoke from the bully pulpit of the London stage. Beckett was an exile in the tradition of Joyce, who felt more at home in Paris than in this country. Only Heaney comes anywhere near fitting the nationalist mold, and his is a much more international vision than de Valera would have begun to recognize.

Wilde, Synge, and Orpen, whose works have defined the past season in Dublin for me, exemplify Irishness as a much less static quality than the nationalist vision would recognize. Wilde in his theatrical works went right to the heart of establishment London to reveal its hypocrisies and insecurities; his Irishness gave him the insight of the outsider in English society. Synge embraced an Ireland that was not really his own by birth and background, becoming a most eloquent spokesman—despite his detractors who accuse him of a kind of stage Irishness—for the old life in the West. Orpen, a cosmopolite like Wilde, moved freely between Dublin and London. Though he engaged the new nationalism in a series of allegorical paintings that scathingly critiqued the religious and cultural narrowness of what was then the new Ireland, for him nationality was not a compelling issue. Synge, if he were to visit today's Ireland, would find that the life he immortalized has become a thing of the past. Wilde and Orpen would, I suspect, be able to navigate the currents of the new and future Ireland with ease.

2

Who Were the Anglo-Irish?

Hybrids, as horticulturists know, sometimes produce the most brilliant blossoms in the garden. Hybridization in human culture, particularly in the arts, can also have memorable results. Anglo-Irish writing, from Maria Edgeworth to William Trevor, has been one of the glories of literary art; but the term "Anglo-Irish" can be confusing, because it is sometimes applied to all literature written in English by Irish writers—as distinguished from literature in the Irish language, which is considerable.

Julian Moynahan, in his comprehensive and satisfyingly readable study *Anglo-Irish: The Literary Imagination in a Hyphenated Culture*, defines his subject as follows: "Anglo-Irish literature is the writing produced by that ascendant minority in Ireland, largely but not entirely English in point of origin, that tended to be Protestant and overwhelmingly loyal to the English crown, and had its power and privileges secured by the English civil and military presence." In political and economic terms the Protestant Ascendancy's golden age came during the last decades of the eighteenth century, when the Irish Parliament was able to assert its power vis-à-vis London as an independent governing body. This coincided with an inspired building boom that made Dublin one of the great Georgian capitals in Europe.

"Something shattering would have to happen," Moynahan writes, "to awaken the Ascendancy to reality and to show its members how they actually stood toward the English and toward their fellow-Irish before a genuine Anglo-Irish literature . . . could get under way." With almost uncanny timing the first demonstrably Anglo-Irish novel, *Castle Rackrent* by Maria Edgeworth, was published in 1800, the fateful year of the Act of Union, when the Ascendancy doomed itself to eventual extinction by voting, under heavy pressure from England, aided by thousands of pounds in bribes and promises of peerages for Irish grandees, for the dissolution of the Dublin parliament.

D uring the period from the late eighteenth century through the early twentieth, the underpinnings of Anglo-Irish power were steadily being eroded. Advocates of Home Rule were making their voices heard in the Parliament at Westminster. The Catholic Emancipation Act of 1829 brought the previously disenfranchised Irish majority into the political realm. Think of the implications of the following statement made by the Chief Chancellor of Ireland in the eighteenth century: "The law does not suppose any such person to exist as an Irish Roman Catholic"! Eighteen thirty-eight saw Parliament deny the (Protestant) Church of Ireland its right to exact tithes from the largely Roman Catholic population, and in the 1860s the Church of Ireland was disestablished altogether. The great famines of the 1840s depopulated the land through starvation, disease, and immigration, bankrupting in the process the landlord class, whose rents depended on the decimated peasantry. These disasters were followed by the Land Wars and finally by Gladstone's Land Law Act of 1881. Inexorably during the nineteenth century "the Ascendancy," in Moynahan's words, "becomes a Descendancy." Its literary golden age came during its long period of decline in the nineteenth and early twentieth centuries.

The literary history of the Anglo-Irish could credibly be said to begin earlier than 1800, with Jonathan Swift for example, but it was *Castle Rackrent* that laid the groundwork for this remarkable but relatively brief tradition. Prominent on the "check list of characteristics, if not a paradigm" that Julian Moynahan draws up as a guide to Anglo-Irish writing is "a focus on the fortunes or misfortunes of the rural proprietors and their families in the isolated estate houses of the Irish country districts as Anglo-Irish power and authority begin their long contraction and decline." The scenes of this body of literature are largely drawn from the countryside, and the rural settings lead naturally to another characteristic: a sense of loneliness and isolation that helps form the ethos that Yeats would define as "Anglo-Irish solitude."

The Anglo-Irish did not create an urban literature. By contrast, James Joyce, a contemporary of Somerville and Ross, wrote one of the great urban novels, *Ulysses* (published three years before *The Big House of Inver* by Somerville and Ross). It's interesting to speculate about the cultural differences that led Joyce to write a walkabout novel, naming his character after a legendary wanderer, at the same time that members of the established Irish ruling class focused on place and habitation. While the term "big-house literature" does not exhaust a taxonomy of their literary output, it goes far in that direction. It is striking how many novels by members of this class—planters and settlers, administrators, country gentlemen, daughters of gentry families—concern themselves with, are even named after, houses.

Starting with *Castle Rackrent*, the big-house novel was distinguished later in the course of its development by books like *The Big House of Inver*. Perhaps its swan song and at the same time its greatest achievement—certainly its most nuanced achievement, and a book where ambivalence attains a kind of sublimity—is *The Last September* by Elizabeth Bowen, where the action of the book takes place in the pivotal year of 1920. "As time passes since her death in 1973," Moynahan writes, "we are beginning to see Elizabeth Bowen as one of the very few great writers of prose fiction at work in Ireland and England between the end of the first World War and the end of the 1960s."

The mention of Bowen is a reminder that a large number of these writers were women. Literature was a nexus where the big houses intersected the psyches of the daughters of these houses. While the sons of Anglo-Irish families typically entered the law or the church, went to work at the bank, or became officers in the armed forces or the colonial administration of the British Empire, the daughters were often left at home to manage the house, which over and over again is described as a burden.

It is worth noting that both Edith Somerville and Elizabeth Bowen used the earnings from their fiction and journalism to shore up the declining fortunes of the family seat, without which Anglo-Irish identity threatened to dissolve, leaving their occupants stranded amongst and undistinguished from the "mere Irish." Their short stories and book reviews paid for paint and plaster, curtains and carpets, sherry and turnips, firewood and horseshoes. The battle between man-made habitation and the punishing Irish weather, where mold will appear on an interior wall overnight, is a recurring motif in this literature. The consciousness of decline and ruination, as in the literature of the American South—equally brilliant and equally brief— gives many of these stories of collapsing houses and old families gone to seed the poignancy of elegy and the dignity of classical tragedy.

As colorful, admirable, and appealing as the authors of these books and the characters in them can be—particularly given that we are viewing the class through its own eyes, with the notable exception of *Castle Rackrent*, where the family retainer recites the narrative of the family he at least nominally serves— it is well to remember that the Anglo-Irish were a ruling class imposed on the native population by the Crown. The fact that land forcibly taken from the Irish beginning in Elizabethan times was then rented back to them remains an injustice that cannot be excused, except perhaps when one notes that it represented the continuation of a feudal system that once prevailed throughout Europe and many other parts of the world. Dated, polemical, and partially discredited as it may be, Daniel Corkery's 1924 classic *The Hidden Ireland* is helpful in providing the other side of the Irish story, as is Brian Friel's *Translations*.

There is evidence of affectionate relations between some tenants and some landlords, and in the countryside even today, some of the old people remember or claim to remember which were the "good" landlords and which were the "bad." Rents were allowed to go into arrears in many cases, and during the Famine some landlords bankrupted themselves in an effort to save their tenants. Two men who died from "famine fever" while nursing their tenants during the Famine were Lady Gregory's father-in-law and Thomas Martin of Ballynahinch, a cousin of Martin Ross. In addition, it is said that the Anglo-Irish landlords were often more humane than the native Irish middlemen or "grabbers," like Roderick Lambert in *The Real Charlotte*, who bought up the old estates during the late nineteenth century and rackrented the tenants.

The flexibility of the landlord-tenant situation on some estates is hinted at in "Oh Love! Oh Fire!" from Somerville and Ross's *Some Experiences of an Irish R.M.*, during a party old Mrs. Knox throws for the tenants. Though well into her eighties, Mrs. Knox dances a jig, much to the delight of her guests. "They say," the narrator relates, "that that jig was twenty pounds in Mrs. Knox's pocket at the next rent day; but though this statement is open to doubt, I believe that if she and Flurry [her grandson] had taken the hat round there and then she would have got in the best part of her arrears."

Still, the Anglo-Irish remained, to a greater or lesser degree, interlopers. Referred to in the Irish language as "strangers" or simply "English," they stoutly regarded themselves as Irish and had very ambivalent attitudes toward England and the English. A good place to get a sense of this dilemma, this source of cultural schizophrenia, is *The Last September* of Elizabeth Bowen. The young heroine Lois looks down on the big house called Danielstown, modeled on Bowen's Court, from the mountains:

> The house seemed to be pressing down low in apprehension, hiding its face, as though it had her vision of where it was. It seemed to huddle its trees close in fright and amazement at the wide light lovely unloving country, the unwilling bosom whereon it was set.

Julian Moynahan, with a good eye for metaphor, comments: "She sees the estate as a jewel; others [the IRA], spying from the mountains and attacking from under the protective dusk of dense trees, see instead the chains by which jewels like Danielstown hung upon the 'unwilling bosom' of the country."

Anglo-Irish estrangement from their country of residence, as strangers in a strange land, was the source both of their existential insecurity and of a heightened awareness that gives their literature its edge. They developed, according to Moynahan, a "fascination, often a nervous one, with the lives of the 'peasantry,' that majority population of native Irish people who live surrounding and subordinate to the landlord class." The title of William Carleton's masterpiece, *Traits and Stories of the Irish Peasantry* (1830–33), is indicative of the "attitude of research" that the Anglo-Irish took toward the lives of the people. And this is one of the attitudes that links the Anglo-Irish to the ruling classes of colonized countries throughout the world.

The less knowledgeable a commentator is, however, the more likely he will be to link the Irish dilemma with colonialism or to speak of the country today as a postcolonial phenomenon when these terms don't quite fit. Whatever one's attitudes about the British Empire, however—and my own are nuanced and ambivalent—even the most convinced Anglophile must shake his head in disbelief at Britain's actions toward Ireland over the centuries: the brutality, for instance, with which Irish partisans in the 1798 Rising (brought to a wide audience by the great historical novelist Thomas Flanagan's best seller *The Year of the French*) were massacred, while the French officers who had led them were billeted in the best hotels in Dublin while awaiting repatriation. Or Britain's studied, Malthusian indifference to the starvation of hundreds of thousands of people during the Famine. More recent examples surrounding the Troubles in Northern Ireland abound, though they have become somewhat less blatant.

The Anglo-Irish were, of course, painfully aware of British callousness and incomprehension. Much of the humor in Somerville and Ross's stories comes from their strategy of placing the visiting Englishman in a position to misinterpret Irish life comically. The Honourable Basil Leigh Kelway in "Lisheen Races, Second-hand," for instance, comes over to Ireland on a junket, "collecting statistics . . . connected with the liquor question in Ireland," telling his friend Major Yeates, now an Irish Resident Magistrate, that "he thought of popularizing the subject in a novel, and therefore intended to, as he put it, 'master the brogue' before his return."

But what were the Anglo-Irish to do? Their very existence depended on being backed up by British might. The assessment of their position offered by a commentator on the famine of 1848 is harsh but has the ring of truth to it:

> They form no class of the Irish people or any other people. Strangers they are in the land they call theirs, strangers here and strangers everywhere, owning no country and owned by none; rejecting Ireland and rejected by England; tyrants to this island and slaves to another; here they stand . . . alone in the world and alone in its history, a class by themselves.

The bleakness of this view shows the background against which the immense achievement of Anglo-Irish literature has been created. Year by year from 1800 on, as their position became less and less tenable, the heart and pluck and humor of those whom Yeats called "the indomitable Irishry" built from words a hybrid body of work that will stand with the world's best.

Anglo-Ireland and its literature have flowered and gone to seed, dried up and blown away. The legacy, though, has to some extent hybridized itself into the continuing vitality of Ireland's literary culture. Seamus Heaney has gone to school both to Carleton and to Yeats. Though there is nothing hyphenated about his own imagination, Heaney like Carleton, Somerville and Ross, Bowen, and Yeats, has sometimes served as an interpreter of his own culture for a larger English-speaking readership. His mediation between the homely and the cosmopolitan, which was at the core of the Anglo-Irish literary project, is given voice in the poem "Making Strange." The poem tells of bringing a visitor to his home country. "I found myself driving the stranger," he writes,

> through my own country, adept
> at dialect, reciting my pride
> in all that I knew, that began to make strange
> at that same recitation.

The Uneasy World of
Somerville and Ross

"Let us take Carbery and grind its bones to make our bread," Violet Martin wrote in a letter to Edith Oenone Somerville in 1889, "and we will serve it up to the spectator so that its mother wouldn't know it." Violet (1862–1915) was then twenty-six years old, and Edith (1858–1949) thirty-one; the two second cousins had recently finished collaborating on their first novel, *An Irish Cousin*, which would be published in London later that year. Violet, who took the nom de plume of Martin Ross, was writing from her family's ancestral home, Ross House, near Oughterard in County Galway. The bones she proposed to grind were those of "that fair and far-away district, the Barony of West Carbery, County Cork," as Edith later called the place in her *Irish Memories*, "the ultimate corner of the ultimate speck of Europe—Ireland." Martin's humorous, off-the-cuff characterization is powerfully suggestive of the nature and purpose of their art.

In Somerville and Ross's world, social hierarchies are strictly observed. "That they were snobs—in one sense of that word," observes Conor Cruise O'Brien almost casually, followed naturally from the fact that they belonged to the Irish landed gentry. They had to look down on other people in order to see them. Or so they sincerely felt. And they wanted to see them clearly, to place them socially: "Catholic middle-class moving up"; "Protestant lower-middle class, stuck"; "Gentleman run wild, with touch of brogue." They wrote on these matters with an almost pedantic care for accuracy, within social conventions which they thoroughly understood and thoroughly approved.

Though they were worlds better off than the mass of the Irish peasantry at the end of the nineteenth century, the Anglo-Irish landed gentry that had at one time ruled the island from their "big houses" was fast losing ground to a newly emergent and resourceful middle class of merchants, professional men, land agents, and the like, who were buying up properties the Anglo-Irish were selling in the wake of recent land agitation. The famines of the 1840s, in which one-quarter of the population either died or was forced to emigrate, also ruined the landlords. As Gifford Lewis makes clear in the introduction to her edition of the Somerville and Ross letters, the Anglo-Irish, including the Martins and the Somervilles, had now, like the rest of the world, to earn their own living. And they did so resourcefully and with élan. Elizabeth Bowen had this to say on the subject in 1940:

> It is, I think, to the credit of big house people that they concealed their struggles with such nonchalance and for so long continued to throw about what did not really amount to much weight. It is to their credit that, with grass almost up their doors and hardly a sixpence to turn over, they continued to be resented by the rest of Ireland as being the heartless rich.

Sir Egerton Coghill and Hildegarde, Lady Coghill, Edith's brother-in-law and sister, went into the photography business and sold their pictures of the rugged West Cork shoreline to the tourist trade. Hildegarde managed a dairy herd and a violet farm from which she shipped flowers all over the British Isles. Violet Martin's mother sold her eggs and greengage plums in the market at Oughterard. In her later years we find Edith Somerville buying Irish horses and traveling to America to sell them while at the same time conducting lecture tours. The sons of these families went into the army, the navy, and the church. Robert Martin, Violet's brother, who should by right have become the master of the Ross estate, which in the seventeenth century had amounted to some 200,000 acres, was a political journalist and writer of popular songs in London. Some of the female cousins became doctors or journalists, or wrote children's books.

The most common solution to financial insecurity for the daughters of impoverished gentry families, though, was marriage. Gifford Lewis, whose *Somerville and Ross: The World of the Irish R.M.* (1985) I draw on heavily here, puts it this way: "Many an English officer took home an Anglo-Irish bride to sighs of relief in many a damp drawing-room." The haven of marriage did not appeal to Edith Somerville: her long engagement to an Oxford don, Herbert Greene, forms a kind of running gag in letters and diaries throughout most of her adult life. Somerville determined early on that she would provide for herself. Soon after the two cousins met, in 1886, their diaries contain items like "Various literary labours till tea time." The collaboration is characterized in its early stages as little more than an amusement: "We began to invent a plot for a penny thriller," Edith wrote in her diary about two years before publication of the book, which its authors and their families called "the shocker." "At it all day, except when we went down to help at the Christmas tree. Shockered far into the night."

Fiction writing appears in the diaries and letters as an amusement akin to the charades, amateur theatricals, jumble sales, charity dances, and hunt balls that made up the social life of Castletownshend, the village where Edith Somerville grew up, and in whose life Violet Martin came increasingly to play a part as the friendship and collaboration grew. "Castle Townshend" (the name is spelled variously), as described in *Irish Memories*, "is a small village in the southwest of the county of Cork, unique in many ways among Irish villages, incomparable in the beauty of its surroundings, remarkable in its high level of civilization, and in the number of its 'quality houses.'" The last point is particularly worth noting. Most of the Anglo-Irish lived at great geographical remove from one another. What made Castletownshend special was the presence of several gentry families who had settled there in the time of Cromwell, prospered, intermarried, attended the same church, and saw one another daily.

D espite one's sense that the work of art must speak for itself, the biography and peripheral works of one's favorite authors, those rare spirits who have left behind living monuments made of words, exercise a powerful fascination. Somerville and Ross were alive during the great days of diary-keeping and letter-writing. Their diaries (which are in the library at Queens University, Belfast) and letters (many of which can be found in the Berg Collection at the New York Public Library) make pleasurable reading in themselves; moreover, one can see how valuable these private writings were to the two cousins as writers of fiction.

At first Edith and Martin lived about 150 miles apart over roads dusty or muddy by season, whose condition can only be imagined—though even today, and even in the summer, can turn a man's thoughts toward religion. Since theirs was a collaborative process in which scenes and sentences by one partner would be reworked and revised by the other, letters were of the utmost value. In letters one of these quite different but complementary sensibilities attempted to explain itself to the other. On the small island of Ireland, postal service was and is more efficient than in the United States—so efficient that return addresses are not routinely written on letters. Very often an anecdote from a letter would later be spun out into a story or an episode in a novel.

In 1886 the two cousins set about writing for fun *The Buddh Dictionary*, a lexicon of words commonly used by their interrelated families, all of whom were directly descended from a distinguished ancestor, Charles Kendal Bushe, Lord Chief Justice of Ireland. Family pride and self-regard apparently led the two young women to identify in themselves and their relatives a Buddha-like self-sufficiency and contentment, which they simultaneously celebrated and satirized as "Buddh." Acquaintances who fit more or less into their social class but who were not Buddhs were "suburbans"—and this included most of those English people to whom the aristocratic residents of Castletownshend rented their houses during the summers to gain some much needed income while they camped out with relatives. Edith Somerville's brother-in-law, a baronet, moved his family onto his schooner for the summer while the big house earned rent. It was cooler on the water anyway.

To decipher Buddh words is to enter a more than hundred-year-old private language of subtle, idiosyncratic, and sometimes mildly off-color wit. "I must decant," a lady might say to her relatives, leaving the room to relieve herself. A Buddh- or Bushe-leg was a limb of unusually large size—a physical trait evidently genetic. A lady's large hat might be "flangey." (Edith Somerville, known for the extravagance of her headgear, appeared at a wedding in 1944, when she was eighty-six, wearing a hat topped by a stuffed seagull.) Some Buddh words were based on Irish: a "flahoola" is defined as "a large loud woman of a stupendous vulgarity." Others derive from Latin: to "absquatulate" was to express oneself loudly and vociferously. Anything *de trop* might be summed up as "Kneebuckles to a Highlander" (who, since he wore a kilt, would not need them).

For reasons that remain mysterious, there are times, places, and people that seem to have more richness, more charm, more character than other times, places, and people. Ireland in the eighteenth and nineteenth centuries must have been just such a place. And the Irish, high and low, were and are such a people. Part of it is their linguistic genius. The sweeping, poetic gesture—often used ironically—is ready to hand: "We walked that half-mile in funereal procession behind the car," says Major Yeates, narrator of the Irish R.M. stories; "the glory had departed from the weather." The homely domestic simile appears with unforced ease: "'What did she say?' Charlotte darted the question at Norry as a dog snaps at a piece of meat."

Of Christopher Dysart in *The Real Charlotte*, a servant declares, "Shure he's the gentlest crayture ever came into a house." (In her memoirs Edith Somerville applies the same characterization to her father.) "Sure a Turk itself wouldn't be a match for her!" someone remarks of a character in the R.M. stories. "That one has a tongue that'd clip a hedge!" Flurry McCarthy Knox (whose last name is emphatically British and Protestant, while his middle name is that of the ancient kings of Munster), scoundrel hero of the Irish R.M. stories, when asked about whether there might be a suitable four-year-old horse for sale, replies, using a trope that is still to be heard in Ireland: "There isn't a four-year-old in this country that I'd be seen dead with at a pig fair."

Between their first novel, *An Irish Cousin*, and their masterpiece, *The Real Charlotte* (1884), came a novel about the Land Wars called *Naboth's Vineyard* and two travel books. *Through Connemara in a Governess Cart*, where they reported on their native Ireland for an English audience, and *To the Vine Country*, which took them to France, were both commissioned by the *Lady's Pictorial* and illustrated with drawings by Edith Somerville, who had studied art in Paris and was a gifted painter and draftsman. She wryly dismisses the activity that engendered the travel books as "Tours, Idle Tours." But in *The Real Charlotte* they achieved what must, consciously or unconsciously, be the goal of all writers: they wrote the book that they alone, by temperament, experience, and gifts, could have brought into being.

Charlotte Mullen is one of the nineteenth century's most complex, unhappy, and convincing villains—sympathetic and repellent at the same time. Mention Somerville and Ross to most readers—those who have heard of them at all—and what will come to mind is a romanticized view of Anglo-Irish life in the days before the Republic, replete with sentimentalized, stage-Irish characters. How far this notion is from the actuality of these authors' vision! They understood human nature and knew their world much too thoroughly for such prettification, and they seem to have been compelled to write the book by some irresistible fascination with the darker side of humanity. In *Irish Memories* Edith Somerville invokes the biblical proportions of this fascination when she writes that "those unattractive beings, Charlotte Mullen, Roddy Lambert, The Turkey-Hen [Lambert's first wife], entered like the plague of frogs into our kneading-troughs, our wash-tubs, our bedchambers."

A contemporary review in the *Lady's Pictorial* shows how far *The Real Charlotte* departed from the reading public's taste in literary accounts of the Irish, with their supposed "happy go-lucky mode of life, the curious mingling of shrewdness and childishness, the vulgarity which is offensive only when it becomes snobbish, and the irrepressible love of fun and frolic. . . ." Yet these very qualities, when rescued from pejorative construance, are just what helps make *The Real Charlotte* such a powerful novel. The late Terence de Vere White, writing in the *Irish Times*, provokes a comparison between it and Joyce's masterpiece: "Leaving the huge whale—*Ulysses*—basking off-shore, what better Irish novel is there than *The Real Charlotte*?"

Somerville and Ross were too grounded in the mud and stables and kitchens of country life to be tempted by Joyce's flirtations with classical myth—and perhaps, unlike Joyce, they were too satisfied with the life they led to go looking for the extra dimension that myth added to his view of urban Irish life during the same period. Otherwise, what these two novels have decisively in common is a vigorous realism, in strong reaction to the sentimentality and florid rhetoric of the nineteenth-century Irish tradition, which Yeats himself only escaped when he was blindsided by modernism.

The realism that offended the genteel literary establishment of their time may be traced to Somerville and Ross's knowledge of all levels of Irish society. As I have pointed out, big-house life in Ireland was not really very grand. The Anglo-Irish had few Bridesheads to boast of. Master and servant lived on terms of mutual interdependency and even intimacy. Gifford Lewis comments: "Hildegarde's Bridget Driscoll and Gungie Minehan, and Edith's Mike Hurly, were members of the household in a way inexplicable to English visitors. Edith once turned her rage on a Drishane house guest because she had 'treated Mike like a servant.'" Their intimacy with the female side of belowstairs life added another dimension for the cousins' fiction:

> Edith and Martin happened to be in many unusual places and wrote about aspects of Irish life previously unseen or unnoticed by the centre-stage male; they enjoyed laundries, kitchens, boot cupboards, ashpits—in short, places frequented by servants, most of whom were women. . . . It was the authors' familiarity with the poor, poverty, dirt and ugliness that repelled many readers of *Charlotte*.

Few other authors have captured so well the sense of the makeshift and slipshod in Irish life. In discussing the work of Maria Edgeworth in his *Irish Classics*, Declan Kiberd makes the following observation:

[The] substitution of one thing (the personal) for another (the public) will become a central technique of *Castle Rackrent*, whether a slate is made to replace a broken window or, indeed, the form of the English novel is replaced by that of the Irish anecdote as more appropriate to a makeshift world. If Gibbon and Fielding produced epics in tragic or comic mode and at appropriate length, here is an oral *glissade* which will narrate the history of four generations in scarcely sixty pages.

The use of anecdote to substitute for the classic Flaubertian short story becomes a notable feature of the Irish R.M. stories.

For readers who fall under the spell of Somerville and Ross's world, the continuity between actual and fictional realms provides many little pleasures. The saga of a mother cat named Jubila and her kittens, recounted in Violet Martin's letters, which coincides with Martin's and her mother's efforts to reclaim and refurbish Ross House after having lived away from it for years, makes very clear how heavily her fiction drew on daily life, and how thoroughly the wit in the stories represented the wit of the letter writers (as well as adumbrating an attitude that today would be called elitist):

> The cat, being in labour, selected as her refuge the old oven in the kitchen, a bricked cavern, warm, lofty, and secluded. Here among bottles, rags, and other concealments she nourished and brought up her young in great calm till the day that Andy set to work at the kitchen chimney. . . . I was fortunately pervading space on that day, and came in time to see a dense black cloud issuing from the oven mouth. I yelled to a vague assembly of Bridgets in the servants hall, all of whom were sufficiently dirty to bear a little more

without injury. . . . For the rest of the day Jubila cleaned herself with her children in the coldest parts of the house, with ostentatious fury and frump . . .

It is not far, as the imagination flies, from the kitchen at Ross to Tally Ho, the residence of Charlotte Mullen. The Tally Ho kitchen, of which the authors write with an almost perceptible shudder, is a species of that minor hell of squalor and disorder that seems to lie in wait for the Protestant middle class whenever it loses its tenuous grip on respectability. Here Charlotte's servant, Norry the Boat, sulks and grumbles against her mistreatment by her mistress while the omnipresent cats roam where they will:

The objects in the kitchen were scarcely more than visible in the dirty lights of a hanging lamp, and the smell of paraffin filled the air. . . . A door at the end of the kitchen opened into a scullery of the usual prosaic, not to say odorous kind, which was now a cavern of darkness, traversed by twin green stars that moved to and fro as the lights move on a river at night, and looked like anything but what they were, the eyes of cats prowling around a scullery sink.

Another world that Somerville and Ross knew about were those parts of Dublin occupied not by the desperately poor, but by those lower-middle-class Protestant clerical workers and minor office functionaries who clung to the coattails of the professions, government, and commerce. When Violet Martin's mother closed Ross House in the early 1870s and took her five daughters to the capital so that they could go to school and meet Dublin society, the young Martin got some taste of a city that must have seemed very much a backwater, particularly in summer, when those who could afford to had gone away to the seashore or the country. Francie Fitzpatrick, the orphaned heroine of the book, who later has the fatal ill luck to get between

Charlotte and her goals, lives here with her aunt and uncle. This is the scene on which *The Real Charlotte* opens:

> An August Sunday afternoon in the north side of Dublin. Epitome of all that is hot, arid, and empty. Tall brick houses, browbeating each other in gloomy respectability across the white streets; broad pavements, promenaded mainly by the nomadic cat; stifling squares, wherein the infant of unfashionable parentage is taken for the daily baking that is its substitute for the breezes and the press of perambulators on the Bray Esplanade or the Kingston pier.

Later in the novel, Francie returns to Dublin in disgrace after her flirtation with the caddish English officer Hawkins in the more elevated society of Lismoyle, where her cousin Charlotte lives. Francie's aunt and uncle have now come down even further in the world and are living in Bray in a shabby little house, which was "just saved from the artisan level by a tiny bow window on either side of the hall door, and the name, Albatross Villa, painted on the gateposts." If genius is attention to detail, the firm of Somerville and Ross never disappoints the reader in its deployment of little touches like "Uncle Robert, arranging a greasy satin tie under his beard at the looking glass, preparatory to catching the 8:30 train to Dublin" and "the fact that Bridget put on the coal with her fingers was recorded on the edges of the plates."

The center of the novel—the center of its action and of the book's moral questioning—is Charlotte Mullen, whom we first meet on the night her aunt dies at Tally Ho, the house Charlotte is to inherit from the old lady. "Probably at no moment of her forty years of life had Miss Charlotte Mullen looked more startlingly plain than now, as she stood, her squat figure draped in a magenta flannel dressing gown." At once it is established how unattractive Charlotte is, how intelligent, and how capable:

> Charlotte took the tiny wrist in her hand, and felt the pulse with professional attention. Her broad, perceptive finger-tips gauged the forces of the little thread that was jerking in the thin network of tendons, and as she laid the hand down she said to herself, "She'll not last out the turn of the night."

"Where's little Francie? You mustn't send her away, Charlotte; you promised you'd take care of her, didn't you, Charlotte?" are old Mrs. Mullen's dying words. "'Yes, yes,' said Charlotte quickly . . . 'never fear, I'll see after her'"—a deathbed pledge that bitterly foreshadows the plot of the novel, because Charlotte's machinations eventually result in the ruination and death of her young cousin. Julian Moynahan points out astutely in *Anglo-Irish: The Literary Imagination in a Hyphenated Culture*, "The house name, from the place Violet Martin stayed during her first visit to Castletownshend, is perfect for conveying the note of false heartiness and cheer that Charlotte often sounds in company, especially among her equals and betters."

What makes Charlotte so compelling a character is that physically and morally unattractive as she may be, she is at the same time impressively capable in practical matters, as well as being the intellectual superior of everyone else in the book:

> Her neighbours never forgot to mention, in describing her, the awe-inspiring fact that she "took in the English *Times* and the *Saturday Review*, and read every word of them," but it was hinted that the bookshelves that her own capable hands had put up in her bedroom held a large proportion of works of fiction of a startlingly advanced kind, "and" it was generally added in tones of mystery, "many of them French."

Charlotte was evidently modeled on a distant cousin of Edith's who had cheated her out of an inheritance, and for the book's authors the key to her motivation was the maxim, "Hell holds no fury like a woman scorned"—a maxim she demonstrates, chillingly, in several different instances. For years Charlotte has been carrying a torch for Roddy Lambert, estate agent for the aristocratic Dysart family—a position Charlotte's father had held. Lambert, having started out as Charlotte's father's protégé, has over the years been Charlotte's as well. She has lent him money, given him advice, and collaborated with him on business deals. There are hints of an earlier flirtation between the two of them, before Roddy married "the turkey-hen" for her money. Roddy is not shy about using his masculine charms to their full advantage, as is clear from the following exchange between them on the possibility of his stabling horses on a small estate belonging to the Dysarts called Gurthnamuckla, which she might take over if a way can be found of evicting its current tenant:

"Well, if you'll get me Gurthnamuckla," said Charlotte with a laugh, in which nervousness was strangely apparent, "you may buy up every young horse in the country and stable them in the parlour, so long as you'll leave the attics for me and the cats."

Lambert turned his head upon its cushion, and looked at her.

"I think I'll leave you a little more space than that, Charlotte, if ever we stable our horses together."

She glanced at him, as aware of the double entendre, and as stirred by it as he had intended her to be. Perhaps a little more than he had intended.

Charlotte's ruthlessness is startling, and the aggregate effect of it takes the reader by surprise, because the authors narrate each action she takes in such an understated manner. Having managed, as the book opens, to inherit her aunt's property by promising to take care of young Francie, she succeeds in triggering a heart attack in Lambert's wife, by agitating the sickly "turkey-hen" when she tells the unfortunate lady of Lambert's infatuation with the beautiful young Francie. While Mrs. Lambert collapses, calling out for her "drops," Charlotte does nothing—instead seizing the opportunity occasioned by the woman's unconsciousness to read, propelled by her obsessive jealousy, Lambert's love letters to Francie. Death held a powerful fascination for Violet Martin, and one can detect her hand in this description of Charlotte's reaction to the death:

> She dropped on her knees beside the motionless, tumbled figure on the floor. "She's dead! She's dead!" she cried out, and as if in protest against her own words she flung water upon the unresisting face, and tried to force the drops between the closed teeth. But the face never altered; it only acquired momentarily the immovable placidity of death, that asserted itself in silence, and gave the feeble features a supreme dignity, in spite of the thin dabbled fringe and the gold ear-rings and brooch, that were instinct with the vulgarities of life.

Several more chilling opportunities remain for "the real Charlotte" to emerge from beneath the comfortable persona she presents to the provincial Irish town where she lives. Later, in the triumphant comedies of the Irish R.M. stories, which would make the firm of Somerville and Ross an Anglo-Irish icon, the two cousins hit on a mode that hid social truths beneath caricature and accommodation. But in *The Real Charlotte*, in their thirties, they managed to touch, uncomfortably, the quick of Irish life at a time of cataclysmic change.

A re distinguished works of art more likely to occur— as received opinion has it—in moments of social tranquility than in times of turmoil and transition? Or, on the other hand, has the world ever seen an age that was not an age of transition? Whatever nostalgia she and her collaborator may have felt toward what Martin called "the quietness of untroubled centuries" in Ireland, their genius lay in evoking the strains of the transitional times in which they lived, when the Protestant Ascendancy, their own class, was well on its way to extinction. I don't recall a single letter or diary entry suggesting that these two women set out to write "political" books. It may simply be that, caught up as they were in the great social changes that characterized their time, they could not do otherwise.

Their major characters are all trying to get on, and if possible, to rise through the shifting currents of change in their country: Lambert, whose "raw Limerick brogue" betrays itself in moments of stress; Francie, who Christopher Dysart thinks "must be a nice girl somehow not to have been more vulgar than she was"; even Captain Hawkins, infatuated with Francie but feeling compelled to marry a boring English girl for her money. And especially the real Charlotte, whose father was a land agent but who is moved to say to Christopher Dysart, "your poor father would tell you if he was able, that the Butlers of Tally Ho were as well known in their time as the Dysarts of Bruff!" "Yes, indeed," she adds:

> "as good a family as any in the country. People laugh at me, and say I'm mad about family and pedigree; but I declare to goodness, Mr Dysart, I think the French are right when they say, *'bong song ne poo mongtir,'* and there's nothing like good blood after all."

I wonder whether Conor Cruise O'Brien's disapproving assessment of Somerville and Ross, quoted earlier, is quite fair. To hold them to the democratic standards of our own age would be to require from these turn-of-the-century women attitudes that in their own times would have seemed utopian and bizarrely unrealistic. Certainly, however class-conscious they were, they were also aware how deeply implicated they and their characters—beneficiaries and victims of the English conquest of the island—were in the ironies and tragedies of Irish history. Francie is thrown from her horse and killed when she and her English officer blunder into a Catholic funeral procession. This happens because "heedless of the etiquette that required that she and Hawkins should stop their horses till the funeral passed," she rides in among the mourners. Startled by the "Irish Cry" of ritual mourning, her horse throws her and breaks her neck. "The faces in the carts were all turned upon her, and she felt as if she were enduring, in a dream, the eyes of an implacable tribunal."

Travels through Somerville and Ross's Ireland

R eaders of Somerville and Ross's novels and Irish R.M. stories will have formed their own mental pictures of the characters and settings found in the writings of the two literary second cousins. Real people resembling their fictional characters, being creatures of the late nineteenth and early twentieth centuries, have long since vanished from the Irish scene. But many places associated with Edith Somerville of County Cork and Violet Martin, penname Martin Ross, of County Galway remain to be visited and savored.

The imposing limestone mass of Ross House, which Martin Ross characterized in a memoir as "a tall, unlovely block, of great solidity," is visible overlooking Ross Lake east of the road between Moycullen and Oughterard north of Galway City. Its owners, George and Elizabeth McLaughlin, have plastered over the bare stone and had it smartly painted. They call the place Ross Castle. The Martins, one of the legendary Tribes of Galway, came to Ireland with Strongbow during the reign of Henry II and became the greatest landowners in Connacht with an estate of some 200,000 acres. They retained their Roman Catholicism until Violet Martin's great-grandfather converted, to marry one of the local Protestant O'Haras. Ross House dates from 1590, but all that remains of the sixteenth-century structure are its groin-vaulted cellars. The three-story Georgian mansion that exists today was built in 1755 following a devastating fire in 1740. The older house is said to have had mahogany floors taken from ships that foundered in the rough seas off the Galway coast.

The house was sold by its last Martin owners in 1925 and suffered another fire in 1930, which gutted the interior. It has been lovingly restored and may be visited for a small fee. The McLaughlins have made a striking mantelpiece in their dining room from an ancient marriage stone they found lying overgrown with weeds outside the stables. The stone joins the Martin coat of arms—a cross flanked on either side by the sun and the moon—with the Lynch crest, whose three shamrocks are a familiar adornment both at Lynch's Castle and St. Nicholas' Church in Galway.

Anyone undertaking a Somerville and Ross pilgrimage might want to stay at nearby Currarevagh House, where Violet Martin attended dances and parties, on Lough Corrib four miles from Oughterard. The proprietor, Mr. Harry Hodgson, has a collection of Somerville and Ross first editions as well as a set of Edith Somerville's illustrations for *Slipper's ABC of Foxhunting*. Violet and her sister Geraldine's drive to the Hodgsons' in August 1888, described in a letter, turned out to be more memorable than the party itself: "We started at nine in the pitch darkness just before moon rise, and as soon as we got into the road remembered with some apprehension that it was the night of the Oughterard races, and the roads would be full of carts with drunken drivers." The hilarious and hair-raising account of the drive, of shouting back and forth to drunken revelers and dodging carts in the dark, became raw material for the carriage wreck in the story "Lisheen Races, Second-hand."

Somerville and Ross drew closely from life. Shreelane—the fictional house of "the Irish R.M.," Major Yeates—"a tall, ugly house of three storeys high, its walls faced with weather-beaten slates, the windows staring, narrow, and vacant," resembles nothing so much as Ross House before its refurbishment. Edith's drawing of the front door of Shreelane, printed in illustrated editions of the *Experiences of an Irish R.M.*, was clearly the front door of Ross.

The most vivid impressions of these two great chroniclers of Anglo-Irish life are to be found not in Galway, however, but in Castletownshend, located in a remote part of County Cork. This seaside town, with its crowds of cousins, its parties, its comings and goings, was altogether more cheerful than Martin's house in the remote Galway countryside. It is still cheerful today. The town's main thoroughfare, which divides to go around "the two trees"—sycamores planted in the middle of the street in what Edith Somerville described as "a sort of giant flowerpot built of rough stones"—descends precipitously to the harbor, which is busy with yachts and sailing and fishing boats. Mary Ann's Bar and Restaurant—dark, low-ceilinged, decorated with nautical maps, ships' bells, coach lamps, an old clock, and local memorabilia—is everything a pub in a seaside town should be.

Drishane, Glen Barrahane, Cosheen, and Seafield, the Somerville, Coghill, and Townshend/Chavasse family houses, are not open to the public. But Mrs. R. M. Salter-Townshend takes guests at the Castle, a Georgian house with neo-Gothic castellations, from which the village takes its name. Two square towers squat at either end of the two-story central block, which was built around 1700. The house is replete with family portraits, an impressive display of coats of arms, old swords, old china, and furniture.

The guest rooms have names, not numbers: the Colonel's Room, Beryl, and Army, which has a small balcony. My room, the Studio, was twice the size of most bed and breakfast or guesthouse rooms. There are enough creaky floors and trophies of past glory to delight any reader of Molly Keane's novels. As I sat at the window of my room, a heron flapped slowly over the water, a yacht came in on sail, a father and son from the village fished off the breakwater. At a little distance from the house stands a tower folly with creeper growing up one side of it.

St. Barrahane's Church, uphill from the Castle, is a little neo-Gothic gem, very simple and Anglican inside, with memorial windows dedicated to the local families—some of them by the twentieth-century master of stained glass, Harry Clarke. Petit-point seat cushions surround a limestone baptismal font placed in a raised alcove on the north side of the nave. Edith Somerville, who was organist and choir-director here for most of her life, designed the fine mosaic pavement in the chancel. She and Martin Ross are buried in an atmosphere of peace and seclusion behind the church on a windy hill above the town and harbor.

The Asymmetrical
George Moore

O nce numbered among the best-known authors
and most controversial literary figures of his day,
George Moore has been relegated to a footnote on the Irish
Literary Revival in the first decade or so of the twentieth century. Moore's most important book remains the three-part *Hail
and Farewell (Ave, Salve, Vale)*, his door-stopper of a memoir
of his life in Ireland during the Revival. Hemingway included
the book in his short list of prose works a young writer must
read. In bringing Moore and his times to life in a copiously foot-
noted biography of more than six hundred pages, *George Moore,
1852–1933*, Adrian Frazier has produced a fascinating picture
of this Anglo-Irish writer, a man of many contradictions, immense initiative, and energy, one of the most multifaceted writers of his own or any time.

Moore was born in 1852, the oldest son of George Henry
Moore, Member of Parliament from County Mayo, a Catholic
landlord, horseman, and famous orator from an old landown-
ing family, who defended the rights of Ireland's impoverished
Catholic tenant class. When his father died in 1870 the young
George found himself heir to Moore Hall, a Palladian mansion
overlooking Lough Carra in the west of Ireland with an estate of

over twelve thousand acres, yielding a sizeable income. The first of many instances of irreverence in a career filled with a determination to shock occurred when the young heir realized that his father's death made him glad, because it "gave me the power to create myself."

Moore's childhood had not been ideal. His appearance was odd, and his parents succeeded in making him feel stupid. From early days on, an air of the ridiculous—in looks, manner, and opinions—attended Moore. But it was a ridiculousness backed by self-confidence. Thus was born Moore the defiant contrarian. "To be ridiculous has always been *mon petit luxe*," he writes in *Salve*, "but can anyone be said to be ridiculous if he knows that he is ridiculous?" The sublime poet W. B. Yeats, his sometime friend and chief foil in his Dublin years, is occasionally described by contemporaries as ridiculous, but was personally oblivious, apparently, to this aspect of himself. By Moore's standards, then, Yeats was truly ridiculous, while Moore, who built his persona on it, was not.

"It is the plain duty of every Irishman," Moore wrote in *Ave*, "to disassociate himself from all memories of Ireland—Ireland being a fatal disease, fatal to Englishmen and doubly fatal to Irishmen." In this rejection he prefigured the young James Joyce. Moore at first thought he wanted to be a painter, and this took him to Paris, where he became not an artist but a critic of art. The young man who had rejected his role as Moore of Moore Hall (which is how in his years of literary eminence his publishers would designate him) had by his mid-twenties become acquainted with Manet and Zola and placed himself in the thick of the new developments in Paris: Naturalism and Impressionism. Manet was fascinated by Moore's strange looks, and the young Irishman became the subject of several works by the great French painter:

Is it my fault if Moore looks like a squashed egg yolk and if his face is all lopsided? Anyway, the same applies to everybody's face and this passion for symmetry is the plague of our time. There is no symmetry in nature.

Manet's *Portrait of George Moore* (1879) is astonishing in its Impressionistic approach to human likeness. The right eye is ringed in burnt umber; around the left is an almost bruised-looking circle of light purple. The chestnut beard is a study in chaos, the ear like a wobbly slice of aubergine. On each side of Moore's head above the ears, his hair is teased out like two extended points of a waxed moustache. His fleshy lips, his frank and curious eyes, express a look of bafflement. In his *Autobiographies* Yeats skewered him as "a man carved out of a turnip, looking out of astonished eyes." Yet behind this "squashed egg yolk," if one looks at it with some knowledge of Moore's character, lie self-possession and determination.

His Paris years were formative. In the cultural capital of the world, the young man who had been an awkward schoolboy only a few years before found himself taken seriously by the leading figures of the French avant-garde. He bought paintings that formed the basis of a distinguished personal collection. In the English-speaking world he would become known as the "discoverer" of Manet and would later write two influential books on what was then the *dernier cri* in art, *Modern Painting* and *Reminiscences of the Impressionist Painters*. Most of all he would adapt from Manet his personal motto, "Be ashamed of nothing but to be ashamed"—a dubious philosophy, but it was what made George Moore who he was.

For Moore the ephebic novelist, exposure to the naturalism championed by Zola provided an all-important orientation for his entire career. Just as he was helping introduce Impressionism to the English art world, he wrote about Zola for the London periodicals. Zola was the model for Moore's realistic novels like

A Mummer's Wife and *Esther Waters*. Early on, he wrote of himself as *un ricochet de Zola en Angleterre*.

Events in Ireland precipitated an end to his Parisian idyll. The formation of the Land League in 1879—the same year Manet painted Moore's portrait in Paris—would change things forever for Irish landlords. Moore's letter to his estate agent shows him in his guise as conservative landowner: "This question of the tenants refusing to pay rent is horrible! What does it mean—communism? If you dont [*sic*] get the rents what is to be done?" Almost as soon as the news came, Moore settled his affairs in Paris and returned to Moore Hall, where, soon after, he declared on the side of Parnell and Home Rule. But his heart was not, and never would be, in Irish politics. He was first and foremost an aesthete and a man who would make his living by writing: "Of all the latest tricks that had been played with French verse," he wrote in a series of letters for *Le Figaro* that was later published in book form as *Parnell and His Island*, "he was thoroughly the master; of the size, situation, and condition of his property he knew [nothing]. Indeed he hated all allusion to be made to it, and he looked forward with positive horror to meeting his tenants."

For the immediate future, Moore's working life lay in London. There he could earn the living that the Land Wars in Ireland were increasingly depriving him of. As a late-nineteenth-century scion of the *rentier* class pursuing authorship as a form of support, he resembles Edith Somerville and Martin Ross. Adrian Frazier gives an exhaustive account of the author's early career as a literary comer in London. The young Irishman was extraordinarily adept, both as a literary politician and, more tellingly, as a tireless writer of poems, reviews, and novels, in making his way in the English capital. "I am working hard for fame," he wrote his mother back in County Mayo, "and I think I shall succeed. I feel that I must conquer. I am conscious that I am a force, rather that I am becoming a force."

Traditionally the route to fame for an Irish writer has led through the capital city of the empire of which Ireland used to be a part. In the eighteenth century the Irish-born playwright Richard Brinsley Sheridan needed the London stage as a platform for his success. In Moore's own times, Oscar Wilde and William Butler Yeats preceded him as Irishmen who mastered the game of literary politics in London. George Bernard Shaw, who knew Moore before he made his name as a novelist, was yet another Irishman who reached the top of the heap in the capital city. Shaw's comments on Moore, as reported by an earlier biographer, are telling:

> "There was always a certain delicacy about George and he knew how to be a gentleman when he wanted to." However, he was "always telling stories about himself and women"; the stories usually ended up with the woman throwing a lamp at George. "If you said," Shaw recalled, "'But George, don't talk such nonsense, you are making it all up,' he was not in the least put out . . . but just said, 'Don't interrupt me,' and went on as before." Shaw lost sight of Moore. Then one day William Archer said he had been reading a wonderful naturalist novel by a new author. Shaw asked who it was. "Well," Archer replied, "his name is George Moore." "'Nonsense,' Shaw replied. 'But I *know* George Moore. He couldn't possibly write a real book. He couldn't possibly do anything.' But there it was. He had written it, and then I began to understand the incredible industry of the man."

High praise coming from one of the most industrious writers who ever lived! As he went back and forth between thriving, late-Victorian London and an Ireland shaken by agitation on behalf of tenants' rights and the drive toward Home Rule under Charles Stewart Parnell, Moore began a lifelong friendship with Edward Martyn, a man whose background and activities paralleled his own. Martyn's estate, Tillyra Castle, lay only a few miles from Coole Park, Lady Gregory's house near Gort, a dozen miles from Galway City. "Edward," in Frazier's words, "was a 'woman-hater,' the contemporary phrase for a man who loved men, though for all that Edward was a misogynist as well."

Though markedly limited in his literary talents, Martyn was a key figure in the Literary Revival. He was present at the meeting at Mount Vernon, Lady Gregory's seaside house in Dooras, near Kinvara, where plans were laid for the "Celtic Literary Theatre," which would become the Irish National Theatre. (Moore was in London writing fiction when this meeting took place.) Martyn wrote his play *The Heather Field* from a synopsis by Moore, and it appeared as part of a twin bill with Yeats's *Countess Cathleen* at the opening of the Irish Literary Theatre, which was to become the Abbey, in 1899. The homosexuality of Martyn's youth appears to have been sublimated into a strict, celibate Catholicism as he aged. In addition to the literary patronage he offered such ventures as the National Theatre, he was a major patron of St. Brendan's Cathedral in the town of Loughrea, not far from Tillyra, which is decorated with outstanding examples of modern Irish stained glass by Irish artists such as Sarah Purser and Harry Clarke.

Nothing could have induced the "slightly fat, slightly balding, and large-booted" Martyn to marry—despite his mother's anxiety on that score and the expensive annexe she built at Tillyra in the 1880s "to suit," as Frazier puts it, "Edward's hypothetical wife." On a personal note, I wangled an invitation to Tillyra some years ago from the owners, a couple from Texas who had traded a large yacht for the place and were unaware of its literary-historical significance. It is as fine an example of the neo-Gothic as you will see, but few people see it because it is not open to the public. By contrast, practically every literary tourist in Ireland goes to Coole Park just down the road, where Lady Gregory's house was torn down years ago. The chief delight of visiting Tillyra, however, is not the "new" part but the twelfth-century tower house, where Edward Martyn retreated from his mother's matrimonial schemes. I quote Frazier's description of the eccentric aesthete-turned-ascetic's domicile:

> Up the steep stair of the tower, on the first stage Martyn had set up his private place of worship, with a seven-foot-tall candlestick, and a wooden chair copied from a picture by Durer; on the next stage was the study, lit by Pre-Raphaelite stained-glass windows just completed in 1883 in London by Edward Frampton: the saints depicted are Chaucer, Milton, Dante, Shakespeare, and Plato. The bedroom at the top had a flagstone floor, a slightly cramped oak four-poster (hardly big enough for two) made in 1616. Beside it was Edward's prie-dieu, kneeler, and prayer rail. Cloistered and encastled, Martyn had built his aesthetic stronghold against his mother's matrimonial plans.

Readers of Yeats's *Autobiographies* will recall that on a visit to Tillyra the great Irish poet, staying in the room in the tower above Martyn's, conducted a seance, during which the spirits, as spirits will, pounded on the table and thrashed around the room. Martyn, disturbed both by the noise and by the intrusion of paganism into his inner sanctum, prevailed upon Yeats to desist.

Moore evidently was less resistant to the idea of marriage than Martyn was, and in 1883–84 he courted Maud Browne, the daughter of his mother's sister. In this brief courtship as in all circumstances, Moore proved himself to be a man on whom nothing is lost. His attendance at the Dublin "season," which centered around the Shelbourne Hotel on St. Stephen's Green and the State Ball at Dublin Castle, where matches were arranged between the marriageable young women and the eligible young men of Irish society, allowed him to do research from the inside on the high-end marriage market in Ireland. While his cousin Maud accepted George as a suitor, her family rejected the match. "I consider everything now over between Maud and me," he wrote his mother, "but I shall never forget the horrible system of terrorism to which she has been subjected." The result of his experiences was *A Drama in Muslin*, which was published in 1886.

The book presents itself as a conventional women's novel of the late Victorian age while at the same time essaying many subterfuges and veiled explorations of unconventional and unsanctioned areas of life. In a plot device suggestive of Maeve Binchy's *Circle of Friends*, it begins tamely enough as the story of a group of Irish schoolmates at the Convent of the Holy Child in England and then follows their adventures as they return to their homes in County Galway and then go up to Dublin for the Castle Ball social season I have touched on above. Old money in the person of Lord Dungory, a vainglorious old roué, cooperates with new money in the person of Mrs. Barton, whose ambition through much of the book is to marry her beautiful daughter Olive to a marquis. Though the marquis's only hope of avoiding financial ruin is to marry someone like Olive, who will bring to the marriage a hefty dowry, he does the improvident thing and marries for love. As befits the tact of the age, we are never told clearly that Mrs. Barton and Lord Dungory are lovers until we overhear a conversation between the two on the train as they return from Dublin to Galway. Even then the reader is shielded from the implications of their conversation unless he or she knows French. The two are discussing the latest outrage, a murder in the Irish midlands whose commission has been facilitated by the lawless conditions that prevailed during the Land Wars.

> "I wonder," said Mrs. Barton, "what those wretches will have to do before the Government will consent to suspend the Habeas Corpus Act, and place the country in the hands of the military. Do they never think of how wickedly they are behaving, and of how God will punish them when they die? Do they never think of their immortal souls?"
>
> "*L'ame du paysan se vautre dans la boue comme la mienne se plait dans la soie.*"

"Dans la soie! dans la soie! oh, ce milord, ce milord!"

"Oui, madame," he added, lowering his voice, *"dans le blanc paradis de ton corsage."*

What makes the novel's political commentary so effective is the effortlessness of it. Moore never strains to make a point, because the living conditions of the peasantry, the oafishness of the provincial Catholic clergy, the frivolity of the *rentier* class were all out in plain view for anyone with eyes to see. Here is how word of the Phoenix Park murders, a pivotal act of terrorism that shocked the ruling establishment in 1882, comes to one gentry dinner table:

> At that moment the butler entered the room with an entree. Speaking to Mr. Barton he said:
>
> "Very dreadful news has just been received in Gort, sir: Lord Frederick Cavendish and Mr. Burke were murdered last night in the Phoenix Park."
>
> The knives and forks dropped clinking on the plates as the entire company looked up with white terror painted on their faces. Mr. Adair was the first to speak:
>
> "This is," he said, "an infamous and lying report that has been put into circulation. . . ."
>
> "It is, unfortunately, quite true, sir; it is in all the Sunday papers."

The agitation for land reform and Home Rule was so unignorable that it seeps inexorably into every conversation in Ireland. It even gives the much-sought-after marquis a chance to escape from the clutches of the marriage his hostess is trying to bribe him into: "I'm afraid I must leave you tomorrow, Mrs. Barton. I shall have to run over to London to vote in the House of Lords."

The novel's most celebrated scene is the procession of carriages headed for the Viceroy's reception at Dublin Castle, seat of British rule in Ireland:

Notwithstanding the terrible weather the streets were lined with vagrants, patriots, waifs, idlers of all sorts and kinds. Plenty of girls of sixteen and eighteen come out to see the "finery." Poor little things in battered bonnets and draggled skirts, who would dream upon ten shillings a week; a drunken mother striving to hush a child that cries beneath a dripping shawl; a harlot embittered by feelings of commercial resentment; troops of labourers battered and bruised with toil: you see their hang-dog faces, their thin coats, their shirts torn and revealing the beast-like hair on their chests; you see also the Irish-Americans, with their sinister faces, and broad-brimmed hats, standing scowling beneath the pale flickering gas-lamps, and, when the block brought the carriages to a standstill, sometimes no more than a foot of space separated their occupants from the crowd on the pavement's edge. Never were poverty and wealth brought into plainer proximity. In the broad glare of the carriage lights the shape of every feature, even the colour of the eyes, every glance, every detail of dress, every stain of misery were revealed to the silken exquisites who, a little frightened, strove to hide themselves within the scented shadows of their broughams: and, in like manner, the bloom on every aristocratic cheek, the glitter of every diamond, the richness of every plume were visible to the avid eyes of those who stood without in the wet and the cold.

"I wish they would not stare so,' said Mrs. Barton; "one would think they were a lot of hungry children looking into a sweetmeat shop. The police really ought to prevent it."

A decade and a half would pass between *A Drama in Muslin* and Moore's return from England to Ireland at the beginning of the new century. This was the period of his blockbuster naturalistic novel, *Esther Waters*, his canvas for exploring those he described to his brother as "the people I love and understand—the dull Saxon. Flesh of my flesh, bone of my bone—how I love that thick-witted race. . . . I want to paint the portrait of the Saxon in his habit of instinctive hypocrisy . . . the Cotton Factory behind him starting from the cricket field." This was also the period of his long affair with Maud Burke, Lady Cunard. Speculation is that Moore was the father of Nancy Cunard; in any case an affectionate friendship between the two developed, and she wrote a memoir of Moore that gives an intimate picture of him at his leisure. When she asked him if she was indeed his daughter he replied, "Oh my Lord! Never ask your mother that!"

During the period of his eminence as an English man of letters, Moore met Yeats in London and began to be drawn, little by little, into the Irish literary scene. Frazier's answer to the question "Why did George Moore, like a cosmopolitan Lord Jim, make a standing jump from all that he had known for the last thirty years into the strange seas of Dublin political life?" is that, in addition to several personal factors, he was motivated by "an ambition to be a playwright with an audience and a fascination with literary adventures (such as the possibility of being the father of a new literature in an ancient language), a sense of rejection as an Irish Catholic by English society and the hope of acceptance within Ireland as a distinguished national figure. Within and above these threadlike factors there was the hovering design of the great spider spinning its self-pleasing thread even while being suspended by it." Moore was going to expose himself to that disease "fatal to Englishmen and doubly fatal to Irishmen," which he had defined Ireland as being. The result was his masterpiece, the three-part memoir called *Hail and Farewell.*

Hail and Farewell, which weighs in at just under seven hundred pages, is a rambling memoir to be dipped into, thumbed through, set down and picked up again later. But for anyone wishing to get the flavor of upper-middle-class Anglo-Irish Dublin when the Irish Literary Revival was coming into flower, it remains the essential on-the-ground book to read, despite Moore's ill-tempered dismissal of the Revival: "There is no literary revival. There is only one man, Mr. Synge, and he has written only one really beautiful play, 'The Well of the Saints.'" It is a book filled with quarrels: Moore's quarrel with the materialistic England to which he owed his success, with his brother, with Yeats, with his lifelong friend Edward Martyn, but particularly with Roman Catholicism. This is a subject on which Moore expatiates at tiresome lengths. It was the major bee in Moore's bonnet, and his animadversions on the Church obviously carried over into his conversation. Nancy Cunard notes: "even those who disliked him or whom he made uncomfortable could not deny that he was a beautiful conversationalist. Yet the subjects, the subjects! Was it really permissible to go on so much, for instance, about Catholicism, in such a flippant vein?"

This quarrel almost sinks *Hail and Farewell*, as it threatens to sink even the novel *A Drama in Muslin*. Some historians argue that the Church sustained the Irish people through centuries of hard times and British domination. Moore felt that it had become a millstone around Ireland's neck. With all its carry-on about Ireland's ancient myths and heroes, the Literary Revival can be seen as a last-ditch effort by the Protestant ruling class, having lost the Land Wars of the nineteenth century, to define Irishness in a way that would eliminate the Catholic Church from the picture, and thus include themselves at the center. "The plot of the trilogy as a whole," Frazier writes, "is really a conceit: Moore comes to Ireland on a mission, like an aesthetic St. Paul or St. Patrick; but his aim is to save the Irish *from* Catholicism. . . . Through the whole trilogy . . . there repeatedly sounds a requiem to the Irish Ascendancy, passing away amid eccentric plans for regeneration, while the Roman Catholic Church builds an empire on its ruins." Having freed themselves from Britain in the War of Independence in the 1920s, many would say that Ireland would later become enmeshed in the struggle to free herself from the domination of the Church. In the first decade of the twenty-first century, it would seem that the Irish have liberated themselves from a second dominating power.

Religion and politics aside, *Hail and Farewell* is a great book of gossip, table talk, and portraits of fascinating people. There was no moment of the day during which Moore stopped being a writer, and it is not surprising that he "spoke of Dublin," as Frazier puts it, "not as home but as his 'workshop.'" His life was "copy." Ely Place, where Moore lived, was a choice address, and he gave memorable dinner parties, with rare wines that seldom made it over to provincial Dublin otherwise. After dinner, one guest noted, "Moore listened, smoking his cigar, and, unlike his guest, seldom lifting the wine-glass to his lips." Moore was a bit of a cad in his books as in his life. The artist Sarah Purser said of Moore, "Some men kiss and tell; Moore tells but doesn't kiss."

George Russell (pen name Æ) wrote to the literary and artistic patron John Quinn in New York: "one half of Dublin is afraid it will be in [*Hail and Farewell*], and the other is afraid that it won't." As with many writers, betrayal came easily to Moore, and his remarks on Edward Martyn's sexual predilections are an early example of "outing." He promised Martyn that "on the subject . . . there is not a word in my book, I assure you." In fact, however, Moore's little ways are a running gag throughout the book. Noting the small harmonium in Martyn's rooms, Moore surmises: "one can only think it serves to give the keynote to a choir-boy." "Every Saturday night," Frazier summarizes, "before the Sunday performance of his specially endowed Palestrina choir at Dublin's Pro-Cathedral, Edward takes a boy home to listen to his singing."

As for Moore himself, Adrian Frazier judges him to be "a homosexual man who loved to make love to women." Anomalous as this definition of George Moore may be, it is no more anomalous than many other things about him, and it may make some sense of the pleasure he took in torturing poor Edward Martyn in print. Moore analyzed his own sexual nature as follows:

> Never before me has the soul of a man been so embroiled with that of a woman, and to explain the abnormality of my sexual sympathy for women, I can only imagine that before my birth there was some hesitation in the womb about the sex. Nevertheless, I was a happy boy and excellent sportsman: once I had a horse between my legs or a gun in my hands, I left behind all those morbid imaginations, all strange desires to travesty women, to wear their little boots and peignoirs.

Frazier comments: "That horse and gun are good: there were plenty of conscious jokes about 'phallic symbols' before Freud."

Born to the life of a country gentleman, Moore quickly surmised that fulfillment for him lay elsewhere. The life of a writer meant renouncing the ideal of the gentleman, which was a powerful force still in Moore's day. Yeats saw and disapproved of Moore's lack of gentlemanly discretion when he first read *Ave*, remarking, "there isn't the smallest recognition of the difference between public and private life" in the book. Moore's weakness for cruel gossip was merely the underside of an artistic credo that leads Frazier to identify his subject as one of the first modernists. Significantly, the first thing Moore did when he went to Paris as a young man was to send his valet home: "his presence stood between me and myself; I wished above all things to be myself. . . . Myself was the goal I was making for, instinctively if you will, but still making for it." He praised Manet because, though the painter had been "born in what is known as refined society," and was "in dress and appearance" an aristocrat, he was savvy enough to "avoid polite society."

Moore as an Irish nationalist differs from others in the movement by his complete lack of idealism and patriotic sentiment. It was not some revolutionary utopian temperament that led Moore to observations on the disgraceful inequalities of Irish life such as those I have quoted from *A Drama in Muslin*. Perhaps it was having been brought up with an insider's view of the frivolity and lack of social responsibility of the Anglo-Irish ruling class that emboldened him in his condemnation of the way power was exercised in the country, but the position was obvious. Moore knew his inherited class had no future—certainly not in Ireland. As a personality, he rises above the times in which he lived, just as he rose above the social position into which he was born. This singular man's greatest creation, over and above the millions of words he wrote in the course of a long, laborious career, was that unique and asymmetrical man, George Moore.

Elizabeth Bowen:
The House, the Hotel,
and the Child

To read Elizabeth Bowen is to enter, both with pleasure and with consternation, the world of the Anglo-Irish in their decline. By the time Bowen was born, in 1899, the shadows of what Mark Bence-Jones has called (in his 1987 book of the same name) the "Twilight of the Ascendancy" had already lengthened. Though she spent most of her adult life in England, and London is in some ways the center of her fictional world, Elizabeth Bowen was the daughter of a County Cork big house called Bowen's Court, which she inherited and, unable to afford its upkeep on her earnings as a writer, eventually had to sell in 1959.

The alienation of the Anglo-Irish landowner, set above and isolated from the "native" population, is a vantage point to which Bowen refers often in writing of Ireland. "I have grown up," she writes in her essay "The Big House" (1940), "accustomed to seeing out of my windows nothing but grass, sky, trees, to being enclosed in a ring of almost complete silence and to making journeys for anything that I want." Visiting these houses today as a guest or a tourist, one feels the uncanny accuracy with which Bowen captures the strangeness emanating from these grey limestone piles. Palladian or neo-Gothic, set starkly against the primal green of the Irish countryside:

> Each house seems to live under its own spell, and that is the spell that falls on the visitor from the moment he passes in at the gates. The ring of woods inside the demesne wall conceals, at first, the whole demesne from the eye: this looks, from the road, like a *bois dormant* with a great glade inside. Inside the gates the avenue often describes loops, to make itself of still more extravagant length; it is sometimes arched by beeches, sometimes silent with moss. On each side lie those tree-studded grass spaces we Anglo-Irish call lawns and English people puzzle us by speaking of as "the park." On these browse cattle, or there may be horses out on the grass. A second gate—(generally white-painted, so that one may not drive into it in the dark)—keeps these away from the house in its inner circle of trees. Having shut this clanking white gate behind one, one takes the last reach of avenue and meets the faded, dark-windowed and somehow hypnotic stare of the big house. Often a line of mountains rises above it, or a river is seen through a break in woods. But the house, in its silence, seems to be contemplating the swell or fall of its own lawns.

The sense of the house "contemplating" its surroundings is pure Bowen—one of many instances of a house as a living entity: an Irish house or just any house. In her novel *The House in Paris* (1949), she writes: "The cautious steps of women when something has happened came downstairs, sending vibrations up the spine of the house." Just how remote, how starved these houses felt when their day had passed, can be gathered from the opening sentences of *The Last September* (1939):

About six o'clock the sound of a motor, collected out of the wide country and narrowed under the trees of the avenue, brought the household out in excitement on to the steps. Up among the beeches, a thin iron gate twanged; the car slid out of a net of shadow down the slope to the house. Behind the flashing windscreen Mr. and Mrs. Montmorency produced—arms waving and a wild escape to the wind of her mauve motor veil—an agitation of greeting. They were long-promised visitors.

Many of the Anglo-Irish found it convenient to forget how they came by their land in the first place. In *Bowen's Court* (1942, revised 1964), her classic family history, and elsewhere, Elizabeth Bowen does not shy away from admitting that her original Welsh ancestor (the name Bowen derives from Welsh *ap Owen,* "son of Owen") was granted land taken from the defeated Irish owners as booty from Oliver Cromwell's campaign to put down the rebellion of the 1640s. At the same time she unapologetically makes a claim for the value of the country-house culture founded by people of her class. This culture, molded in the age of Gandon and Swift and Burke, retained in its architecture and literary style the clean lines of classicism. And Bowen saw in big-house life, too, a ritualistic element that harks back to the Middle Ages. How the housemaid Matchett in *The Death of the Heart* (1938) prepares for the night in the London establishment that she serves is informed by her English country house training:

> About now [i.e., about 10:30 P.M.], she served the idea of sleep with a series of little ceremonials—laying out night clothes, levelling fallen pillows, hospitably opening up the beds. Kneeling to turn on bedroom fires, stooping to slip bottles between sheets, she seemed to abase herself to the overcoming night. The impassive solemnity of her preparations made a sort of an altar of each bed: in big houses in

which things are done properly, there is always the religious element.

As its last owner, Elizabeth Bowen describes Bowen's Court, built in 1776, as "a high bare Italianate house" and elsewhere as a "great bare block," "severely classical." Like Newbridge in County Dublin, Castle Ward in County Down, the ruin of Tyrone House in County Galway, and many another Irish big house, Bowen's Court, which was pulled down in 1960, was an austere rectangle of limestone that dominated the landscape from its imposing elevation.

For the full flavor of the Anglo-Irish in their ridin', fishin', and shootin' prime, the reader should turn to Somerville and Ross, who picture an Anglo-Irish ruling class characterized by vigor, *sang-froid*, eccentricity, and a habit of command, at ease with their neighbors among the native Irish. As we saw in the previous chapter, theirs is a world where a favorite hunting dog wipes his muddy paws on a priceless Persian rug, where the squire goes on a tear with the poacher. The Resident Magistrate of Somerville and Ross's stories adjudicated—often with hilarious results—the disputes of the Catholic majority, while other members of this group functioned in the Irish economy as large farmers, bankers, merchants, and administrators. The never less than outspoken Edith Somerville reprimanded her brother, who had written her that he had come to regard himself as English: "Nonsense about being 'English'! I don't mind if you say 'British' if you like. . . . My family has eaten Irish food and shared Irish life for nearly three hundred years, and if that doesn't make me Irish I might as well say I was Scotch, or Norman, or Pre-Diluvian!"

The attenuation and malaise one feels among Bowen's characters spring, historically, from the growing isolation of the Anglo-Irish in an Ireland increasingly bent on controlling its own destiny and increasingly successful in moving toward that goal. Only four years after Bowen was born, the Wyndham

Act—engineered by George Wyndham, Chief Secretary for Ireland at the turn of the last century—was passed, enabling landlords to sell their farms to their tenants in transactions financed by the government, with an added bonus of 12 percent paid by the British treasury. By 1914 three-fourths of the former tenants had bought the lands they farmed, leaving landlords with only their big houses and a few hundred acres of surrounding land. This put them in the position of being (relatively) rich men living in islands of leisure, with no useful function in what would become the new nation. "The story is told," writes Mark Bence-Jones, "of how when Wyndham was walking through one of the gaming rooms at Monte Carlo a few years after the passing of his Act, he was greeted by an Irish peer of his acquaintance who pointed to the large pile of counters in front of him and said gratefully: 'George, George, the Bonus!'"

I would not want to suggest that such irresponsible attitudes toward the ownership of property in a poor country were typical: in landed or monied classes the socially responsible and the scrupulous always coexist cheek by jowl with the callous and the profligate. *The Last September*, set in 1920 during the Troubles of that period, is Bowen's most sustained look at the predicament of Anglo-Irish big-house people—caught between the nationalist agitation of the Irish with whom, temperamentally, they feel they have much in common, and the protection of the British military, whom they really don't like very much. Perhaps because of their hyphenated position between England and Ireland, the Anglo-Irish have produced several masters of the comedy of manners—Oscar Wilde, Richard Brinsley Sheridan, and William Trevor among them. Bowen's writings are sprinkled with delicious little moments of social comedy, and the latitude she allows herself in using the omniscient point of view lets us see into the minds of widely incompatible characters whose thoughts are inaccessible to each other. Here, in *The Last September*, we have a British officer's wife, Mrs. Vermont, and an

Irish lady, Mrs. Carey, conversing at a tea and tennis party at a country house called Danielstown:

> "Hoity-toity!" thought Betty Vermont (she never used the expression aloud, as she was not certain how one pronounced it: it was one of her inner luxuries). Turning to Mrs Carey (the Honourable Mrs Carey), who sat on her other side, she said frankly:
> "Your scrumptious Irish teas make a perfect piggy-wig of me. And dining-room tea, of course, makes me a kiddy again."
> "Does it really?" said Mrs Carey, and helped herself placidly to another slice of chocolate cake. She thought of Mrs Vermont as "a little person" and feared she detected in her a tendency, common to most English people, to talk about her inside. She often wondered if the War had not made everybody from England a little commoner. She added pleasantly: "This chocolate cake is a specialty of Danielstown's. I believe it's a charm they make it by, not a recipe."
> "Things do run in families, don't they! Now I am sure you've all got ghosts."
> "I can't think of any," said Mrs Carey, accepting another cup of tea.

Just three years before the date when *The Last September* takes place, Edith Somerville wrote in *Irish Memories* of "English people whose honesty and innocence would be more endearing, if they were a little less overlaid by condescension." The patronizing tone adopted seemingly unconsciously by the English when speaking about the Irish shows little sign of abating even in our own day. The revulsion and hostility occasioned by IRA bombs going off near the Bank of England, by the mortar attacks on Heathrow Airport, were made all the more virulent by the sense that one was being betrayed by people who had been considered to be loyally subservient. I have heard the same language from Israelis of the kibbutz generation who speak of "our Arabs" who then become "the terrorists."

Speaking to an Anglo-Irishwoman, Mrs. Vermont will naturally presume that they are both of the same breed, unaware how complicated questions of identity were for the Anglo-Irish, who thought of themselves as Irish, while to their tenants they were "the English." This was brought home to me recently in a conversation with a friend from Connemara who, despite her republican politics, was a great fan of Elizabeth Bowen. I was speaking to her of the ease with which Bowen used French words in her writing. "Yes of course," my friend said. "That would have been typical for an Englishwoman of her time."

To return to our conversation between Mrs. Vermont and Mrs. Carey, here are the terms in which the English officer's wife commiserates with her Anglo-Irish acquaintance concerning the armed rebels in the hills above her house:

"All this is terrible for you all, isn't it? I do think you're so sporting the way you just stay where you are and keep going on. Who would ever have thought the Irish would turn out so disloyal—I mean, of course, the lower classes! I remember Mother saying in 1916—you know, when that dreadful rebellion broke out—she said 'This *has* been a shock to me; I never shall feel the same about the Irish again.' You see, she had brought us all up as kiddies to be so keen on the Irish, and Irish songs. I still have a little bog-oak pig she brought me back from an exhibition. She always said they were the most humorous people in the world, and with hearts of gold. Though of course we had none of us ever been in Ireland."

If you add to the isolation common to members of her class in the twentieth century the peculiar circumstances of Elizabeth Bowen's childhood, you find yourself face to face with an individual perilously, heroically it seems to me, cut off from nurturing influences. Her father, Henry, broke with a family tradition that expected the master of Bowen's Court to live there and manage the affairs of the estate. He studied law, eventually becoming an examiner of landlords' titles for the Irish Land Commission, and set up housekeeping in Dublin. After suffering a nervous breakdown apparently brought on by overwork, Henry Bowen succumbed to a mental illness that lasted for the rest of his life. His daughter responded with a "campaign of not noticing," which may be related to the subtlety and indirectness of her fiction: the reader must often follow barely detectable nuances in the development of character and plot. Not uncommonly in Bowen's work, something that is never mentioned—or that is alluded to only ten pages later—may be the most important thing going on in the story.

"I had come out of the tension and mystery of my father's illness, the apprehensive silence or chaotic shoutings," Bowen would later write, "with nothing more disastrous than a stammer." Artists in any field must turn defects into distinctions, and she would turn her speech impediment to advantage. As an internal British Council memo regarding Bowen as a lecturer put it in 1950: "She is a *most* successful lecturer with a *most* successful stammer."

With Henry Bowen confined to a mental hospital near Dublin, his wife and daughter left for England, where they bounced from one relative and one rented house to another. In 1912 her mother told her sister-in-law, "I have good news, now I'm going to see what Heaven's like." She had cancer, and she died when Elizabeth was thirteen. As Victoria Glendinning writes in her biography, "One of the words at which her stammer consistently baulked her was 'mother.'"

From her first novel, *The Hotel* (1927), to her last, *Eva Trout* (1968), the isolated or orphaned girl is a recurring character in

Bowen's fiction: the girl who lives much of her life in hotels, the girl who gets fobbed off on relatives. In *The Death of the Heart*, Bowen's best-known novel, Portia, the isolated, in-the-way girl, with her outsider's point of view, reminds one of the way Robert Lowell writes of himself as a child: "I wasn't a child at all— / unseen and all-seeing, I was Agrippina / in the Golden House of Nero." The conflict with which *The Death of the Heart* opens is initiated when Portia's sister-in-law, Anna, finds and reads her diary, which contains disturbing though vague comments about Anna and St. Quentin, Anna's presumed lover. I say "presumed" because Bowen is not one to make such relationships explicit. "Fancy her watching me!" St. Quentin exclaims. "What a little monster she must be. And she looks so aloof." Anna responds: "She does not seem to think you are a snake in the grass, though she sees a good deal of grass for a snake to be in. There does not seem to be a single thing that she misses."

Portia Quayne is the daughter of a love-match. Her father, an older man, has fallen in love with Irene—this is his daughter-in-law Anna telling the story—"A scrap of a widow, ever so plucky, just back from China, with damp little hands, a husky voice and defective tear-ducts that gave her eyes always a rather swimmy look." How unerringly Bowen places her characters in these thumbnail sketches: "[Irene] had a prostrated way of looking at you," continues Anna,

> "and that fluffy, bird's-nesty hair that hair pins get lost in. At that time, she must have been about twenty-nine. She knew almost nobody, but because she was so plucky, someone had got her a job in a flowershop. She lived in a flatlet in Notting Hill Gate. . . . I often think of those dawns in Notting Hill Gate with Irene leaking tears and looking for hairpins, and Mr Quayne sitting up denouncing himself. . . . She would not be everyone's money. You may be sure that she let Mr Quayne know that her little life was from now on entirely in his hands. By the end of those ten days he

Elizabeth Bowen

cannot have known, himself, whether he was a big brute or St George."

No fool like an old fool, of course, and Mr. Quayne confesses the affair to his wife. "Mrs. Quayne was quite as splendid as ever: she stopped Mr. Quayne crying, then went straight down to the kitchen and made tea." Before he knows it, the poor man has been kicked out of his comfortable country house and finds himself living out the rest of his life on a reduced income with his new little family of three in hotels, pensions, and rented villas in the least fashionable parts of the Riviera. Portia's half-brother and his wife, Anna, take the orphan to live with them after both her parents have died. "A house *is* quiet, after a hotel," Portia tells her brother. "In a way, I am not used to it yet. In hotels you keep hearing other people, and in flats you had to be quiet for fear they should hear you."

Perhaps it is the habit of keeping quiet and listening that has sharpened Portia's attentiveness to the nuances of life in her new surroundings. "Mother and I got fond of it, in some ways. We used to make up stories about the people at dinner, and it was fun to watch people come and go." This outsider's point of view—cold-eyed, without illusions—places Portia beyond the cosy circle of civilized mutual accommodation practiced by Anna and Thomas, and thus makes their visitor a dangerous presence.

What Portia's inner wounds might be, we are never quite sure. Of her mother, the child's constant companion, we learn little, even about the circumstances of her final illness. We only catch a glimpse—poignant for anyone who has ever lived on the cheap in Europe during the off-season—of the last little pension where they lived in Switzerland:

they always stayed in places before the season, when the funicular was not working yet. . . . Their room, though it was a back room facing into the pine woods, had a balcony; they would run away from the salon and spend the long wet afternoons there. They would lie down covered with coats leaving the window open, smelling the wet woodwork, hearing the gutters run. Turn abouts, they would read aloud to each other the Tauchnitz novels they had bought in Lucerne. Things for tea, the little stove and a bottle of violet of methylated spirits stood on the wobbly commode between their beds, and at four o'clock Portia would make tea. They ate, in alternate mouthfuls, block chocolate and *brioche*. Postcards they liked, and Irene's and Portia's sketches were pinned to the pine walls.

And finally we see them leaving:

When they left that high-up village, when they left for ever, the big hotels were just being thrown open, the funicular would begin in another day. They drove down in a fly, down the familiar zigzag, Irene moaning and clutching Portia's hand. Portia could not weep at leaving the village, because her mother was in such pain. But she used to think of it while she waited at the Lucerne clinic, where Irene had the operation and died: she died at six in the evening, which had always been their happiest hour.

In Anna's relations with Thomas Quayne, one guesses there is something of Elizabeth Bowen's own marriage to Alan Cameron, an ex-army officer who bored the London literary crowd—perhaps deliberately, as a way of getting even for being ignored—by telling long war stories. One anecdote that Victoria Glendinning repeats has a guest at a Bowen's Court party, while searching through the old house trying to find a lavatory, opening a door and finding Alan Cameron "alone in a small room eating his supper off a tray." Thomas chafes in his study with a large whiskey while Anna has her tête-à-têtes with her friend St. Quentin and the *enfant terrible* Eddie, whose relations with Anna are even more equivocal than what the reader surmises about those with St. Quentin. The situation might remind someone who has read Bowen's biography of Mr. Cameron's complaints about the "Black Hats"—so called from the rows of men's hats hanging in the hall of their house in Regent's Park when he would come home from his office at the BBC—who visited his wife. Theirs was a complex and interesting marriage in which romance was less a factor than a mutual dependence and affection. "I never saw real strain or needling between them," May Sarton writes, "never for a second. Love affairs were a counterpoint."

Perhaps drawing parallels between marriages, fictional and real, even after husband and wife are dead, is an exercise in frivolous presumption. In *The Death of the Heart*, at any rate, Anna is rattled by her young sister-in-law's observant eye. "I cannot stand being watched. She watches us." Bowen renders the tense accommodation between Anna and Thomas with her own keen eye:

> She posted herself at the far side of the fire, in her close-fitting black dress, with her folded arms locked, wrapped up in tense thoughts. For those minutes of silence, Thomas fixed on her his considering eyes. Then he got up, took her by one elbow and angrily kissed her. "I'm never with you," he said.
>
> "Well, look how we live."
>
> "The way we live is hopeless."
>
> Anna said, much more kindly: "Darling, don't be neurotic. I have had such a day."
>
> He left her and looked round for his glass again. Meanwhile, he said to himself in a quoting voice: "We are minor in everything but our passions."
>
> "Wherever did you read that?"
>
> "Nowhere: I woke up and heard myself saying it, one night."

"How pompous you were in the night. I'm so glad I was asleep."

In a house galvanized by these tensions, only Matchett, the impassive family retainer, one of the best serious portraits of a servant in fiction since Proust's Françoise, has very definite ideas about what is to be done with Portia. And with Bowen's beautifully specific imagination, the details of Matchett's standards ring with authenticity:

> Matchett's ideas must date from the family house, where the young ladies, with bows on flowing horsetails of hair, supped upstairs with their governess, making toast, telling stories, telling each other's fortunes with apple peel. In the home of today there is no place for the miss: she has got to sink or swim. But Matchett, upstairs and down with her solid impassive tread, did not recognize that some tracts no longer exist. She seemed, instead, to detect some lack of life in the house, some organic failure in its propriety. Lack in the Quaynes' life of family custom seemed not only to disorientate Matchett but to rouse her contempt—family custom, partly kind, partly cruel, that has long been rationalised away. In this airy vivacious house, all mirrors and polish, there was no place where shadows lodged, no point where feeling could thicken.

Portia, like Bowen's other orphans, is in dire need of affection, unequipped by her experience with the means to ask for love. She turns to the massively self-controlled Matchett, whose very name tells us how stiff and contained a creature she is. A poignant scene in *The Death of the Heart* has Matchett sitting on Portia's bed, reluctantly drawn into the sort of confidential talk Portia ought to be having with her sister-in-law if Anna were not so cold:

Elizabeth Bowen

"She had a right, of course, to be where I am this minute," Matchett went on in a cold, dispassionate voice. "I've no call to be dawdling up here, not with all that sewing." Her weight stiffened on the bed; drawing herself up straight she folded her arms sternly, as though locking love for ever from her breast. Portia saw her outline against the window and knew this was not pique but arrogant rectitude—which sent her voice into distance two tones away. "I have my duties," she said, "and you should look for your fond-ofs where it is more proper."

Matchett is only one of the servants who appear in Bowen's pages—though a distinction should be made between Irish servants and English servants, in houses and in books. Irish people curiously manage to be both egalitarian and hierarchical at the same time. Hierarchical because traces of a feudal society endured perhaps as late as the 1950s on this island with its large estates, its bogs and mountains and months of rain. The Middle Ages were slow to disappear in a "land of saints and scholars" and large landholdings, where even today, driving through the Irish countryside, the visitor is struck by long stretches of demesne walls, perforated every so often by neglected baronial gates and Gothic gate-lodges. Egalitarian, perhaps because traditionally the Irish are religious people whose church teaches that all souls are equal in the eyes of God.

And perhaps also because the man saddling the horse of his jumped-up Anglo-Irish squire or squireen may have, or fancy he has, noble blood running in his veins. The Kerry poet Aogán O'Rahilly (1670–1726), of whom Brendan Kennelly has written, "O'Rahilly *is* a snob, but one of the great snobs of literature," wrote a contemptuous putdown of the new Cromwellian adventurers who had conquered Ireland and usurped the land of the Irish nobility, using the house, as Bowen habitually does, as an emblem of a way of life:

That royal Cashel is bare of house and guest,
That Brian's turreted house is the otter's nest,
That the kings of the land have neither land nor crown
Has made me a beggar before you, Valentine Brown.

These lines are from Frank O'Connor's translation of the Irish lament "A Grey Eye Weeping," where O'Rahilly characterizes himself in a haunting synecdoche as "an old grey eye, weeping for lost renown." The last line, in which the English name Valentine Brown would undoubtedly sound even more contemptible in the context of the Gaelic words of the original, recurs as the burden of each stanza in the poem. Kennelly comments: "O'Rahilly himself would have considered 'Valentine' a ridiculous name for anyone calling himself a gentleman, and as for 'Brown,' he would as soon have addressed a 'Jones' or a 'Robinson.'" I mention O'Rahilly and his great poem of hauteur and despair because he lived in the next county over from Elizabeth Bowen's County Cork, and because the people he so eloquently despised were of the same ilk as the Bowens. Valentine Brown will enter our story again later in the book.

The persistent anxiety underlying the claims of the Ascendancy to legitimacy, the fear that despite all their pretensions they were never really an aristocracy, leads, according to Declan Kiberd in his *Irish Classics*, to a sense of caricature that often pervades portrayals of the master-servant relationship in Anglo-Irish fiction:

This may be because each is acting a part, whether that of 'master' or 'servant', yet neither can be convinced of or convincing in their role—the former because they know in their bones that they are usurpers and the latter because they can never forget that they were the ones usurped. . . . The rather cramped dimensions of Castle Rackrent (its kitchen is scarcely three paces in length; its doors open directly onto the village street) suggest a middle-class dwelling masquerading as a castellated ancestral seat. Edgeworth knew that the bourgeois planters were unconvincing aristocrats. In the political vacuum of pre-1782 Ireland, there was little to do except elaborate a personality, for neither master nor servant had hands on levers of significant power.

Bowen never committed the modern heresy—inspired, I suppose, by a kind of romantic Marxism—of wanting to become a member of the working class. She never for a moment considered servants—or the "suburban" Mrs. Vermont, of the bog-oak pigs and the tendency to talk about her "inside"—to be her social equals. In the eyes of many readers this makes her a snob. Even as sensible a reader as Elizabeth Bishop, in a letter to Robert Lowell expressing reservations about the Boston poet Anne Sexton, criticizes Bowen for her gentility:

> Anne Sexton I think still has a bit too much romanticism and what I think of as the "our beautiful old silver" school of female writing, which is really boasting about how "nice" *we* were. V. Woolf, E. Bowen, R. West, etc.—they are all full of it. They have to make quite sure that the reader is not going to misplace them socially, first—and that nervousness interferes constantly with what they think they'd like to say.

I think Bishop mostly has it wrong. Bowen to a large extent took the world as she found it, and was more interested in her characters as people with likes and dislikes, and especially with a desperate and often frustrated need for love, than as exemplars of social class.

When politics arises in Bowen's novels—and it rarely does—it is seen as a form of emotional desperation. Here is part of an exchange from *The House in Paris* between Karen, who has grave doubts about her impending marriage, and her upper-middle-class Aunt Violet. The time would be the early 1930s.

"Things one can do have no value. I don't mind feeling small myself, but I dread finding the world is. With Ray I shall be so safe. I wish the Revolution would come soon; I should like to start fresh while I am still young, with everything that I had to depend on gone. I sometimes think it is people like us, Aunt Violet, people of consequence, who are unfortunate: we have nothing ahead. I feel it's time something happened."

"Surely so much has happened," said Aunt Violet. "And mightn't a Revolution be rather unfair?"

"I shall always work against it," said Karen grandly. "But I should like it to happen in spite of me."

Except for saying she wants to work *against* the revolution, how much Karen sounds like the young W. H. Auden and his generation!

The "lack of life" Matchett regretted would not, I suspect, have been found at Bowen's Court when Elizabeth Bowen was mistress there. Something of the insouciance, the gay defiance of adversity, to be found at all levels of Irish society can be seen in Bowen's remark from the essay I have quoted:

the big house people were handicapped, shadowed and to an extent queered—by their pride, by their indignation at their decline and by their divorce from the countryside in whose heart their struggle was carried on. . . . These big house people admit only one class-distinction: they instinctively "place" a person who makes a poor mouth.

The strengths of Bowen's big-house people—pluck, style, common sense, decency, and a sense of community—are what several of her orphans and heart-wounded girls yearn for, often without even being aware of it. A question Bowen implicitly asks over and over is: What precisely is the emotional damage inflicted on her orphaned heroines (herself presumably included) by the circumstances of their lives? In "The Easter Egg Party" (1946), Hermione, taken in for a long visit in the country by two maiden ladies who are friends of her recently divorced mother, frustrates the ladies' desire to help her. "Their object was to restore her childhood to her," the story begins. But there is some basic human generosity, some sense of give and take, that she has simply missed out on. A spoiled child, she can appreciate things only by owning them: "'I think those lambs are pretty,' said Hermione, suddenly pointing over a wall. 'I should like a pet lamb of my own; I should call it Percy.'" After she demands to leave the sisters' home, seeing that they refuse to cater to her self-centeredness, she leaves a sadness behind her, because they realize her childhood is beyond the power of their wholesome kindness to restore: "The sisters seldom speak of her even between themselves; she has left a sort of scar, like a flattened grave, in their hearts."

As implied by the age and nature of many of her characters, Bowen's novels and stories are songs of innocence and experience. The innocence is not necessarily pure, and the experience may be benign or sinister. In *The House in Paris*, surrounded by a lie that the tyrannical Leopold, the illegitimate child of a troubled and unfortunate affair, is willing to tell, Henrietta, the settled, "normal" child, finds herself thinking: "'But we're children, people's belongings: we can't—' Incredulity made her go scarlet. . . ." Leopold observes cynically: "'Nobody speaks the truth when there's something they must have.'" Emma, beginning an affair in "Summer Night" (1941), realizes: "Yes, here she was, being settled down to as calmly as he might settle down to a meal." Portia in *The Death of the Heart*, because she is such a sacrificial lamb, is easy prey for the heartbreaker Eddie, Anna's young protégé. The novel, as its title implies, is almost an allegory, a Unicorn Tapestry in which the "pure"—

Portia, Thomas—are victimized by the worldly and corrupt: Anna, St. Quentin, Eddie.

Unstrung by Eddie's betrayal, and disoriented by Anna's rejection of her, Portia takes the extraordinary step of going to the decent, avuncular old Major Brutt, a demobbed colonial ex-army officer who is floundering around trying to find his way in the fast-changing Britain of the thirties, living in an attic room of a cheap hotel in the Cromwell Road. After she has told the major how unhappy she is with her brother and sister-in-law, he asks quietly what she wants to do:

> "Stay here with you," she said. "You do like me," she added. "You write to me; you send me puzzles; you say you think about me. . . . I could do things for you; we could have a home; we would not have to live in a hotel. . . . I could cook; my mother cooked when she lived in Notting Hill Gate. Why could you not marry me? I could cheer you up. I would not get in your way, and we should not be half so lonely."

Eva Trout, the young heiress and title character of Bowen's last, rather odd, and not very satisfactory novel, buys through the mail, in a similar effort to settle herself, a seaside house—sight unseen. When she descends on the small town to take possession, she startles the real-estate agent by her rather mad-seeming peremptoriness.

> "Now," she announced, looking round for her charioteer, "I want to go home."
> "*Home*?" Cried he, fearing all was lost.
> "Where is my house?"

Ireland and England, house and hotel, innocence and experience, the child and the world—these are the boundaries between which Elizabeth Bowen's fiction runs its subtle and sinuous course. With a touch of the worldly French moralist, she is fond of delivering maxims reminiscent of Madame de Sévigné. And thinking about the way she mediates between her classic polarities, one might ponder the following formulation from the last part of *The Death of the Heart*: "Happy that few of us are aware of the world until we are already in league with it."

William Trevor: "They Were As Good As We Were"

The fictions, careers, and milieux of Somerville and Ross, then Elizabeth Bowen, and finally William Trevor provide a history in brief of the Anglo-Irish from the mid-nineteenth century to the present. Trevor was born and raised a Protestant in provincial Ireland, went to school there, attended Trinity College, Dublin; a quarter of the pieces from his *Collected Stories* are set in Ireland or are peopled with Irish characters living abroad, usually in England. He himself has for many years lived and written in Devon. The term "Anglo-Irish" usually calls to mind either the early-twentieth-century members and descendants of the Protestant Ascendancy, such as Yeats, Lady Gregory, and Synge—prime movers in the Irish Literary Revival; or it brings to mind the fiction written by Somerville and Ross, Elizabeth Bowen, and more recently, Molly Keane. A somewhat imprecise Celtic mythologizing tendency is evoked in the case of the Revival; decrepit country houses, hunt balls, and a Faulknerian preoccupation with lineage in the other writers mentioned. Bowen was a master of a somewhat neurasthenic inwardness associated with the last years of the Ascendancy.

Even after distinguishing the differences among the writers I have mentioned, to associate Trevor with the milieu conjured up by the term "Anglo-Irish" can be misleading. For one thing, the Anglo-Irish tradition itself has become increasingly attenuated since the nineteenth century. As early as the 1860s, in Somerville and Ross's early days, Gladstone's disestablishment of the (Protestant) Church of Ireland and his Land Acts—and later those of Balfour—in response to the agitations associated with Parnell, together with Conservative adoption of land reform policies, drastically liberalized the landlord-and-tenant system that had ruled the island since the Tudors revoked the legitimacy of the native Irish nobility, forcing them to swear fealty to and draw their legitimacy from the Crown.

The history of Ireland after the land reform movement was one of Protestant flight to England, North America, and elsewhere in the face of an Ireland that increasingly defined itself, especially under de Valera's Irish Republic, as Gaelic, agrarian, and Catholic. These were the attenuated conditions in which Elizabeth Bowen wrote. The Protestants who have remained in the Irish Republic since her time are an isolated remnant. (The terms "Protestant" and "Catholic," of course, imply social distinctions as much as matters of faith.) Trevor's understanding of the lives of Irish Protestants may be seen as emblematic of a broader identification with an element of humanity psychologically marginalized, passed-over, alienated. And since Trevor's characters and settings are in fact often English rather than Irish, he might more accurately though more long-windedly be identified as "Protestant-Irish and English."

Yet Trevor's Irish characters and situations have never excluded the Catholic Irish, so he is by no means "Anglo-Irish" in the way that Bowen was. Trevor's fiction candidly recognizes that until quite recently, life for the majority of those who live in Ireland, particularly in the provinces, has been an unending struggle to make ends meet within a farming economy that offers little diversion. Bridie, in Trevor's early story "The

Ballroom of Romance," cares for her widowed father who is handicapped with an amputated leg, on a small farm like so many in the country. The narrowness of this life, particularly back in the 1940s and '50s, is from an American point of view almost impossible to grasp.

As drab as life in the nearby town is, Bridie still fantasizes about it: "The town had a cinema called the Electric, and a fish-and-chip shop where people met at night, eating chips out of a newspaper on the pavement outside. In the evenings, sitting in the farmhouse with her father, she often thought about the town, imagining the shop-windows lit up to display their goods and the sweet-shops still open so that people could purchase chocolates or fruit to take with them to the Electric cinema. But the town was eleven miles away, which was too far to cycle, there and back, for an evening's entertainment." Instead she cycles once a week to a roadhouse called the Ballroom of Romance, to dance and socialize with the same crowd of bachelors and spinsters who frequent the place, trying to attract the attention of the drummer in the band, Dano Ryan. Dano is not interested, however. "Once, at the end of an evening, she'd pretended that there was a puncture in the back wheel of her bicycle and he'd concerned himself with it while Mr Maloney and Mr Swanton waited for him in Mr Maloney's car. He'd blown the tyre up with the car pump and had said he thought it would hold."

While there is plenty of dry humor in Trevor's writing, he seldom condescends to his characters, but pays laconic tribute to their stoicism and decency. Bridie's evening at the Ballroom of Romance is revealed, but only at the end of the story, to have been her last night there. When the dance hall closes, she allows the old bachelor Bowser Egan to accompany her and even to kiss her in a field along the way, having in the reticent and coded manner of these tradition-bound people indicated he would marry her once his mother dies, leaving him the small farm where mother and son live.

William Trevor

Marriage, as is often the case in these Irish stories, represents a resigned acquiescence in the understanding that, as Dr. Johnson put it, "Life has little to be enjoyed and much to be endured." After the chaste and sad little exchange in the field, Bowser and Bridie mount their bikes and part. Without any flourish of exultation or self-pity, Bridie has made a major decision in her circumscribed life. "She rode through the night as on Saturday nights for years she had ridden and never would ride again because she'd reached a certain age. She would wait now and in time Bowser Egan would seek her out because his mother would have died. Her father would probably have died also by then. She would marry Bowser Egan because it would be lonesome being by herself in the farmhouse."

In "The Property of Colette Nervi," a story published some twenty years later, another rural Irish marriage of convenience—between a farmer and the daughter of a shop-keeper—is made affordable with money the farmer has stolen from a purse French tourists have left sitting on top of their rental car. The French people have come to look at the little settlement's one touristic claim to fame, Drumgawnie Rath, "a ring of standing stones that predated history." One irony in the story is that tourists will come from all over Europe to see these unimpressive stones, which "a visitor who had spent the whole afternoon examining them and had afterwards returned to the shop to verify the way to the Rossaphin road had stated that they were the most extraordinary stones of their kind in the whole of Europe. 'I think he was maybe drunk,' Dolores' mother had commented, and her father had agreed." The stolen money will allow Henry Garvey, who will inherit a decrepit old farm, to marry the crippled Dolores, who will inherit the shop at the crossroads, in a marriage ceremony where the arm-support of the crutch will be decorated in white lace. "Dolores thought she'd never seen a crutch look so pretty, and wondered if it was a marriage tradition for crippled brides, but did not ask." This last phrase is emblematic of the repressive society that Trevor chronicles, where so much is understood and so little is expressed.

"An Evening with John Joe Dempsey" gives us an insight into the life and mind of a character thoroughly out of sync with the pieties and repressions of his town. The story begins with John Joe's being sent by his widowed mother on an errand to the combination pub/grocery store that one still finds in rural Ireland. "Mr Lynch, now a large, fresh-faced man of fifty-five who was never seen without a brown hat on his head," who works as a clerk in a meal business, lives with his seventy-nine-year-old mother, and spends his evenings drinking in Keogh's public house, buys the fifteen-year-old boy his first bottle of stout and decides to give him some advice, starting off with some stories about the "glory girls" of London, where Mr. Lynch was stationed while serving with the British army. The preamble to Mr. Lynch's words of wisdom would capture any boy's attention:

> "If your daddy was alive today, he would be telling you a thing or two in order to prepare you for your manhood and the temptations in another country. Your mother wouldn't know how to tackle a matter like that, nor would Father Ryan, nor the Christian Brothers. Your daddy might have sat you down in this bar and given you your first bottle of stout. He might have told you about the facts of life."

John Joe knows exactly what he wants to hear about: "Did one of the glory girls entice yourself, Mr Lynch?" To John Joe's intense disappointment, though, and in one of the wry twists that William Trevor specializes in, the point of the story is that faced with "the glory girl," it turns out that Mr. Lynch has a vision of the Blessed Virgin. "'As soon as the glory girl said we'd drink the beer before we got down to business I saw the statue of the Holy Mother, as clear as if it was in front of me.'" "'I couldn't repeat,' he added, 'what the glory girl said when I walked away.'"

William Trevor

What a bring-down for the young man! Typical of Trevor's comic sense is Mr. Lynch's summing-up remark: "'I was telling you a moral story,' he said reprovingly. 'The facts of life is one thing, John Joe, but keep away from dirty women.'" Not to worry. John Joe has at fifteen learned to say what is expected of him:

> "You have pimples on your chin," said Mr Lynch in the end. "I hope you're living a clean life, now."
> "A healthy life, Mr Lynch."
> "It is a question your daddy would ask you. You know what I mean? There's some lads can't leave it alone."
> "They go mad in the end, Mr Lynch."

John Joe's mother and everyone else wonders why the lad spends so much time in the company of the town idiot, a dwarf named Quigley. Brother Leahy questions him sharply about the dwarf: "'Tell me this, young fellow-me-lad, what kind of a conversation do you have with old Quigley?' They talked, John Joe said, about trees and flowers in the hedgerows. He liked to listen to Quigley, he said, because Quigley had acquired a knowledge of such matters." But even Mr. Lynch is astute enough not to believe that. John Joe's private view is that "Quigley, a bachelor also, was a happier man than Mr Lynch. He lived in what amounted to a shed at the bottom of his niece's garden. Food was carried to him, but there were few, with the exception of John Joe, who lingered in his company." Like John Joe himself, Quigley spends most of his time thinking what it would be like to have sex with the ladies of the town, spying on them, and spinning fabulous tales about their intimate lives: "Quigley's voice might continue for an hour and a half, for there was hardly a man and his wife in the town whom he didn't claim to have observed in intimate circumstances. John Joe did not ever ask how, when there was no convenient shed to climb on to, the dwarf managed to make his way to so many exposed upstairs windows. Such a question would have been wholly irrelevant."

In a series of hilarious vignettes, Trevor retails John Joe's fantasies, each of which, simmering just beneath the surface of his imagination, involves his being seduced by one of the married ladies of the town. When his mother gives him his father's old fountain pen as a birthday present, he finds himself writing, as a way of testing the pen, "It's hot in here. Wouldn't you take off your jersey? 'That's a funny thing to write,' his mother said. 'It came into my head,'" is John Joe's reply.

The end of "An Evening with John Joe Dempsey" follows the main character to his room, where he "looked with affection at his bed, for in the end there was only that." Our sympathies are with the boy, because in the face of the town's repression and compromise, his fantasy life embodies his only sanity: "He travelled alone, visiting in his way the women of the town, adored and adoring, more alive in his bed than ever he was at the Christian Brothers' School, or in the grey Coliseum [the cinema], or in the chip-shop, or Keogh's public house, or his mother's kitchen, more alive than ever he would be at the sawmills. In his bed he entered a paradise: it was grand being alone."

The closest Trevor gets in his short stories to the atmosphere that might be called, in the terms I have suggested above, "Anglo-Irish," is the poignant piece "The Distant Past," which tells the story of an old brother and sister who live on in their dilapidated Georgian manor house, with its leaky roof and family crest and Cross of St. George worked into Irish linen and displayed in the front hall—all that is left of an estate called Carraveagh. "The Middletons of Carraveagh the family had once been known as, but now the brother and sister were just the Middletons, for Carraveagh didn't count any more, except to them." On the day of Queen Elizabeth's coronation in

1952 they had driven into town with a small Union Jack displayed in the rear window of their car.

The Church of Ireland (Anglican) Middletons have always enjoyed affectionate relations with the Catholic Irish of the town, their loyalties to the imperial past being smiled on as harmless eccentricities. Of the display of the flag on coronation day, "'Bedad, you're a holy terror, Mr Middleton!' Fat Cranley laughingly exclaimed, noticing the flag as he lifted a tray of pork steaks from his display shelf." Part of the irony is that Fat Cranley, during the Irish War of Independence, had actually fought against the British, showing up at Carraveagh with a shotgun in expectation of a battle with British troops, and locking up the family in an upstairs room. But as the Troubles of the Easter Rising and Civil War period faded into memory the town could laugh about those events, the Middletons amiably taking their place as "harmlessly peculiar," cobwebby museum pieces who gave the town a bit of tone. Everyone has been able to accept the transition through which the Middletons have gone from being part of the ruling class to being two old relics of the past. "On Fridays when they took seven or eight dozen eggs to the town, they dressed in pressed tweeds and were accompanied over the years by a series of red setters, the breed there had always been at Carraveagh."

As the old brother and sister have declined in the world, the new Ireland has prospered, becoming less a poor province of Britain and more a part of Europe, with a growing tourist trade: "the wife of a solicitor, a Mrs Duggan, began to give six o'clock parties once or twice a year, obliging her husband to mix gin and Martini in glass jugs and herself handing round a selection of nuts and small Japanese crackers." Trevor effortlessly sketches a three-paragraph history of the newly prosperous Irish Republic. As for the Middletons, "Dimly, but with no less loyalty, they still recalled the distant past and were listened to without ill-feeling when they spoke of it and of Carraveagh as it had been, and of the Queen whose company their careless father had known."

The trouble arises when the distant past stops being distant. "We can disagree without guns in this town" has been gospel here, "the result of living in a Christian country." "That the Middletons bought their meat from a man who had once locked them into an upstairs room and had then waited to shoot soldiers in their hall was a fact that amazed the seasonal visitors." Then the new Troubles begin, with Protestant attacks on Catholic neighborhoods, the rebirth of the old IRA as a brutal revolutionary force, the Protestant paramilitaries—as bad as the IRA or worse—the murders and retaliations. Since the town lies a scant sixty miles from the border, tourism falls off and the town's hard-won prosperity starts to ebb. The Middletons start being snubbed: "It was as though, going back nearly twenty years, people remembered the Union Jack in the window of their car and saw it now in a different light. It wasn't something to laugh at any more, nor were certain words that the Middletons had gently spoken, nor were they themselves just an old, peculiar couple." The humor, the affection, the very human accommodation between old antagonists—all of them caught between conflicting social forces over which they have no control—disappear now, in a past that has suddenly become present. "Because of the distant past they would die friendless. It was worse than being murdered in their beds."

Irish society retains certain postcolonial qualities, certain signs of a people still shaking off the shadows of foreign domination. Attitudes toward government and toward secular authority figures, for example, are still strikingly ambivalent. But the English and the Scots were always too close to the Irish to be thought of as colonizers in the classic model. Trevor brings a subtlety of insight to the relations between Ireland and "the other island." Take Norah and Dermot of "Another Christmas."

Irish by birth, they have emigrated to Fulham shortly after their marriage and are now permanently settled in England. "Their children spoke with London accents. Patrick and Brendan worked for English firms and would make their homes in England. Patrick had married an English girl. They were Catholics and they had Irish names, yet home for them was not Waterford." In this they typify many Irish people who live in England.

The crisis of the story arises from the unspoken understanding that their landlord, Mr. Joyce (why he has an Irish name is not explained), will for the first time in years not be coming to Christmas dinner. They understand this, and Norah is planning to deliver a present to him, sensing he won't come, though Mr. Joyce has not said he will not come, and Dermot insists, "I'd say there was no need to go round with the tie. I'd say he'd make the effort on Christmas Day." The estrangement has come about because of words spoken while the three were watching a television news report of "another outrage"—an IRA bombing. When Mr. Joyce had said, "He couldn't understand the mentality of people like that . . . killing just anyone, destroying life for no reason," Dermot had commented "that they mustn't of course forget what the Catholics in the North had suffered. The bombs were a crime but it didn't do to forget that the crime would not be there if generations of Catholics in the North had not been treated as animals."

Can anyone who knows his history disagree with that? The story dramatizes how the lives of these London Irish are impinged upon by the Troubles. Norah, caught between two nations, "felt she should be out on the streets, shouting in her Waterford accent, violently stating that the bombers were more despicable with every breath they drew, that hatred and death were all they deserved." At the same time her husband faces the possibility of losing his job as a meter-reader for North Thames Gas because men with Irish accents make people nervous these days. Still Norah resents his statement about Irish history because "Their harmless elderly landlord might die in the course of that same year, a friendship he had valued lost, his last Christmas lonely." We can see how many families, friendships, and lives are affected by the conflict in the North, which now thankfully seems largely resolved.

Politics, history, and social class engage Trevor's imagination not in and of themselves, but because of the way they affect people's lives. Though Northern Ireland or even Ireland does not appear to be an obsession for him, Trevor has written other stories that get right into the belly of the beast. In two cases the main character is a woman. Attracta, the Protestant school-teacher in an eponymous story, has somehow managed to put into the back of her mind the death of her own parents when she was three years old—they were shot down by mistake in an ambush the Nationalist insurgents had planned for the Black and Tans. In the aftermath the man responsible for the ambush became Attracta's protector, and Attracta only learns the facts of her parents' death when she is eleven, from a bitter, some-what deranged old man in the town.

She has managed somehow to repress all feelings toward the Troubles of the 1920s until by chance she reads in a newspaper of the suicide of an Englishwoman whose husband, an army of-ficer, was murdered by the IRA, who decapitated him and sent his head to her in the mail. Then Attracta loses control of what she has repressed all these years, goes off her head and tries to talk to her pupils about the horror that lies just beneath the sur-face of Irish history, the horror that most people successfully ignore. The next day the Protestant archdeacon kindly con-vinces Attracta to take early retirement.

In "Beyond the Pale," Cynthia, an Englishwoman on vaca-tion in Northern Ireland with her husband, his mistress of many years, and her husband's best friend, becomes hysterical after hearing the story of a local Irishman's former girlfriend who has been killed by a bomb explosion in England in some obscure plot between the rival terrorist groups. The man drowns himself in the sea just outside the hotel where the foursome vacation;

this spot was where he and his girlfriend had come as children. This sends Cynthia off on a mad ramble about Irish history, in the course of which she spills the beans about her husband's affair. His mistress, who narrates the story, is naturally more upset about this revelation than about the tragedies of Irish history: "Why couldn't it have been she who had gone down to the rocks and slipped on the seaweed or just walked into the sea, it didn't matter which? Her awful rigmarole hung about us as the last of the tea things were gathered up—the earls who'd fled, the famine and the people planted. The children were there too, grown up into murdering riff-raff."

The stickiest problem of Irish history is, writ large, the same impulse that Trevor worries relentlessly in many if not most of his stories—the impulse to hide, to suppress, to lie. I have dwelt on the specifically Irish and Irish-English sides of Trevor's work, but his preoccupation with repression and with loaded secrets is by no means limited to the national and ethnic context. He gives human nature a wide berth, sometimes turning an amused eye on our duplicities, more often adopting a severe if not bitter tone. Disillusionment is the characteristic mode of this most acute observer of the human condition.

The seasoned reader of Trevor's work, upon opening a story called "A Happy Family," braces himself for the "attitude adjustment" that is surely waiting in the wings, even at the moment when ordinary human contentment is being evoked in passages like this: "I remember sitting in the number 73 bus, thinking of the day as I had spent it and thinking of the house I was about to enter. It was a fine evening, warm and mellow, the air heavy with the smell of London. The bus crossed Hammersmith Bridge, moving quite quickly towards the leafy avenues beyond." In a house in those leafy avenues lives a woman who will soon begin receiving phone calls from a Mr. Higgs, who uncannily knows all the secrets of her life, a caller who turns out to be imaginary—the midlife version of an imaginary childhood figure. When the woman has to be put away, her husband cannot help being disconcerted by the fact that their daughter also has an imaginary friend: "I stopped the car by our house," the story ends, "thinking that only death could make the house seem so empty, and thinking too that death was easier to understand. We made tea, I remember, the children and I, not saying very much more."

In the world inhabited by William Trevor's characters, the happy family is either transitory or illusory, or simply does not exist. In one of my favorite stories, "Mr McNamara," Trevor creates over the space of four pages a golden picture of childhood in an Irish town in the Midlands, in a family which is content despite having come down in the world. "As a family we belonged to the past. We were Protestants in what had become Catholic Ireland. We'd once been part of an ascendancy, but now it was not so. Now there was the income from the granary and the mill, and the house we lived in: we sold grain and flour, we wielded no power. 'Proddy-woddy green-guts,' the Catholic children cried at us in Curransbridge. 'Catty, Catty, going to Mass,' we whispered back, 'riding on the devil's ass.' They were as good as we were." The family consists of a son and three daughters, "and Flannagan in the garden and Bridget our maid, and the avuncular spirit of Mr McNamara."

The parents are as good a pair as one could hope for: "when they disagreed or argued their voices weren't ever raised. They could be angry with us, but not with one another. They meted out punishments for us jointly, sharing disapproval or disappointment. We felt doubly ashamed when our misdemeanours were uncovered." The father is a large, "bulky" man who drinks from an extra-large teacup. What is the significance, we wonder, of his having a special knife and fork, "extra-strong because my father was always breaking forks"?

Throughout the narrator's childhood there are the father's visits to Dublin, a regular feature of which would be his visits to the bar of Fleming's Hotel with his friend Mr. McNamara: "The whole thing occurred once every month or so, the going away in the first place, the small packed suitcase in the hall, my father in his best tweed suit. Flannagan and the dog-cart. And the returning a few days later: breakfast with Mr McNamara, my sister Charlotte used to say"—because during breakfast the morning after he returned, the father would recount all the Dublin news, along with Mr. McNamara's views on it all, and the endlessly complicated though rather ordinary stories of Mr. McNamara's family, who live in a house "in Palmerston Road, and the dog they had, a spaniel called Wolfe Tone, and a maid called Kate O'Shea, from Skibbereen."

Mr. McNamara even sends the boy a thirteenth-birthday present. Trevor has a delightful way of making a detail stand out. "One by one my presents were placed before me, my parents' brought from the sideboard by my mother. It was a package about two and a half feet long, a few inches in width. It felt like a bundle of twigs and was in fact the various parts of a box-kite. Charlotte had bought me a book called *Dickon the Impossible*, Amelia a kaleidoscope. 'Open mine exceedingly carefully,' Frances said. I did, and at first I thought it was a pot of jam. It was a goldfish in a jar." How much these details tell us of the care with which life was managed in this household! "Open mine exceedingly carefully" is redolent of the long-vanished rectitude and precision of language of the English and Anglo-Irish middle classes. Mr. McNamara's gift, though, is the best of all: a little dragon made of brass, with "two green eyes that Frances said were emeralds, and small pieces let into its back which she said looked like rubies." The boy is enjoined to write a thank-you note. "Give me the letter when you've done it," his father says. "I have to go up again in a fortnight."

But his father dies the next day—"a grim nightmare of a day, during all of which someone in the house was weeping, and often several of us together." Interestingly, Mr. McNamara, through the mother's intercession, is not informed. "My father and Mr McNamara had been bar-room friends. [Mother] pointed out: letters in either direction would not be in order." From then on, the boy's mission in life is to grow up and replace his father as owner of the granary and mill, and to further his education he is sent to a Protestant boarding school in the Dublin mountains. Eventually he works up his courage to make up an excuse to go into Dublin—"'An uncle,' I said to the small headmaster. 'Passing though Dublin, sir'"—so that he can see Fleming's Hotel for himself.

The inevitable occurs. In one of the most exquisitely bitter-sweet scenes in fiction, the boy cycles up to Fleming's Hotel and goes in. "A tall grandfather clock ticked, the fire occasionally hissed. There was a smell of some kind of soup. It was the nicest, most comfortable hall I'd ever been in." He proceeds into the bar, empty except for the barman and "a woman sitting by the fire drinking orange-coloured liquid from a small glass. Behind the bar a man in a white jacket was reading the *Irish Independent*." The boy manages to be served a bottle of ale, his first encounter with the stuff, and as he drinks it, waiting for Mr. McNamara to appear, he notices that the woman is looking at him, and he wonders in his naïve way if she might be a pros-titute: "A boy at school called Yeats claimed that prostitutes hung about railway stations mostly, and on quays. But there was of course no reason why you shouldn't come across one in a bar. . . . Yet she seemed too quietly dressed to be a prostitute."

Eventually the woman gets up and leaves, "and on her way from the bar she passed close to where I was sitting. She looked down and smiled at me." After she has left, the boy asks the barman who she is. And when the man says, "That's Nora Mc-Namara," the reader finds he is really not surprised, remember-ing the little brass dragon—which is more a woman's gift than a man's—and the mother's insistence that Mr. McNamara not be notified of her husband's death, suggesting that she shared with him the fiction of "Mr." McNamara's identity.

William Trevor

What is perhaps even more absorbing than this discovery is the boy's bitter reaction to it. As much as the boy resents his father's having given the other woman's gifts to his children, "yet somehow it was not as great as the sin of sharing with all of us this other woman's eccentric household, her sister and her sister's husband, her alcoholic aunt, a maid and a dog"—the violation of the family's sanctity that comes from the intrusion of another reality into their midst, introduced under false pretenses. He relives all of it at home on Christmas morning:

I hated the memory of him and how he would have been that Christmas morning; I hated him for destroying everything. It was no consolation to me that then he had tried to share with us a person he loved in a way that was different from the way he loved us. I could neither forgive nor understand. I felt only bitterness that I, who had taken his place, must now continue his deception, and keep the secret of his lies and his hypocrisy.

To be an adult is to be able to keep a tough secret. The boy has become a man.

William Trevor's keen eye illuminates the lives of the Irish, the Anglo-Irish, and also the English. The sequence of stories called "Matilda's England" is one of the best treatments of the English experience of World War II that I have ever read. But his vision transcends, as I have suggested, the various contexts within which he places his stories. Taken as a whole, his fiction makes a strong assertion about human nature, as an observer of which Trevor is unsparing, not given to the epiphanies we associate with other great Irish short-story writers such as James Joyce and Frank O'Connor. There is humor here, and certain moments that glow with the enjoyment of life, perfectly rendered into beautiful prose. But reading these stories one after the other can be a sobering and chastening experience. They have kept me awake at night. The reader is not advised to read consecutively, as I have done over the past several months, the twelve hundred pages of *The Collected Stories*. These are meant to be absorbed one at a time. But once the stories become part of one's mind and life, there's no shaking them.

William Trevor

3

Listening to Irish
Traditional Music

Unofficial clubs whose only dues are the price of a drink, impromptu stages for the flights of fancy and rhetoric Irish talkers are renowned for, pubs also provide a setting for traditional Irish music, which since the early 1960s has enjoyed a worldwide revival. The term "traditional" is to be preferred over "folk music," which in Ireland calls up images of guitar strummers in Aran sweaters singing "Danny Boy" and "There's Whiskey in the Jar." What follows is a brief primer for readers who may be new to the music. The Belfast poet Ciarán Carson, himself an accomplished traditional flautist, has written two extraordinary books on the subject: one is an excellent little book written for the Appletree Pocket Guide series; the other is the classic *Last Night's Fun*, a brilliant memoir and meditation not only on the music itself but on the life lived around the music—one of the most amazing books ever to come out of Ireland. The chapter on breakfasts is worth the price of the book on its own. As in the case of many great books, its true subject is memory. In terms of what you can learn about Irish culture from one book, it ranks with David Thomson's great memoir, *Woodbrook*.

Each of Ireland's four provinces, indeed each of its thirty-two counties, has its own songs, its own variations on well-known melodies. But most aficionados of the music would agree that the punter could do far worse than to head for the West of Ireland, and especially for the counties of Galway and Clare, with their fishing and farming villages perched on the shores of Galway Bay, still not quite overwhelmed by condominiums, their rocky fields where sheep graze above the sea. You might, some blustery Saturday night or slow Sunday afternoon when the air is tangy with sea salt and fragrant with turf smoke, notice in the window of an out-of-the-way pub a hand-lettered sign announcing a music session. Walk in and if luck is with you, you could hear music that will take your breath away.

As with Irish weather, finding the music is very much a matter of being in the right place at the right time. There is, to be sure, a fair amount of just plain bad music—hotel lounge "ballad sessions," for example, designed for tourists. And not everyone who plays the fiddle or the button accordion plays it well. But the real thing is present in abundance and enjoys great popularity among those who know. The musicians who have been responsible for the trad revival feel that in breathing life into this old music, they are preserving a part of their heritage threatened with extinction by drum machines and synthesizers. Older people remember the music from their youth, and cherish it. The generations mix in Irish pubs, and often I have seen a young fiddler pause between tunes and ask some grizzled old farmer to "give us a song." The publican will do his best to get a little attention from the crowd, and a pure voice, unaccompanied, will lilt out, in the *sean-nós* (old style) manner, an ancient ballad of thwarted love, hard times, or emigration.

Traditional music has a way of sounding sprightly and melancholy at the same time. The tunes, most of which derive from a very old folk tradition, were first written down in the eighteenth century. Though it has become listening music, it began like jazz as dance music, as the names for different types of tunes—hornpipe, jig, reel, Kerry polka—suggest. If your luck holds, some of the locals at a session will get up and dance a few "sets." Set dancing, similar to square dancing but with fancier footwork, is said to have been brought back from France in the early nineteenth century by Irish soldiers returning from the Napoleonic Wars. The origins of sets danced in Irish pubs and kitchens can be traced back to the French court of the eighteenth century. The soldiers also brought back tunes, including slow airs like the haunting one whose name, "The Wounded Hussar," hints at its origins.

Traditional music is largely instrumental. The similarity between Irish traditional music and traditional American folk music is not fortuitous, since Irish music was one of the formative influences on the music played in the mountains and hollers of the American Southeast. Heading the list of favored instruments is the fiddle, played with minimal vibrato. Two great contemporary masters of the fiddle are Martin Hayes and Tommy Peoples, both from Clare. Then comes the accordion or "box" as it is usually called. Once you've heard someone like Jackie Daly or Martin O'Connor play the instrument, all associations with polkas and church socials will disappear. Particularly in music originating in County Clare, you will also hear the concertina. Various stringed instruments including banjo, guitar, and bouzouki are used, also the wooden or silver flute. In quieter moments musicians will bring out the tin whistle, which can be surprisingly expressive and various. The beat is sometimes laid down by the bodhrán, a shallow, hand-held drum similar to the Middle Eastern tar, played with a little stick and particularly effective accompanying the flute.

Old-fashioned Irish pubs, unlike the imitations of them that have sprung up all over the world, tend to be modest, unprepossessing places. The Victorian gin palaces one sees in England, with their stained glass, polished mahogany bars, and elaborately tiled floors, are rare in Ireland. In the old days the pubs got so smoky you'd come out with enough secondhand smoke to fill a cancer ward. Now all that has changed and you can breathe freely while listening to music. A typical evening begins late, usually around ten o'clock, and can easily go on till two in the morning in small towns, where pub closing hours are not rigidly enforced. The blinds will be drawn at dark and the doors closed at 11:30, but once you're inside you can stay until the publican decides to put everyone out.

The musicians gather in a corner of the pub around a low table crowded with drinks. Half the pub will chatter away obliviously, so if you've come to listen, arrive early to make sure you get a good seat. Irish people are naturally courteous on the whole and are unlikely to come out and tell you if you are making a nuisance of yourself, so a word about pub etiquette may be in order. Though there may be free stools or chairs in the area where they are playing, don't sit with the musicians. The empty places are being saved for other musicians and friends who will show up later. A session is not a preplanned performance, but rather an informal, evolving musical happening. If you wish to tape a session, ask permission, which will usually be granted. The best tactic is to make yourself as unobtrusive as possible— the less you intrude upon the atmosphere, the more you'll get a taste of its essence.

One very acceptable way for a punter to show his appreciation for the music is to buy the musicians a round of drinks. Just tell the bartender you're standing a round; he or she will know what everyone is drinking, will carry the drinks over and discreetly announce that this round is on you. Don't expect to be thanked with much more than a wink and a nod, though— getting a few free pints is considered a musician's privilege.

The round of drinks you buy for a group of musicians, incidentally, may be the only one you buy in Ireland that will not be reciprocated. First-time visitors often get the impression that the Irish are very generous people. And maybe they are, but the name of the game is reciprocity: you are expected to take turns buying drinks. Mental notes of whose turn it is to buy a round are kept, and though no one will ever be so rude as to say so, you will be considered to "have no nature in you" if you don't hold up your end of the bargain. I used to drink two or three nights a week with the same group at the Ould Plaid Shawl in Kinvara, and it was uncanny the way everyone would remember whose turn it was to buy the next round. Nothing was ever said, but everyone knew.

A visitor to Ireland could spend a pleasant week in Galway and north Clare, seeing the country by day, dining on local seafood and visiting the pubs by night. As I picture in my mind traditional music pubs from the city of Galway down to the village of Doolin in County Clare—a fifty-mile distance traversed by the coast road, which winds through rugged and scenic countryside—Naughton's in Galway comes first to mind.

Tigh Neachtáin (Naughton's) occupies the ground floor of a medieval townhouse. With its steeply battered walls, curiously arched windows, and Gothic oriel overlooking the intersection of Quay and Cross streets, the building itself is fascinating to look at. Inside, the pub is one of the coziest in Ireland, divided as it is into half a dozen "snugs" where one can savor a quiet pint in solitude or enjoy a romantic conversation. Naughton's has played host over the years to a fine group of younger musicians including the virtuoso box player Dermot Byrne, as well as Brendan Larrissey, Sharon Shannon, and Seán, Cora, and Breda Smyth—all accomplished fiddlers. The Quays, across the street, used to be a Galway institution; the great tin whistle player Seán Ryan was a regular there in the old days. But now the pub has been rebuilt and expanded into a kind of mega-pub that fools no one but the tourists. Walk up Lower Dominick Street for one long block, then jog left and turn right and you will find yourself in the vicinity of two very reliable music pubs: the Crane Bar and the Galway Shawl. These places are always a good bet for a session.

Heading south from Galway on the Limerick highway (N18), turn right at Kilcolgan (Moran's on the Weir, famous for its oysters, makes a good lunch stop). I never eat here without thinking of these lines from Seamus Heaney's poem "Oysters":

Our shells clacked on the plates.
My tongue was a filling estuary,
My palate hung with starlight:
As I tasted the salty Pleiades
Orion dipped his foot into the water.

The poem is said to have been brought on by a meal consumed in the first snug on the right as you enter. It continues:

We had driven to that coast
Through flowers and limestone
And there we were, toasting friendship,
Laying down a perfect memory
In the cool of thatch and crockery.

Continue south toward Kinvara on the N67. Winkles Hotel, which had a history of attracting some of the best musicians, including Jackie Daly, probably the best pure accordion stylist in Ireland, who used to live near Kinvara and now lives in Clare, has recently given way to condominiums and a shopping center complex. God help us. Different pubs have sessions on different nights of the week: Connolly's on the quay, the Ould Plaid Shawl on the main street. Green's is where the great singers gather one night a week.

Head in the direction of County Clare up the main street until you are almost out of town, and look for Tully's. Here the sessions occur more sporadically than elsewhere, but this pub is many people's favorite place to listen to music in Kinvara. Frankie Gavin and Alec Finn can be heard here from time to time. In the manner of old-fashioned country pubs, you enter through the small grocery store that opens onto the street. In times past the logic was that Herself did the shopping while Himself drank a pint. Tully's has a beautiful old wooden bar that curves around the room about chest-high, as well as superb acoustics and the warmest stove in town. At this writing, the pub is closed, but one hopes it will open again soon.

From Kinvara, follow the N67 southwest into County Clare, looking for the red-and-blue signs picturing a lobster and a pint of Guinness that direct you to Linane's in Newquay, a mile or so off the main road. This charming pub, situated on an estuary on the south shore of Galway Bay, is relaxed and untouristy even in July and August, though it lost a bit of its charm when it was expanded a few years ago. On Friday nights I often used to hear Seán Tyrrell, who sings and plays the bouzouki.

Get back on the N67 and follow it down to Ballyvaughan (Claire's Restaurant and Monk's Pub are both excellent for lunch or dinner), where you can either follow the coast road (N477) around scenic Black Head or shorten your trip by staying on the N67 to Lisdoonvarna, then cutting over to Doolin on the coast.

Doolin is unpleasantly overcrowded during the summer by virtue of being one hour's drive from Shannon Airport and also a short ferry ride from the Aran Islands. Except that I know you will not consider your trip to Ireland complete unless you go to Doolin, I would warn you away from the town altogether. But since you are going there despite what I say, my first recommendation for music would be McGann's, which draws a young crowd from Doolin's several hostels. O'Connor's, which is picturesquely located overlooking the sea, also has music every night during the high season.

Flann O'Brien:
No Laughing Matter

My best guess is that "the luck of the Irish" is a phrase that originated in America. When one contemplates the lives some of the best Irish writers have led in and out of the pubs of Dublin during the past half-century or so, "curse" comes to mind as a better word than "luck." Hence the sobering title of Anthony Cronin's superb biography, *No Laughing Matter: The Life and Times of Flann O'Brien.*

O'Brien, a novelist and satirist, was actually three in one—an entity the novelist Dermot Bolger has called "that wondrous multi-layered mind which singularly comprised the Unholy Trinity of Flann O'Brien, Brian O'Nolan and Myles na Gopaleen." Can any other writer have gone by so many different names over the course of a lifetime? Myles (one instinctively wants to call him by the first name of the nom de plume he adopted for the long-running column he wrote for the *Irish Times* starting in 1940) was born into the riverrun of modern Ireland in 1911. A writer of O'Brien's cut is imaginable only in a country that could never quite make up its mind what exactly it was. Those were days when, from Paris, Joyce and then Beckett exercised their colossal absence, when Brendan Behan played the stage Irishman to great effect in New York and Dublin, while Myles and the poet Patrick Kavanagh were twin eminences who between them dominated Dublin's literary pubs.

By choice of his father, who was an upper-level civil servant, Irish was the language of the household in which the young Brian O'Nolan grew up. This linguistic decision represented a patriotic cultural gesture—not unusual among educated families of the emerging nation, who wished to turn their backs on the language of their English nemesis. When he himself became a civil servant, the subject of this biography was sometimes Brian O'Nolan and sometimes Brian O Nualláin. Though he came to loathe the civil service, his job became a necessity: his father died young, and it fell on O'Nolan's shoulders to support a family of twelve.

Though drink was at first a recreation, no doubt his later dependence on it owed something to the tedium of his job, much of which involved sitting in the Dáil, or Irish parliament, listening to the tedious speeches of politicians. "For some seven years my duty as a Private Secretary necessitated almost daily attendance at Leinster House. Garrulity is a feeble word to describe what I encountered in Dáil Éireann. . . ." When one of his superiors in the civil service warned him avuncularly about his increasingly frequent recourse to a public house near his office— "You were seen going into the Scotch House"—O'Nolan replied, "You mean I was seen *coming* into the Scotch House." He died in his mid-fifties from throat cancer brought on by a lifetime of heavy drinking and smoking.

O'Nolan emerges from Cronin's account as a example of a classic Dublin type often seen in the old days but uncommon in today's Ireland: the disappointed man. During the years of life that are the most productive for many writers, O'Nolan went through a creative silence during which he wrote no fiction, a period that lasted twenty years. His nom de plume, the Irish name Myles na Gopaleen—which means "Myles of the little ponies"—was presumably a bilingual pun on the little naggins of whiskey he liked to carry around in his pockets when he went to the racetrack and to the *Irish Times* offices; or else the surname alludes to the race horses he followed avidly.

Even today his column, "Cruiskeen Lawn" or "little brimming jug," enjoys iconic status among Irish readers. The column's popularity must have something to do with the character called "the brother," who expressed something of the letdown many people felt upon finding that the euphoria of Independence did not last—an instance of national postpartum depression. Another of O'Brien's books, *An Béal Bocht* or "the hungry mouth," has lent its name in the last few years to a popular pub in the Bronx that functions as a literary center for recent immigrants and other lovers of Irish poetry. A contemporary heir to "Cruiskeen Lawn" was the column "Days and Nights in Garavan's," written by the fictional Morgan O'Doherty (Jeff O'Connell) for the *Galway Advertiser*.

And yet, brilliant as it is, "Cruiskeen Lawn" appears not to have satisfied its author, who was a novelist of startling originality. Patrick Kavanagh's repeated judgment may have been right: "That poor little na gCopaleen [Kavanagh uses the pedantic form of the genitive plural that Myles had at first favored when signing his columns] has never found a myth that would carry all the stuff in his column, that would lift it on to a creative plane."

Since Irish was his first language, it is not hard to see why his disillusionment about Irish would have hit O'Nolan so hard. "It is common knowledge," Myles observed bitterly, satirizing Eamon de Valera's vision of an Ireland where happy Gaelic-speaking peasants farmed blissfully and comely maidens danced at the crossroads, "that certain categories of Irish speakers are boors. They (being men) have nuns' faces, wear bicycle clips continuously, talk in Irish only about *ceist na teanga* [the language question] and have undue confidence in Irish dancing as a general national prophylactic. . . ."

An article by Elaine Black headed "We never have to speak a word of Irish again" in the June 10, 2006, *Irish Times* made me think of O'Nolan. The article was part of an "exam diary" being written for the paper by a schoolgirl taking her Leaving Certificate, the culmination of secondary education for Irish students, which determines their options for college and careers. "I know there's supposed to be a renaissance in the Irish language these days, but 68 students in one Sligo school were dancing on Gaelige's (Irish's) grave today," Ms. Black writes. "We were all so delighted at the idea that we would never have to speak a word of Irish again that we barely noticed the sound of Hector sobbing into his colcannon." Her attitude toward the language, which has perhaps more to do with the unimaginative way Irish is taught than with any inherent response to its merits, is more or less typical of many secondary-school students.

The survival of Irish is a vexed question; all over the world endangered languages decline and disappear almost daily before the juggernaut of world languages like English and Spanish. And yet the Irish government is no more adept today than it was in de Valera's day in making Irish popular. Last summer on holiday in Dingle, we were puzzled to see placards everywhere declaring "Dingle, a town where democracy is denied." The reference was to a decision made by the government declaring that road signs in all Gaeltacht areas should be written only in Irish. The Irish name for Dingle is An Daingean. On country roads, locals had painted out An Daingean and painted in the anglicized name, Dingle.

Years ago, walking though lashing rain to the ruins of the old church at Kilmalkedar near Dingle, three of us met a procession of mourners coming from a funeral in the old graveyard that lies around the church. They greeted us in Irish and we did our best to respond. That encounter lives in my memory as a moment of perfect cultural unity: the black-clad mourners, the ruins of the twelfth-century sandstone church, and, yes, the saturated green fields that lay all around under the lashing rain, the words of greeting spoken in the ancient language of the island. Such moments are familiar to those who love Ireland. Even Flann O'Brien—Brian Nolan or Brian O Nualláin, Myles na Gopaleen, whatever name he answers to in Heaven or in Hell—must have known transcendent moments like this. No doubt his sense that the Irish dream had been spoiled by small-mindedness, greed, prejudice, and stupidity made his bitterness even more profound.

Sadder than his disillusionment with the radical ethno-centricity of de Valera's approach to nation-building was O'Nolan's inability to acknowledge his masterpiece, *At Swim-Two-Birds*, which he dismissed as "mere juvenalia." The book, which appeared in 1939, might lay claim to being the first postmodernist novel written in English. Graham Greene, whose job it was to review the manuscript for a publisher, neatly summed up its plot as follows: "you have (a) a book about a man called Trellis who is (b) writing a book about certain characters who (c) are turning the tables on Trellis by writing about him." Trellis loses control over his characters only when he falls asleep. These devices, which would seem to owe something to Gide and Pirandello, have less novelty value today than they had then. But unlike today's postmodernism, O'Brien's book has the freshness and sprightliness of a joke being told for the first time.

For me the delight and charm of the book lie not so much in its overall premise as in the author's brilliance as a satirist and parodist. In one character, Finn MacCool, O'Brien parodies the ancient Irish poetry he would have read in school, which can only speak in high, traditional style of matters such as the wanderings of the mad king Sweeny. This mixes hilariously with the other characters' more mundane quotidian interests. Here are the characters of Trellis's novel talking among themselves:

I will relate, said Finn.

We're off again, said Furriskey.

The first matter that I will occupy with honey-words and melodious recital, said Finn, is the reason and the first cause for Sweeny's frenzy.

Draw in your chairs, boys, said Shanahan, we're right for the night. We're away in a hack.

Hilariously, Finn's interlocutors, ordinary middle-class Dubliners, tolerate Finn as a harmless long-winded eccentric. O'Brien's parodies of their own garrulousness are exact and delightful. He captures the repetitiveness and unconscious buffoonery of their speech with unerringly precise mimicry. Shanahan glosses one of Finn's tales as follows:

. . . The upshot is that your man becomes a bloody bird.

I see, said Lamont.

Do you see it, Mr. Furriskey, said Shanahan. What happens? He is changed into a bird for his pains and he could go from here to Carlow in one hop. . . .

That was always one thing, said Shanahan wisely, that the Irish race was always noted for, one place where the world had to give us best. With all his faults and by God he has plenty, the Irishman can jump. By God he can jump. That's one thing the Irish race is honored for no matter where it goes or where you find it—jumping. The world looks to us there.

The best comedians are, famously, often the saddest men. In a column written less than a month before his death, Myles wrote that anybody "who has the courage to raise his eyes and look sanely at the awful human condition . . . must realize finally that tiny periods of temporary release from intolerable suffering is the most that any individual has the right to expect." Anthony Cronin notes, "He died peacefully and rather unexpectedly on 1 April 1966, April Fools' Day."

Brian Friel: Transcending the Irish National Pastime

HUGH: Indeed, Lieutenant. A rich language. A rich literature. You'll find, Sir, that certain cultures expend on their vocabularies and syntax acquisitive energies and ostentations entirely lacking in their material lives. I suppose you could call us a spiritual people.

OWEN: (Not unkindly; more out of embarrassment before the Lieutenant) Will you stop that nonsense, Father?

HUGH: Nonsense? What nonsense? . . . Yes, it is a rich language, Lieutenant, full of the mythologies of fantasy and hope and self-deception—a syntax opulent with tomorrows. It is our response to mud cabins and a diet of potatoes; our only method of replying to . . . inevitabilities. (To OWEN) Can you give me the loan of half-a-crown?

"How these people blather on!" the London *Sunday Times*'s drama critic, John Peter, wrote about a recent production of *The Plough and the Stars* by Seán O'Casey. Irish playwrights have, over the years, confirmed the nation's reputation for talk by mounting plays that live or die through their characters' ability to keep an audience enthralled by language. From *The School for Scandal* by Sheridan (one forgets he was Irish) to *The Importance of Being Earnest* by Wilde, to Beckett's *Waiting for Godot*, we remember the great Irish plays for their dialogue rather than for the inventiveness of their dramatic structure. One tends to think of Beckett as an international phenomenon rather than as an Irishman; but how quintessentially Irish he was to put his characters in trashcans or bury them up to their necks in sand so that, their movements severely restricted, they were free to spellbind with their talk! After hundreds of years of invasion, military occupation, economic plundering, and systematic attempts to eradicate their native religion and culture, what has been left to the Irish other than talk? Talk is the national pastime.

Among the myriad ironies of Irish history is that even after the colonizing British managed virtually to stamp out the Gaelic language, the Irish went to work on English itself and transformed it into the colorful hybrid, sometimes called Hiberno-English, that is spoken on the island today. This variety of English, though it largely uses standard vocabulary, has taken on the rhythms, syntax, intonations, and often even the grammar of Irish, which, though almost extinct, has managed to inseminate another linguistic organism with its inventiveness, its evasions and qualifications, its elaborate and ambiguous courtesies.

While his focus on language places him firmly within Irish theatrical tradition, Brian Friel's insistence that language is a tool of oppression both from above and from within has put the politics of language at the center of his concerns. This emphasis is unprecedented on the Irish stage. Seamus Deane in *Celtic Revivals* makes the point that Friel, growing up in Londonderry, a Northern city plagued by chronic unemployment and sectarian tensions between the Protestant descendants of British settlers and the native, Catholic Irish, grew up in a world where failure and frustration were a constant, and politics was a given. Friel, unlike writers from more comfortable backgrounds who

157

"discover" politics and see it as a solution, regards politics as part of the problem, as basic as bad weather.

Despite modernization and the growth of a new spirit of optimism in Ireland following the economic boom of the 1960s and the country's entry into the European Community, the stereotype—amounting almost to a cultural icon—of the brilliant failure, the great talker who accomplishes nothing, still persists. No other Irish writer has been as forthright as Friel in identifying talk, not as a way to charm, but as a temperamental response to, and compensation for, failure—itself seen as resulting from centuries of defeat and suppression. While Friel and the other writers associated with the Field Day Theatre Company have made a point of addressing themselves first to their Irish audience, his plays make clear to the non-Irish playgoer what oceans of sentimentality and prejudice keep us from seeing the Irish in their true complexity.

Beyond his political analysis of the national passion for talk, to which I shall return, Friel stands out among Irish playwrights by his deft touch with theatrical devices and dramatic structure. In a production of *Philadelphia, Here I Come!* (1964) the audience may not at first realize, unless they have read the play, or unless they are serious types who arrive at the theatre early and study the program before the house lights go down, that the two young men they see talking on stage are, as Friel's notes put it, "two views of the same man." What the audience apprehends are two characters unnervingly familiar with each other's thoughts and lives—or rather with that single life they constitute as private and public aspects of the same character. Considerable time passes before we notice that Gar (Private) is invisible to the other characters and that, in the words of the stage notes, Gar (Public) "never sees him and never looks at him. One cannot look at one's alter ego."

Friel's employment of this and similar devices is both bold and simple. The confidence of his dramatic imagination is apparent in *Dancing at Lughnasa*—pronounced "LOO-nah-sah"—(1990), a triumph in its Abbey Theatre premiere and winner of the Olivier Theatre Award for Best Play of 1990 in London. As the play opens, Michael stands downstage, reminiscing to the audience about his childhood, to one side of the set's rendering of an Irish country kitchen, where the family spends much of its time.

The kitchen in the original Abbey production was realistic, but set at an angle to the audience, with its front and side walls removed so that the space outside the house was not blocked from the vision of either actors or audience. Gerard McSorley, who played Michael at the Abbey, wore a good but rumpled linen suit and the dark shirt and solid-colored tie of someone in the arts, journalism, or advertising. It was clear both from his dress and his accent that he had come some distance from his Donegal upbringing. As the action of the play begins, the child Michael has to be imagined as sitting on the ground outside the cottage, making kites. His mother and aunts address him and respond to him, though the child is invisible and his remarks are assumed rather than heard.

More radical and more difficult, since the illusion must be carried off not visually but by dialogue alone, is the pretense that most of the characters in *Translations* (1981)—though of course the play is in English—speak Irish, which is their only language other than a smattering of Greek and Latin they learn from their "hedge" schoolmaster. Dialogue like the following is a bit disorienting:

> MAIRE: Sum fatigatissima.
> JIMMY: Bene! Optime!
> MAIRE: That's the height of my Latin. Fit me better if I had
>   even that much English.
> JIMMY: English? I thought you had some English?
> MAIRE: Three words . . .

In *Living Quarters* (1978), using the non-naturalistic character Sir as an omniscient guide who stage-manages the Butler family through their shared catastrophe, Friel deconstructs plot as a device for revealing the truth. Such ploys, sometimes outlandish but very clear-cut once the audience has accepted the illusion, give Friel's plays a satisfying crispness on the stage, a reassuring sense that what we are witnessing is guided by a sure hand.

Faith Healer (1980) deserves mention here because it represents a crucial moment in Friel's development. In his early days, his short stories appeared frequently in *The New Yorker*, and perhaps their popularity owed something to the American taste for the occasional glass of Irish sentimentality. In *Philadelphia*, the play that established Friel's reputation on the New York stage, Gar (Private)'s palaver smoothed over, in performance at least, dark truths about the desperate conspiracy in rural Ireland to strangle any attempt to rise above the stultifying influence of the Church, the schools, and a class structure that is all the more rigid for the short distance there is between its cellar and its attic. But Friel later got himself branded as a Republican—with suggestions of being an IRA supporter and an exponent of violence—and he suffered at the box office as a result.

Faith Healer may be seen as a gesture of defiance by Friel as an artist. The play has no political surround. Nor has it a conventional dramatic structure. Instead it daringly organizes itself around four monologues, delivered in turn by the play's three characters. Radical in construction, it is at the same time utterly traditional, utterly Irish one might say—because it depends completely on the Irish genius for captivating an audience, whether in a pub, in someone's kitchen, or in the theatre, by telling a story. The easy approach to the leading role would be to play Frank Hardy, the play's eponymous main character, as a charlatan. The problem is that Frank is not really a fake. He has the gift—on certain nights. I should think the actor would find the parallels to his own art a challenge, and more. James Mason played the role in its first production, at the Longacre Theatre in New York in 1979.

I saw the late Donal McCann—whom moviegoers will remember as Gabriel in John Huston's film of Joyce's story "The Dead"—as Frank in the 1990 Abbey revival. What one could never forget about his performance was the stillness, the sense of nothingness almost, from which his rendering of the character sprang. As he stood motionless on the bare stage, risking the longest pauses I have ever heard and getting away with them, one glimpsed the abyss from which the human enterprise proceeds. Ralph Fiennes attempted the part in a revival at Dublin's Gate Theatre in 2006, and the production was then taken to Broadway; but no one who had seen Donal McCann in the role would say there was any comparison.

The sense that the play represented, for its author, not merely a comeback but a definition of himself as an artist, is borne out by resemblances between the faith healer and the playwright or fictionalist. "It wasn't that he was simply a liar," his wife Grace says about Frank, "it was some compulsion he had to adjust, to refashion, to recreate everything around him. Even the people who came to him . . . yes, they were real enough, but not real as persons, real as fictions, his fictions, extensions of himself. . . ."

The high-spirited banter of Gar (Private) in *Philadelphia* consists of asides audible only by stage convention: remarks Gar (Public) makes to himself. They delight the audience because they remind us of our own inner commentaries. For Gar O'Donnell himself, though, they serve a complex and ambivalent function. Interior dialogue is, first of all, a survival mechanism in this character who exists as his father's employee in the family grocery and dry-goods business in a small town in Ireland in the 1950s. On the other hand, his rich inner life facilitates Gar's further isolation because, providing as it does an outlet for his humor, cynicism, idealism, ambition, and hostility, it prevents him from openly confronting his frustrations in the public arena.

While in performance the fine talker familiar from Irish life and literature has his way with the audience, who leave the theatre under the spell of his charm, all that fine talk constitutes, Friel suggests, a kind of pathology—a character's means not only of surviving psychically through what Skinner in *Freedom of the City* (1974) calls "defensive flippancy," but of managing to keep any hard self-analysis from penetrating his defenses. Casimir in *Aristocrats* (1980), a dotty fabulist, lives in a world of his own invention, wherein his ancestors rub elbows with the famous, as at the birthday party for Balzac in Vienna that he "remembers" his grandfather telling him about:

> Everybody was there: Liszt and George Sand and Turgenev and Mendelssohn and the young Wagner and Berlioz and Delacroix and Verdi—and of course Balzac. Everybody. It went on for days. God knows why Grandfather was there—probably gate-crashed.

A foil to this highly amusing blather is Tom Hoffnung, an American academic doing research on "Recurring cultural, political and social modes in the upper strata of Roman Catholic society in rural Ireland since the act of Catholic Emancipation," as he puts it. To which Casimir, taken aback, replies, "Good heavens. Ha-ha." Tom, with the utmost tact, questions the veracity of Casimir's fables: "A few details, Casimir; perhaps you could help me with them?" Even when he catches Casimir out in all sorts of improbabilities and patent lies, Tom remains gentle and apologetic: "I make little mistakes like that all the time myself. My mother worked for the Bell Telephone Company and until I went to high school I thought she worked for a Mr. Bell who was my uncle for God's sake. . . ." Casimir manages to fabulize even this, getting a huge laugh from the audience by saying a few minutes later, "I suspect he may be a very wealthy man: his uncle owns the Bell Telephone Company."

Friel's characters often maintain fictions about themselves, using talk as a way of supporting these fictions. As in the classic English mystery novel of the 1930s, the action of these plays takes place within a closed community—usually adhering to the classical unities of time, place, and action. The friction of interaction between characters wears these fictions away, and the secret that lies behind the fiction is revealed. In *Translations* the action occurs in the classroom of an Irish "hedge" school of the 1830s; in *Freedom*, in the Lord Mayor's parlor in the Guildhall, Derry; in *Faith Healer*, on a stage that simulates the provincial hired halls where Frank Hardy failed or succeeded in working his healing magic. The three characters in *Faith Healer*, Frank, Grace, and their cockney manager, Teddy, form a family of sorts.

An observer of Irish society might be tempted to identify the Church as the nation's most potent institution. But Tom, the family priest in *Living Quarters*, occupies (though not in his own view) a position only a step above Commandant Frank Butler's personal servant:

> SIR: [reading from a ledger in which he has written out the family's story] "'Is Uncle Tom coming with us?' they'd say. And he did. Always. Everywhere. Himself and the batman—in attendance."
> TOM: That's one way of—
> SIR: "—and that pathetic dependence on the Butler family, together with his excessive drinking make him a cliche, a stereotype. He knows this himself—"

When the Canon, played by Derry Power in the Second Age production of *Philadelphia* I saw in Dublin a few years ago, first appeared on stage, his white hair and lobster-red face triggered an immediate shock of recognition, as Gar (Private) muttered "Bugger the Canon!" Like Uncle Tom in *Living Quarters*, this priest is a harmless old parasite whom no one takes seriously. Here he is arriving for his nightly game of draughts with S. B. O'Donnell:

> CANON: She says I wait till the rosary's over and the kettle's on . . . hee-hee-hee.
> S.B.: She's a sharp one, Madge.
> CANON: "You wait," says she, "till the rosary's over and the kettle's on!"

The schoolmaster, another brick in the wall of the Irish village, gives Gar, as a going away present, a book of his poems ("I had them printed privately last month. Some of them are a bit mawkish but you'll not notice any distinction") before touching him up for the loan of ten shillings on his way to the pub.

But the observer I invoked in the previous paragraph would be mistaken if he gave the Church pride of place among Irish institutions. The family, that prototype of the closed community, is the prime focus of Brian Friel's analytical dissection of Irish society. Why the family is an even mightier force in Ireland than elsewhere may be explained in part by the country's history. Though there were petty kings in Ireland as far back as its history can be traced, Ireland never had the centralized government of countries like England. Loyalty always meant loyalty to a clan. When Ireland became part of the British Empire, the family provided one of the few available defenses against the redcoats and the landlord.

I have mentioned that the three characters in *Faith Healer* constitute an impromptu family, and that Tom in *Living Quarters* clings pathetically to the Butler family. Likewise, Madge, the housekeeper in *Philadelphia*, gives Gar the maternal love he never received from his mother, who died three days after giving birth to him. The play's central pathos, though, resides in Gar's and his father S. B.'s inability to connect. The moment that Gar remembers fondly from childhood involves a blue boat in which father and son once went fishing. When Gar finally brings himself to mention the boat, this is his father's response:

> S.B.: (Justly, reasonably) There was a brown one belonging to the doctor, and before that there was a wee flat-bottom—but it was green—or was it white? I'll tell you, you wouldn't be thinking of a punt—it could have been blue—one that the curate had down at the pier last Summer—

Once Gar has gone to bed on his last night at home before emigrating to America, his father tenderly relates to Madge some moments he recalls from Gar's childhood. But they can never say these things to each other. The bonds between parent and child are parodied in the play when Gar (Public) discusses with his friend Joe his decision to emigrate:

> JOE: Lucky bloody man. I wish I was you.
> PUBLIC: There's nothing stopping you, is there?
> JOE: Only that the mammy planted sycamore trees last year, and she says I can't go till they're tall enough to shade the house.
> PUBLIC: You're stuck for another couple of days, then.

To put broader political issues in a larger context, Friel's favorite ploy is to bring an "expert," like Tom Hoffnung in *Aristocrats*, on stage—or, in *Freedom*, Dr. Dobbs, another American professor, who announces: "I'm a sociologist and my field of study is inherited poverty or the culture of poverty or more accurately the subculture of poverty." Dr. Dobbs's ideas simplify the characters, but do not ultimately distort them. That the subculture of poverty provides the chronically poor with strategies for self-definition and survival will meet with little disagreement.

But a balance of viewpoint is achieved by the presence and the dialogue of characters who actually come from "the subculture of poverty," and who are more likely to be talking about things like how their feet hurt, or whether the horses they bet on have won or lost. These characters are not, however—some of them, at any rate—incapable of analyzing their own predicaments:

> SKINNER: If I'm sick, the entire wisdom of the health authority is at my service. And should I die, the welfare people would bury me in style. It's only when I'm alive and well that I'm a problem.

Dancing at Lughnasa's cultural explorations are both broader and more dramatic than anything Friel had attempted before. Early in the play the casual language of the characters establishes a framework of "civilized" Christian contempt for all that is "pagan," non-European, uncontrollable. The new wireless set, which Maggie, the joker of the family, at first wants to call "Lugh, after the old Celtic God of the Harvest" (this is the narrator Michael's voice), has thrown the household into disarray here in the summer of 1936. One of the sisters calls two of the others, who have hiked up their skirts and are dancing, "A right pair of pagans, the two of you." But the "voodoo" radio is not alone in disrupting this tightly controlled household. Living a short distance from the fictional town of Ballybeg (where most of Friel's plays are set), the Mundys are townies who hold themselves above the country people—particularly the back-country folk who celebrate the druidic festival of Lughnasa. "Pagan" influences, though, seep irresistibly into the Mundys' lives.

Some of the play's funniest moments are provided by Michael's Uncle Jack, a priest who has been repatriated from Africa not, as we at first are told, because of poor health, but because during his years in the mythical country of Ryanga, he has been converted to the wisdom of the "pagan" religion the natives follow. Jack often finds himself using the pronoun "we" when describing Ryangan customs: "That's what we do in Ryanga when we want to please the spirits—or to appease them: we kill a rooster or a young goat." Significantly, Jack has come to think in Swahili and is having a hard time recovering his English: "When Europeans call, we speak English."

In answer to Maggie's having asked whether, if they went to Ryanga, Jack could find husbands for the four sisters, Jack replies: "I couldn't promise four men but I should be able to get one husband for all of you." Not a bad solution to the Mundy sisters' problems, since "the husband and his wives and his children make up a small commune where everybody helps everybody else and cares for them." The schoolteacher Kate's response brings the house down:

> KATE: It may be efficient and you may be in favor of it, Jack, but I don't think it's what Pope Pius XI considers to be the holy sacrament of matrimony. And it might be better for you if you paid just a bit more attention to our Holy Father and a bit less to the Great Goddess . . . Iggie.

A few moments later, Michael's errant father Gerry, dancing with one of Michael's mother's sisters to the tune of "Anything Goes," hints that group marriage might suit him very well. Later we learn that he has another wife and family in Wales. So in this and other ways Jack may be correct in saying "In some respects [the Ryangans are] not unlike us."

Having identified the family as his characters' major frustration, Friel asks: as constricting, as repressive, as the family may be, where would we be without its support? Kate, head of the predominantly female family, puts it this way:

> You work hard at your job. You try to keep the home together. You perform your duties as best you can—because you believe in responsibilities and obligations and good

order. And then suddenly, suddenly you realize that hair cracks are appearing everywhere; that control is slipping away; that the whole thing is so fragile it can't be held together much longer. It's all about to collapse, Maggie.

That provincial Irish life is hag-ridden by failure and small-mindedness, that the country still has a long mile to go before shaking off its postcolonial mentality, in no way diminishes the humor, good-heartedness, and courage of its people. Certainly it makes little sense to speak of Ireland as Ben, the Episcopalian from America, speaks of the United States: "It's just another place to live, Elise: Ireland—America—what's the difference?" On the one hand Ireland's best and brightest have traditionally tended to leave, at the same time asking themselves, in Camden Town, South Boston, the Bronx, and Sydney: "God, Boy, why do you have to leave? Why? Why?", as Gar asks himself on the eve of his departure from Ballybeg, only to answer his own question: "I don't know. I—I—I don't know." For the exiles in Friel's plays, according to Seamus Deane, "their ultimate perception is that fidelity to the native place is a lethal form of nostalgia." If emigration opens up a dream world of infinite possibility, home is where everything is known. Frank Hardy, returning to Ireland, sensing he will die there, concludes, "At long last I was renouncing chance."

And yet for all that, Friel sees in Ireland an authenticity of culture and personality, an integral society, unchanged in many ways since the Middle Ages. In *Philadelphia*, Friel identifies Ireland—and he is only partly ironic here—with the ancien régime, having Gar O'Donnell recite as a recurrent motif Edmund Burke's paean to pre-Revolutionary France: "It is now sixteen or seventeen years since I saw the Queen of France, then the Dauphiness, at Versailles; and surely never lighted on this orb, which she hardly seemed to touch, a more delightful vision. . . ."

Brian Friel

A play is not a tissue of ideas, however, or even of words, but rather a spectacle, an experience. Leaving a Brian Friel play, looking for a taxi or hurrying to the pub before closing time, one is less likely to feel depressed by the puritanical repressiveness of small-town Ireland than heartened by an impression of the human spirit asserting itself in the face of impediments: Gar's mordant asides; the risky improvisations of Skinner, who just before stepping outside into Guildhall Square in Derry, where he will be slaughtered by automatic weapons fire from British troops, signs himself in the visitors' book in the mayor's office: "Freeman of the city." And when one remembers *Dancing at Lughnasa*, one smiles, thinking of the play's most celebrated (and significantly, almost wordless) scene, where the Mundy sisters, inspired by music from their "voodoo" radio, break into spontaneous dance, a pure expression of defiance and transcendence.

Seamus Heaney's "Middle Voice"

The convenient fit between poetry and politics suggested by the coupling of Seamus Heaney's 1995 Nobel Prize with the peace process in Northern Ireland is not so neat as the journalism I have read on the subject would have us believe. Not only is Heaney not a product of the Northern Ireland conflict, his is a sensibility that seeks to assuage (one of his favorite words) and to heal. It would not be true to say, as Auden wrote of Yeats, that "mad Ireland hurt you into poetry." Unlike the early Auden, whose genius was sharpened by the revolutionary currents of the 1930s, Heaney would prefer, it seems to me, not to have lived in what his younger contemporary Eavan Boland has called "a time of violence." On the other hand, if Heaney is seen as a symbol of rapprochement and healing, then the political symbolism of his Nobel Prize is brilliantly apt.

Seamus Heaney has never evidenced the kind of cultural parochialism represented, for example, by the tragic destruction of Dublin's Georgian architecture since the 1950s in the name of anticolonialism. He seems to have gleaned from his own reading and from his education at Queens University in

Belfast a sense that the English literary tradition was his to do with what he chose. When he once, rightly, bristled at being placed in an anthology of British poetry, he averred that if he were going to be placed among the *English* poets, that would be another matter—defining his work in terms of the language rather than of a political entity. In "The Ministry of Fear" from the sequence "Singing School," this is how he puts it in the 1975 collection, *North*, assessing what it was like to apprentice as a writer in Northern Ireland:

> Ulster was British, but with no rights on
> the English lyric: all around us, though
> We hadn't named it, the ministry of fear.

In the short poem "Holly" from *Station Island* (1984), while the experience rendered in the poem comes straight out of an Irish childhood, Heaney doesn't hesitate for a moment to marshal the full resources of English, both linguistic and cultural. It is one of many poems in which this poet struggles to reconcile the journey that has brought him from a farm in County Derry to his position as one of the most honored literary figures in the English-speaking world. The remembered scene couldn't be homelier: a childhood Christmastime expedition in search of greenery to decorate the house, when "the ditches were swimming, we were wet / to the knees, our hands were all jags // and water ran up our sleeves." Fast-forward to adulthood:

> Now here I am, in a room that is decked
> with the red-berried, waxy-leafed stuff,
>
> and I almost forget what it's like
> to be wet to the skin or longing for snow.
>
> I reach for a book like a doubter
> and want it to flare round my hand

a black-letter bush, a glittering shield-wall
cutting as holly and ice.

The poem is a lament for the intensity of childhood enthusiasms, even for childhood discomforts. The book he reaches for
would be a substitute for those intensities. I find it striking that
as a metaphor for the "cutting" sharpness he seeks, Heaney
comes up with an image from Anglo-Saxon celebrations of war,
the "shield-wall" familiar to readers of poems like "The Battle of
Maldon."

This is a literary heritage few Irish poets have claimed as
their own. The thrust of the Irish nativist movement since Independence has been to recover a cultural heritage suppressed
under English rule. Few modern poets have taken the course of
actually writing in Irish as, for instance, Máire Mhac an tSaoi,
Michael Hartnett, Nuala Ní Dhomhnaill, Michael Davitt, and
Liam Ó Muithile (as well as Micheal O'Siadhail in his early
books) have done; but few, I think, would range so freely in the
cultural territory of "the oppressor." Even the Anglo-Irish Yeats
and others in the Celtic Revival movement looked for cultural
references to the battles of Cuchulain or some other figure out
of Irish myth. Heaney's counterthrust finds a rough parallel in
the poetry of Derek Walcott, who emerged in the Caribbean
from another outpost of the former British Empire. The approach here has been to make free with one's linguistic heritage
and not be programmatic about where it came from. As op-
posed to many ideological approaches that come to mind,
Heaney's way with the material may be seen as commonsensical
and workmanlike.

"Making Strange," another poem from the 1984 collection,
shows Heaney engaged in the same kind of cultural mediation.
Here the conflict transpires at first not within the poet, but in a
triangular configuration involving two other people he brings together on his native turf:

I stood between them,
the one with his travelled intelligence
and tawny containment,
his speech like the twang of a bowstring,

and another, unshorn and bewildered
in the tubs of his wellingtons,
smiling at me for help,
faced with this stranger I'd brought him.

The use of language here is pure Heaney, with its well-rubbed, determinedly unabstract adjective "tawny," and its tight, masterly simile, "like the twang of a bowstring." What other poet could set the scene so sure-handedly and with so little fuss?

It's easy to imagine the farmer scratching his head and rocking back and forth in his mud-spattered Wellington boots, contemplating this sleek exotic his friend the poet has presented him with. An article and interview with Heaney by James Campbell in the *Guardian* review section for 27 May 2006 provides an interesting biographical note into the genesis of the poem:

> The poem "Making Strange" describes an incident in which Heaney picked up the American poet Louis Simpson from the airport. "And we stopped at a public house about 150 yards from where I grew up. We were standing on the street at the pub and my father came up—'unshorn and bewildered / in the tubs of his wellingtons'—and in a sense I was almost introducing him as subject matter." The memory provokes the amused self-awareness that underlies many of his jokes and asides. "Or I could see that Simpson would see him as that."

Having set up the dramatic face-to-face between these two, Heaney leaves them for a moment and goes within. Or rather, "a

cunning middle voice / came out of the field across the road . . ."
The voice's message goes right to the heart of the divided experience dramatized in "Holly," because it says "Be adept and be dialect . . . love the cut of this travelled one," and calling forth the Old Testament's most memorable symbol of alienation, the voice says, "call me also the cornfield of Boaz." Keats also alludes to the story of Ruth and Boaz in "Ode to a Nightingale." The immortal Bird's voice is "Perhaps the self-same song that found a path / Through the sad heart of Ruth, when, sick for home, / She stood in tears amid the alien corn."

Elsewhere Heaney writes that in school he took on the Latin pen-name "Incertus," with a soft *c* to underscore his innate shyness. And here the middle voice is a voice of encouragement and departures, urging him on to

'Go beyond what's reliable
in all that keeps pleading and pleading,
these eyes and puddles and stones,
and recollect how bold you were

when I visited you first
with departures you cannot go back on.'

Just as in Keats's poem, there is a bird here also—not the grand Romantic nightingale, though, but a common Irish bird of field and stone wall: "A chaffinch flicked from an ash," bringing him out of his reverie. Heaney is master of actions that bring two worlds together, enhancing them both. The poem stubbornly asserts the departures Heaney has earned for himself; but paradoxically it is the homely things of farm and field that he has been able to "make strange."

As for the political ramifications of Heaney's middle voice, it is worth quoting from a short piece he wrote for the BBC periodical, *The Listener*, back in 1971:

For some people in this [Northern Irish] community, the exercise of goodwill towards the dominant caste has been hampered by the psychological hoops they have been made to jump and by the actual circumstances of their lives within the state, British and all as it may have been. A little goodwill in the Establishment here towards the notion of being Irish would take some of the twists out of the minority. Even at this time it is difficult to extend full sympathy to the predicament of that million among us who would ask the other half-million to exalt themselves by being humbled.

Even granted that this was written for a British audience, what restraint, what dignified irony there is in this passage! While faulting the British majority for bullying the Irish minority, he evenhandedly acknowledges the "twists" in the psychology of the dominated caste. And note the use of "caste" itself, pointing out an inflexible social structure in a province where advancement for the Catholic Irish is all but impossible.

Having gone back more than a decade from *Station Island* to the early days of the recent Northern Ireland conflict, I'll range forward again to *North* (1975), Heaney's most explicit comment on the Troubles. Readers hoping for a passionate defender of the Republican cause were not going to find it in Heaney, whose sympathy was with the victims on both sides. And as he notes in "Whatever You Say Say Nothing," language itself, including his own, is one of the victims:

Yet I live here, I live here too, I sing,

Expertly civil-tongued with civil neighbours
On the high wires of first wireless reports,
Sucking the fake taste, the stony flavours
Of those sanctioned, old, elaborate retorts:

'Oh, it's disgraceful, surely, I agree,'
'Where's it going to end?' 'It's getting worse.'

Contemplating the ironic use of "sing" in this passage, one might consider its distance from Keats's nightingale and Yeats's golden bird in "Sailing to Byzantium": "set upon a golden bough to sing / to lords and ladies of Byzantium / Of what is past, or passing, or to come."

Among the several reconciliations that concern Heaney is that between male and female, even the male and female elements within one personality. In his 1978 essay "Yeats As an Example?", he sees such a blending taking place in Yeats toward the end of his life:

> On the one hand, Yeats lies under Ben Bulben, in Drumcliff Churchyard, under that dominant promontory which I like to think of as the father projected into the landscape, and there is perhaps something too male and assertive about the poem that bears the mountain's name and stands at the end of the *Collected Poems*.

Heaney proposes as a more fitting conclusion the poem "Cuchulain Comforted," written shortly before the death of Ireland's earlier Nobel Prize-winning poet. "It is a poem deeply at one with the weak and the strong of the earth"—and here one thinks of Heaney's own response to the Troubles—"full of a motherly kindness toward life, but also unflinching in its belief in the propriety and beauty of life transcended into art, song, words."

In "The Harvest Bow," a poem written about the same time he would have been writing the essay on Yeats, Heaney enunciates an artistic credo based on the Irish folk-craft of weaving lapel decorations and crosses out of wheat straw left over from the harvest. The first lines—"As you plaited the harvest bow / You implicated the mellowed silence in you"—introduce a "you" whose identity is never specified: his father or grandfather perhaps? In "Cuchulain Comforted" Yeats has his hero, "a man / Violent and famous" who "strode among the dead," humble himself and sew a shroud for himself in the underworld. Heaney says nothing explicitly to indicate that the "you" is male, except that he has "lapped the spurs on a lifetime of game cocks" and that he carries a stick, "Whacking the tips of weeds and bushes." He makes with his practiced fingers "A throwaway love-knot of straw."

Quietness, mellowness, love have been—in Heaney's lovely use of a latinate word for its etymological suggestions—"implicated," or folded into, the harvest bow to the extent that it becomes a talisman: "I tell and finger it like braille, / Gleaning the unsaid off the palpable." The words are rich with connotations: That he can "tell" the object, likens it to a rosary; that he is "gleaning" something off it, shows that where its maker has reaped, he comes along behind like Ruth and picks up what remains, which is what it means to glean. Twentieth-century poetry is rich with objects used as sources of meaning: William Carlos Williams's red wheelbarrow, Elizabeth Bishop's toy horse and ballerina from "Cirque d'Hiver," Robert Lowell's father's battered chair from "91 Revere Street," Sylvia Plath's menacing elm in her poem of the same name, the laundry in Richard Wilbur's "Love Calls Us to the Things of This World." But I can think of no poem that uses an object more evocatively than "The Harvest Bow" does. Heaney can almost literally see into it:

> And if I spy into its golden loops
> I see us walk between the railway slopes
> Into an evening of long grass and midges,
> Blue smoke straight up, old beds and ploughs in hedges,
> An auction notice on an outhouse wall—
> You with a harvest bow in your lapel . . .

This poet, "Incertus" no longer, even has the confidence to come right out—in defiance of conventional twentieth-century poetic practice —and draw an explicit meaning from the harvest bow, quoting from Coventry Patmore:

> *The end of art is peace*
> Could be the motto of this frail device
> That I have pinned up on our deal dresser—
> Like a drawn snare
> Slipped lately by the spirit of the corn
> Yet burnished by its passage, and still warm.

If the Nobel Prize committee registered the message of this "frail device" when it linked Seamus Heaney with the excruciatingly slow but hopeful rapprochement between the Unionist and Nationalist communities in Northern Ireland, then its decision was a wise one indeed.

Derek Mahon:
Exile and Stranger

Ireland over the past few decades has been the breed-
ing ground for a dozen or so notable poets. One of
them, Seamus Heaney, has become world-renowned, and rightly
so. A quite different poet, equally worthy of attention, is Derek
Mahon, a near-contemporary of Heaney's, born in 1941, two
years later than the Nobel Laureate. He has not, through most of
his career, been especially prolific. His carefully winnowed *Selected Poems* (1991) contains most of the essential early Mahon;
my focus in this chapter will be on two favorites of mine, *The
Hudson Letter* (1995) and *The Yellow Book* (1997)—fresh, witty,
and often coruscating, at once classic and demotic.

Like Heaney, Mahon was born and raised in Northern Ireland. Unlike his more celebrated contemporary, he is city-
bred, a native of Belfast; and he is culturally a Protestant. While
Heaney attended Queens University in Belfast, Mahon went
south to Dublin, where he studied at Trinity College, then on to
the Sorbonne. Heaney left the North for residence in Dublin
and professorships at Harvard and Oxford, but his work is justly
noted for its rootedness in the rural world of his childhood.
Mahon on the other hand has lived outside Ireland for years at a

time, working in London as a journalist, playwright, and screen-writer.

During his London years he was variously theatre critic for *The Listener*, poetry editor of the *New Statesman*, and features editor at *Vogue*. His career in England somewhat parallels that of his poetic mentor, Louis MacNeice, also a Northern Protestant who was a producer in London for the BBC. He has also been active as a translator from French—Gerard de Nerval, Villon, and others—as well as from classical texts. His versions of *The School for Wives* and *The School for Husbands* (titled *High Times* in Mahon's version) have been mounted on the Dublin stage. For several years his home base was New York, where he lived in the West Village—Perry Street, as I recall—taught at New York University, and wrote *The Hudson Letter*. The poet he most re-sembles may be W. H. Auden. Like Joyce and Beckett, Auden and MacNeice, Mahon has led a life of exile and estrangement. By 1996, though, he had returned to Dublin to live in the "attic flat" he mentions in *The Yaddo Letter* (1992), above "the damp gardens of Fitzwilliam Square."

A pandemic flaw of the American poem, inherited from Whitman, is a determination to make the grand gesture, to exhibit the monumentality exemplified by *Leaves of Grass*. Celebrating one's soul all too often leads to windbaggery. More recently we have been plagued by a fuzzy mysticism not far removed—though its practitioners would not appreciate the comparison—from the sentimental vapors of late Victorian verse. By contrast, Mahon's work is reticent, witty, and bracingly hard-edged. Most refreshingly he does not attempt the de ri-gueur transcendental moment at the end of a poem, where most American writers feel called upon to hit high C. Few poets in the United States would close a poem, as Mahon closes "A Light-house in Maine," which may be found in his *Selected Poems*, as simply as this: "You turn a corner and / There it is, shining / In modest glory like // The soul of Adonais. / Out you get and / Walk the rest of the way." The plain-spokenness, the unraised voice, are quite in keeping with the look of the lighthouse in its New England setting.

"Afterlives," dedicated to another Ulster poet, James Simmons, and announcing "I am going home by sea / For the first time in years," comments on the civil strife in the northern province: "the faith does not die // That in our time these things / Will amaze the literate children / In their non-sectarian schools . . ." The relation in which Mahon stands to the city of his birth is essayed tentatively and bemusedly:

> And I step ashore in a fine rain
> To a city so changed
> By five years of war
> I scarcely recognize
> The places I grew up in,
> The faces that try to explain.
>
> But the hills are still the same
> Grey-blue above Belfast.
> Perhaps if I'd stayed behind
> And lived it bomb by bomb
> I might have grown up at last
> And learnt what is meant by home.

Two notes glancingly struck here—the northern landscape and the occluded hint of personal distress—I shall briefly comment on later.

But the first thing to notice is Mahon's handling of the verse. If, within the insular (or to use the poet's own formulation, "era-provincial") world of late-twentieth-century American practice, to praise a poet for technical expertise sounds like faint praise, it only proves how far and how damagingly our poetry has drifted from its traditional moorings in the simple but hard-to-achieve act of writing well. Ezra Pound says somewhere that technique is proof of sincerity. Only those who have made the effort can know how difficult it is to produce an epigrammatic bombshell like the last, seven-line iambic pentameter stanza of "Knut Hamsun in Old Age," which challenges a high-flown assertion of Yeats's:

> One fortunate in both would have us choose
> 'Perfection of the life or of the work'.
> Nonsense, you work best on a full stomach
> As everybody over thirty knows—
> For who, unbreakfasted, will love the lark?
> Prepare your protein-fed epiphanies,
> Your heavenly mansions blazing in the dark.

For readers whose knowledge of the techniques of verse is rusty, it might be well to point out Mahon's use of both full- and half-rhymes here to bind the stanza together: choose/knows/epiphanies; work/lark/dark. But what about "stomach"? Does that partially rhyme with "work/lark/dark," or is it a free-floater like "war," "recognize," and "behind" in the passage I quoted from "Afterlives"? Mahon's patent mastery of rhyme and meter allows him to leave some rough edges showing, some informalities of technique. Every good versifier, from Shakespeare on, knows that strict adherence to "the rules" is the poetic equivalent of Emerson's "hobgoblin of little minds."

An essential if unspoken requirement for poetry in rhyme and meter is that it must sound natural. Yeats has the last word on the subject: "A line will take us hours maybe; / Yet if it does not seem a moment's thought, / Our stitching and unstitching has been naught." There is a world of difference between the rough edges visible in the verse of masters like Yeats, Auden, MacNeice, Heaney, Michael Longley, and Mahon on the one hand, and today's young converts to "form" who set great store by following the rules. Robert Pinsky begins the first chapter of his handbook, *The Sounds of Poetry: A Brief Guide*, with the following one-sentence paragraph: "There are no rules."

It is instructive to see how Mahon puts a poem together. "Day Trip to Donegal" at first seems to be a straightforward narration of an excursion to the wild maritime county mentioned in the title: "We reached the sea in early afternoon, / Climbed stiffly out. There were things to be done, / Clothes to be picked up, friends to be seen." His account of the trip clips right along; typically, he wastes little time setting the scene and providing atmosphere. This narrative economy sets Mahon's poems apart from those of Seamus Heaney, who describes places atmospherically and spends more time evoking the sense of place.

Here is how Mahon describes Donegal: "As ever, the nearby hills were a deeper green / Than anywhere in the world, and the grave / Grey of the sea the grimmer in that enclave." The famous greenness of the Irish landscape stands in contrast here to shades of that color elsewhere; the poem assumes that the reader comes, like the poet himself, from somewhere else. Mahon paints the sea's greyness not in terms of color value, but morally, in terms of its grimness. When the party leaves Donegal, the drive back is rendered crisply, in a six-line stanza made up of three couplets:

> We left at eight, drove back the way we came,
> The sea receding down each muddy lane.
> Around midnight we changed-down into suburbs
> Sunk in a sleep no gale-force wind disturbs.
> The time of year had left its mark
> On frosty pavements glistening in the dark.

From the blowsy soul-celebrations and philosophical maunderings found in much contemporary American poetry, one turns to sharp-edged verse like this with relief and delight. "Give me a ring, goodnight, and so to bed . . ." the evening ends. And what is the aftermath of this little excursion? A disturbing dream image takes us by surprise:

> At dawn I was alone far out at sea
> Without skill or reassurance—nobody
> To show me how, no promise of rescue—
> Cursing my constant failure to take due
> Forethought for this; contriving vain
> Overtures to the vindictive wind and rain.

The bad dream is the flip-side of the liberating Donegal landscape and seascape. The aesthetic that Yeats frames in "The Fisherman" comes to mind: he sought to write a poem, Yeats says, "as cold and passionate as the dawn." The wild, exhilarating impact of the previous day's experience has changed, by morning, to desolation. The use of generalized attributes, "skill or reassurance," is apt in context. Nothing more specific feels called for. And the plaintive "nobody / to show me how" is simply put and affecting.

Personal glimpses like this can be harrowing; Mahon more characteristically looks outside himself, as he does in "Lives," dedicated to Seamus Heaney, where the speaking voice comes from an "I" whose identity changes throughout the poem. The voice emanates first from an ancient relic, "a torc of gold"; "a labourer / Turned me up with a pick / In eighteen fifty-four // And sold me / for tea and sugar / In Newmarket-on-Fergus." Later the "I" is "a bump of clay // In a Navaho rug." One might make a stab at identifying this shape-shifting essence: a certain quality of authenticity, a product of folkways that are evaporating from the world. As the poem ends, the voice challenges the hyper-rationalized humanity that is taking over, by throwing down the following gauntlet:

Derek Mahon

And if in the distant

Future someone
Thinks he has once been me
As I am today,

Let him revise
His insolent ontology
Or teach himself to pray.

An exile by choice like Auden, Mahon shares with the older poet a tense awareness that he is writing in a time of crisis, shouldering the responsibility to speak publicly on pressing issues of the day. In the last stanza of his elegy "In Carrowdore Churchyard," subtitled "at the grave of Louis MacNeice," are found these Audenesque phrases that bring the natural and personal worlds together with the *res publica*: "From the pneumonia of the ditch, from the ague / Of the blind poet and the bombed-out town you bring / The all-clear to the empty holes of spring . . ."

Mahon shares MacNeice's fatalism and lacks the early Auden's hopefulness that we may eventually be able to cure our many inherent ills. He would never issue an early-Auden bromide like "We must love one another or die." (In fairness it must be noted that Auden himself later backed away from that easy formulation.) If his frequent attempts to grapple not only with the roots of the Troubles in Northern Ireland but with other issues fail to offer solutions, at least they convince the reader of their genuineness, often expressed, as in "The Attic," in the form of a disclaimer: "I who know nothing / Scribbling on the off-chance, / Darkening the white page, / Cultivating my ignorance."

In Ireland, with its layers of history and prehistory, the modern observer often feels like an archaeologist. One of Mahon's consistent concerns is the contrast between this country's violent, heroic past and its modern, ordinary present. Mahon's best-known poem that contemplates this contrast is "Glengormley," which leads off the selection from his work in Paul Muldoon's *Contemporary Irish Poetry*. It takes its title and setting from a middle-class suburb of Belfast. Mahon is at his poised, satirical best, effortlessly encompassing broad expanses of cultural history. Here is the first stanza:

> Wonders are many and none is more wonderful than man
> Who has tamed the terrier, trimmed the hedge
> And grasped the principle of the watering can.
> Clothes-pegs litter the window-ledge
> And the long ships lie in clover; washing lines
> Shake out white linen over the chalk thanes.

"Now we are safe from monsters," the poem goes on to say. The saints and heroes of earlier days are gone:

> And much dies with them. I should rather praise
> A worldly time under this worldly sky—
> The terrier-taming, garden-watering days
> Those heroes pictured as they struggled through
> The quick noose of their finite being. By
> Necessity, if not choice, I live here too.

In a later poem, "Rathlin," Mahon contemplates the violent history of an island off the coast of Northern Ireland: "A long time since the last scream cut short—" the poem begins, "Then an unnatural silence; and then / A natural silence . . ." Returning to the mainland from the island in a motorboat, he concludes the poem with a thought that yokes the violence and chaos of the future: "We leave here the infancy of the race, / Unsure among the pitching surfaces / Whether the future lies before us or behind."

Derek Mahon

Given his cosmopolitan stance, his generalizing rhetoric, and the urban setting of many of his poems, it comes as something of a surprise that Mahon responds so keenly to the natural world. Nature is not at the center of his vision, as it has been in Irish poetry for centuries, but it turns up here and there, and always delightfully. He has a particular appreciation for the limestone-bedded, deforested littoral landscape: "Out there you would look in vain / For a rose bush; but find, / Rooted in stony ground, / A last stubborn growth / Battered by constant rain / And twisted by the sea-wind . . ." There are no pastoral escapes in this realist's world, but neither is the freshness of bird and flower denied. Here, from "Ford Manor," is a little house near London that retains its saving remnant of natural life even when dominated by reminders of industrial civilization:

> Even on the calmest nights the fitful
> prowl of planes is seldom still
> where Gatwick tilts to guide them home
> from Tokyo, New York or Rome;
> yet even today the earth disposes
> bluebells, roses and primroses,
> the dawn throat-whistle of a thrush
> deep in the dripping lilac bush.

The thrush singing in the lilac bush comes across as vividly as any natural image from the world of haiku. The musicality of rhythm and rhyme enhance the poem's lyricism. The varied rhyming of these couplets is the work of someone with an extraordinary ear. The way the unaccented second syllable of "fitful" rhymes with the accented "still" creates a subtle rhythm, avoiding the clunky effect sometimes produced when two monosyllables rhyme fully. The same music occurs with the rhyme between "disposes" and "primroses"; since the accent of the latter comes on the first syllable, the rhyme achieves a nicely floating effect sometimes referred to by students of prosody as "hovering accent." Finally the slight difference in vowel sounds between "thrush" and "bush" adds to the delicacy of the thrush singing in the lilac right after the rain.

*T*he Hudson Letter, a poetic sequence published in 1995 against a personal background of alcoholism, divorce, and writer's block—of which his recourse to translation is probably symptomatic—represents a rebirth for Derek Mahon. The iambic pentameter couplets are more brilliant than ever, and there's a wonderful lightness of spirit in the lines. Even the *cri de coeur*, "Oh, show me how to recover my lost nerve!" sounds like the exclamation of someone who has already accomplished that recovery. Whatever lapses he has recovered from, in this book he is clearly back on his feet again. This is a jaunty Mahon, delighted by life in New York City:

> The lights go out along the Jersey shore
> and, as Manhattan faces east once more,
> dawn's early light on bridge and water-tower,
> Respighi's temperate nightingale on WQXR
> pipes up though stronger stations throng the air,
> a radio serendipity to illustrate
> the resilience of our lyric appetite,
> carnivalesque or studiously apart—
> on tap in offices, lofts and desperate 'hoods
> to Lorca's 'urinating multitudes'
> while I make coffee and listen for the news
> at eight, but first the nightingale. Sing, Muse.

Passages like this, good-humoredly satirical, inspired by the life of the metropolis, illustrate poetry's power to celebrate the quotidian, suffusing it with a sense of quiet joy. An observer overlooking the street bears interested witness as "out of the blue, / 'out there', under the fire-escape, some psycho / sends up a stream of picturesque abuse / directed, evidently, at my 4th-floor window, / his reasoning trenchant, complex and abstruse—". Or later, "Dawn; the kick-start as some heroine / draws on her gloves for the Harley-Davidson dream trip / to Provincetown, Key West or Sunset Strip." These cadences are at least as old as the urban poetry of Jonathan Swift and Alexander Pope, but how freshly they render the energies of Manhattan!

The Hudson Letter may be seen as an interlude, since the sequence removes Mahon from his regular stomping grounds in Belfast, Dublin, and London. On the other hand, since New York is to some extent the creation of Irish immigrants, it's as much the Irish poet's turf as anyone else's. Garcia Lorca's "Poet in New York," which Mahon alludes to above, is after all one of the city's defining works. A versified letter from one Bridget Moore to her mother in Cork puts the experiences of this recent Irish émigré in historical perspective: "I get each Sunday off and use the privilege / to explore Broadway, the new Brooklyn Bridge / or the Statue of Liberty, copper torch on top / which, wd. you believe it, actually lights up . . ."

It would hardly work, however, to place Derek Mahon among the "huddled masses." Though his humanity is large enough to include Bridget Moore, this poet-in-exile gives us two more apt self-images: W. H. Auden in "Auden on St. Mark's Place," and John Butler Yeats, W. B. Yeats's father, who spent his last years in New York, in "Imbolc: JBY." Addressing the ghost of Auden in Greenwich Village, Mahon writes: "you prescribe a cure / for our civilization and its discontents / based on *agapé*, Baroque opera, common sense / and the creative impulse that brought us here, / sustaining us now as we face a more boring future." Mahon himself prescribes no cures.

Though he searches and ponders, though like Auden and Freud he is a keen student of "our civilization and its discon-

tents," part of his authenticity derives from his honest bafflement—a reminder that poetry of the highest order is as much
about what we do not know as what we know. In working toward
a definition of this most adept and yet finally unfinished poet, we
might want to include our voices in the question Mahon asks of
John Butler Yeats: "may we add / that you were at home here and
in human nature? / —But also, in your words, lived and died /
like all of us, then as now, 'an exile and a stranger'?"

Toward the end of the last century Mahon returned to
live in Dublin. If *The Hudson Letter* reports on life in
exile, *The Yellow Book* represents an exile's return. (I use the
terms "exile" and "return" in a relative sense: given the ease of
air travel between New York and Dublin, Mahon would have
been able to go back and forth freely.) With the fastest-growing
economy in Europe, the Irish society that the returning Mahon
finds—this applies to Dublin in particular—is changing in ways
he finds repellent. In New York he could remain detached, con-
descendingly tolerant:

> an amateur immigrant, sure I like the corny
> humanism and car-stickers—'I [heart symbol] NY'—
> and yet remain sardonic and un-*chic*,
> an undesirable 'resident alien' on this shore,
> a face in the crowd in this 'off-shore boutique' . . .
> ("Global Village," *The Hudson Letter*)

In Dublin the changes hit too close for comfort. He sees his
own neighborhood becoming "a Georgian theme-park for the
tourist." In his scorn of "the pastiche paradise of the postmodern," Mahon inscribes the most devastating and curmud-
geonly heroic couplets and quatrains now being written.
    But he is more than a satirist of "an age of sado-mone-
tarism." As the millennium turned, Mahon was pushing sixty

and thus arriving at an age where elegy becomes one's habitual mode of experiencing the world. In "To Eugene Lambe in Heaven" in *The Yellow Book*, he vividly evokes several "scenes" that readers who were there will enjoy—London in the "swinging 60s," for instance:

> At a time of drag and Pop Art, hair and clothes,
> Beardsley prints, floral design and rainbow hues,
> of Quant and Biba, Shrimpton and Twiggy, lurid tights,
> gratuitous gesture, instant celebrity, insolent pose . . .

"Oft in the stilly night," he concludes this reminiscence, "I remember our wasted youth."

"At the Shelbourne" is a verse account of the Dublin hotel, for decades a social and literary landmark. In this poem Mahon speaks in the voice of Elizabeth Bowen, who returned from London during World War II to evaluate Irish attitudes toward the war for the British government. As a returned traveler, Mahon occupies a somewhat analogous position, "spying on my own past"—but he reports only to himself, and by extension, to the reader who looks over his shoulder.

The setting for most of these bleak meditations is his austere room at the top of his building in Dublin: "My attic window under the shining slates / where the maids slept in the days of Wilde and Yeats", I quoted in an earlier essay. In his lofty retreat he resembles his own characterization of Schopenhauer, in "Schopenhauer's Day": "he stares from the window at his idea of the world, / its things-in-themselves . . . / the earth and he were never on intimate terms."

The Yellow Book, its title alluding to the fashionable magazine of the 1890s for which Wilde and others of "the decadents" wrote, and in which Aubrey Beardsley published many of his drawings, implicitly draws a parallel between the fin de siècle periods of the last century and of our own. Oscar Wilde, Elizabeth Bowen, Schopenhauer, Baudelaire, along with well-known and obscure Irish literary figures from the 1950s—these become the poet's platonic companions in the worlds of thought and memory where he lives at one remove from the actual city of Dublin, which for a man of his tastes becomes less and less habitable. His opinion of mankind is buttressed by evocations of other kindred spirits, like the Roman poet Juvenal, whose tenth satire Mahon renders as "The Idiocy of Human Aspiration." Readers who share this poet's view that we are living in a world where idiocy is on the rise and folly reigns, will find Derek Mahon excellent company.

Derek Mahon

The Future of Irish Poetry?

F ew readers would question Seamus Heaney's position as the preeminent Irish poet of the second half
of the twentieth century. But few of us have a good grasp of who
his successors may be, which poets those of us with an interest
in Irish writing might want to read next, which poets readers in
future years are likely to see as filling the shoes of Heaney and
his peers. Because he does have peers—poets just as reward-
ing as Heaney for those who love poetry but equally below the
radar for readers who have room on their reading lists for only
one poet at a time from the literature of a country other than
their own. Heaney is, and has been, but one of a group of tal-
ented poets to emerge from Northern Ireland in the 1960s. He
tends to be grouped with Michael Longley, Derek Mahon, and
James Simmons, with younger Northern poets such as Mebdh
McGuckian, Paul Muldoon, and Ciarán Carson following in
their footsteps. And beyond these names, Ireland both north and
south continues to distinguish itself in the field of poetry.

In 2005 Wake Forest University Press published *The Wake
Forest Series of Irish Poetry*, volume 1, the first in a projected
series of anthologies of Irish poetry. I know of no better place to
start learning about what has been happening recently on the

poetry scene in Ireland. The poets chosen by Jefferson Holdridge for this anthology are Harry Clifton, born in 1952; Dennis O'Driscoll, born in 1954; David Wheatley, born in 1970; Sinéad Morrissey, born in 1972; and Caitríona O'Reilly, born in 1973.

It is illuminating to read these poets against a background of those who preceded them in Ireland. One thing W. B. Yeats, Louis MacNeice, Patrick Kavanagh, and Seamus Heaney, four major poets in the generations preceding the current one, had in common was their preoccupation with their native country both as a nation and as a place. This is not surprising, but when asked to define Ireland, each would have given a different answer.

Yeats as a young man delved into Irish mythology and folklore as a member of the Celtic Revival movement, dreamed of an independent Ireland, and was a major participant in the effort to define the young nation once it came into existence. He was a Senator in the Free State and spokesman for a broad and tolerant national self-definition which took into account the diversity of religions and ethnic strains that had gone into creating modern Ireland. Yeats's definition of Ireland ultimately lost out to the narrow and destructive nationalism that ultimately ushered in the repressive climate of de Valera's Ireland, which I have alluded to here and there—an insular, priest-ridden society, which managed to outlaw divorce and contraception and ban most major works of modern Irish literature.

Though most of his career was spent in London, where he worked for the BBC, Louis MacNeice experienced the excesses of religious intolerance firsthand as the son of an Anglican clergyman growing up in an Ulster characterized by bigotry and ignorance on both sides of the cultural divide. Commenting on the old cliché about Ireland as a "land of saints and scholars," he wrote in "Autumn Journal":

The land of scholars and saints:
    Scholars and saints my eye, the land of ambush,

Purblind manifestoes, never-ending complaints,
    The born martyr and the gallant ninny;
The grocer drunk with the drum,
    The land-owner shot in his bed, the angry voices
Piercing the broken fanlight in the slum,
    The shawled woman weeping at the garish altar.

Patrick Kavanagh's focus on the local can be seen as a re-action against Yeats's lofty rhetoric and grand ideas about the emerging Irish nation. Unlike Yeats, Kavanagh just went about his business as a poet and did not engage in polemics except in-directly. One should bear in mind that historically, the idea of Ireland as an entity, a focus of individual identity, began to jell only with the drive toward Home Rule and independence in the nineteenth century. Most Irish people would still tend to identify themselves, except when traveling abroad, in terms of locality within Ireland rather than as broadly Irish—as a Kerryman, or a Sligo woman or Connemara woman, or a Dub; each of these identifications has a particular flavor to it, just as in the United States you would never confuse a Mississippian with a down-easterner from Maine or a New Yorker. Kavanagh, a farmer in County Monaghan before he migrated down to Dublin, was a firm believer in the value of the local. There is a Zen-like sim-plicity in his assertion that "To know fully even one field or one lane is a lifetime's experience . . . A gap in a hedge, a smooth rock surfacing a narrow lane, a view of a woody meadow, the stream at the junction of four small fields—these are as much as a man can fully experience." His sonnet "Epic" is worth quoting in full for the confident and sly way it comments on the centrality of the local:

I have lived in important places, times
When great events were decided, who owned
That half a rood of rock, a no-man's land

Surrounded by our pitchfork-armed claims.
I heard the Duffys shouting 'Damn your soul'
And old McCabe stripped to the waist, seen
Step the plot defying blue cast-steel—
'Here is the march along these iron stones'.
That was the year of the Munich bother. Which
Was more important? I inclined
To lose my faith in Ballyrush and Gortin
Till Homer's ghost came whispering to my mind.
He said: I made the Iliad from such
A local row. Gods make their own importance.

Louis MacNeice in the sequence "The Closing Album" wrote a poem with some interesting parallels to "Epic." In "Cushenden," as in Kavanagh's "Epic" with its tongue-in-cheek mention of "the Munich bother," the war is referred to slyly and ironically, but more ambiguously than in the Monaghan man's poem. "Cushenden" (a town in County Antrim) introduces us to "Limestone and basalt and a whitewashed house / With passages of great stone flags" where everything is cozy and serene. It could be nothing more than an evocation of a house in a seaside village in Northern Ireland until the last two lines of the poem, which bring the BBC into the room. Here are the last two stanzas of the poem:

Forgetfulness: brass lamps and copper jugs
And home-made bread and the smell of turf or flax
And the air a glove and the water lathering easy
    And convolvulus in the hedge.

Only in the dark green room beside the fire
With the curtains drawn against the winds and waves
There is a little box with a well-bred voice:
    What a place to talk of War.

The Future of Irish Poetry?

Seamus Heaney may be said to have picked up the reins from Kavanagh and to have kept ploughing the same field, only with greater resources and a wider purview. The bluster and silliness of "Epic" are antithetical to Heaney's caution and sense of tact. In "Bogland" he has approached the subject of national self-definition indirectly, famously contrasting the American sense of "manifest destiny," which defined itself by pushing farther and farther into the western frontier, in a horizontal movement, to the vertical, introspective direction of the Irish:

Our pioneers keep striking
Inwards and downwards,

Every layer they strip
Seems camped on before.
The bogholes might be Atlantic seepage.
The wet centre is bottomless.

In "The Haw Lantern" he turns the homely hawberry into an emblematic lantern for the Irish people:

The wintry haw is burning out of season,
crab of the thorn, a small light for small people,
wanting no more from them but that they keep
the wick of self-respect from dying out,
not having to blind them with illumination.

If MacNeice, Kavanagh, Heaney, and Yeats each defined Ireland differently, still, there is an attitude toward their native country that is typical of all of them. It need hardly be said that the sense of place has traditionally been as strong in Ireland as anywhere in the world. The mystique of landscape spoke powerfully to Yeats; it appears early in the poetry written by the young man living in London, dreaming of Sligo, in almost every poem he wrote—"The Stolen Child," for instance:

Where the wandering water gushes
From the hills above Glen-Car,
In pools among the rushes
That scarce could bathe a star . . .

And one cannot fail to respond to the sense of place in middle
and late Yeats; in "My House" from "Meditations in Time of
Civil War," to give another example:

An ancient bridge, and a more ancient tower,
A farmhouse that is sheltered by its wall,
An acre of stony ground,
Where the symbolic rose can break in flower,
Old ragged elms, old thorns innumerable,
The sound of the rain or sound
Of every wind that blows . . .

I hardly need to quote from Heaney and Kavanagh, poets
whose evocations of local landscape are the meat and drink of
poetry. Even the work of the acerbic and cosmopolitan Mac-
Neice and Derek Mahon, who was strongly influenced by the
older poet, are at times drenched with a love of the landscape, as
witness this stanza from MacNeice's "Train to Dublin":

I give you the smell of Norman stone, the squelch
Of bog beneath your boots, the red bog-grass,
The vivid chequer of the Antrim hills, the trough of dark
Golden water for the cart-horses, the brass
Belt of serene sun upon the lough.

When we come to the new poets, those included in the
Wake Forest anthology, that old sense of Ireland seems to have
gone up in smoke. It would seem that now, as a prosperous
member of the European Union, host to waves of immigration
from Eastern Europe and elsewhere, Ireland is just like every-

where else. Harry Clifton's poetry raises several questions of poetic identity. Is Clifton an Irish poet? Certainly: he was born and educated in Ireland and spent most of his first twenty-five years there. On the other hand, he also lived briefly in South America as a boy, and from the ages of about twenty-five to almost fifty-five he spent more time away from Ireland than in it. He has taught English in Nigeria, England, France, and Italy, worked for the Irish Civil Service in refugee aid programs in Thailand, and lived in Paris for many years. In 2004 he returned to this country and now lives in Dublin. Yet if Beckett was Ireland's first European playwright, Derek Mahon and Harry Clifton may be the country's first European poets.

The sense of rootedness in Ireland as a place is just not there in Clifton's work. That doesn't mean he is lacking in a sense of place—simply that his sense of place attaches more to landscapes like the one evoked in "The Desert Route," a bizarre, inbetween territory near the border of, one supposes, two Saharan countries. The focus on geometry and abstraction in the desert superhighway's "lines of purpose" is characteristic of Clifton's philosophical cast of mind:

> . . . the camel trains,
> The slow asphalting-gangs
> On the superhighway, laying down
> Lines of purpose, almost merging
>
> At times, almost parallel,
> Except at the border, where a soldier
> With three stripes, wishing himself elsewhere
> Is waving the landrovers on.

The self in Clifton's poetry is attenuated, impersonal, a kind of philosophical equivalent of the Existentialist figures in Giacometti's sculptures. Clifton's poem "Reductio" is an homage to the sculptor. But Giacometti's spirit informs the self presented in "The Waking Hour":

> . . . I float upwards, from my own depths,
> With a woman beside me
> Wondering, wondering am I real
> Or an angel trapped in the glass of a bedside prayer
> And have I come into her life, and will I stay there
>
> With the other objects, nailed to the wall
> Like permanence, or habit,
> Achieving humanity, averaging out
> Between sacred and profane, through the long attritions
> Marriage and work ordain. . . .

Marriage, too, is one of Clifton's preoccupations. "The Better Portion" tells of a couple whose harmonious routines are shattered by a sudden eruption from the wife's subconscious, reminiscent of Sylvia Plath's disturbed and disturbing self-discovery when she suddenly found herself able to articulate the depth of her rage toward her dead father. Here are the last two stanzas of the poem:

> Suddenly
> One evening, she talked a blue streak
> From half-past-eleven
> To four-fifteen, then fell asleep
> Like a stone disappearing into the deep.
> All this comes from nowhere,
>
> He told himself, flabbergasted
> And unmanned, with the working surface
> Of marriage all around him
> To hold on to—heart and head,
> The better portion neither disputed

In all their years of breaking bread
Before she emerged, from the underworld.

In America the intellectual as hero—Jean-Paul Sartre,
Walter Benjamin—is not a familiar figure. Figures such as Igna-
zio Silone, Søren Kierkegaard, Thomas Merton, haunt Clifton's
work like familiars; he addresses them, contemplates their lives
as object-lessons. Going further back, Saint Augustine ("Reading Saint Augustine") and his world exert a particular fascination:

As for myself, I was desperate to get back
Behind Augustine's *City of God*
To a time before our time, of plunder and sack,
Where the word Apocalypse was clearly stated.

The acts of reading history, and thinking about history, have
seldom been presented so vividly and palpably. He puts this ancient world in the context of his own life:

Eleven thirty. Carthage and Thagaste
Long since fallen, knew their gods had failed.
Alaric and his Huns had stove them in
Like Rome before them. Adeodatus the bastard
Of Augustine, and Augustine himself, were dead.
All that was left, now, was the *City of God*.
The orgies, the pomaded boys, the love-ins,
All were over. Outside, sirens wailed—
A truck rolled by, the windowglass vibrated.
Otherwise all was normal. In your room
Another sentence formed. . . .

The effect of these poems, with their cool surfaces and lack
of obvious affect, is a certain disengagement. If we compare
Clifton's stance with those of his predecessors, we might wonder

why, finally, his poetry feels so different from theirs. Yeats, Kavanagh, MacNeice, Heaney all in their own ways maintain a certain distance and reserve. Perhaps Clifton's work simply shows us how much the world has changed, how glaringly its inequalities, brutality, and exploitation impress themselves on someone who has put himself in a position to see firsthand what is happening in other parts of the world—other cultures that MacNeice, Heaney, and Kavanagh would seem to have had little interest in, while Yeats mined other cultures such as those of Byzantium, China, and Japan for their mythic value. I have been emphasizing the specifically European identity of these poems. To show how deep and how informed and genuine this identification is, I need to quote one poem in its entirety. To read it in bits and pieces is to miss out on the wealth of connections Clifton is able to make, in bringing to the continent of Europe that bracing and powerful sense of place Kavanagh and Heaney brought to their Irish poems.

Taking the Waters

There are taps that flow, all day and all night,
From the depths of Europe,
Inexhaustible, taken for granted,

Slaking our casual thirsts
At a railway station
Heading south, or here in the Abruzzo

Bursting cold from an iron standpipe
While our blind mouths
Suck at essentials, straight from the water table.

Our health is too good, we are not pilgrims.
And the nineteenth century
Led to disaster. Aix, and Baden Baden—

Where are they now, those ladies with the vapours
Sipping at glasses of hydrogen sulphide
Every morning, while the pump-house piano played

And Russian radicals steamed and stewed
For hours in their sulphur tubs
Plugged in to the cathodes of Revolution?

Real cures, for imaginary ailments—
Diocletian's, or Vespasian's.
History passes, only the waters remain,

Bubbling up, through their carbon sheets,
To the other side of catastrophe
Where we drink, at a forgotten source,

Through the old crust of Europe
Centuries deep, restored by a local merchant
Of poultry and greens, inscribing his name in Latin.

Dennis O'Driscoll brings to his poetry a distinctiveness
that could perhaps only be attained by someone who
has, on the one hand, read a tremendous amount of poetry and
who, on the other, is unhampered by an academic study of literature. Commentators on his work tend to stress the latter influence: O'Driscoll studied law and has worked for decades as
an Irish civil servant—not stationed abroad like Harry Clifton,
but in the heart of Dublin. Part of his distinctiveness is that you
will hardly ever encounter in his work the poem-in-a-setting that
is a staple of the genre—the kind of writing that begins with the
poet positioned in a particular place, where the poem unfolds as
a meditation occasioned by that positioning. When I open Paul
Muldoon's anthology, *Contemporary Irish Poetry*, at random, the

first poem I find is Thomas Kinsella's "Mirror in February," which begins "The day dawns with scent of must and rain, / Of opened soil, dark trees, dry bedroom air." "The Other Side" by Seamus Heaney begins, "Thigh-deep in sedge and marigolds / a neighbour laid his shadow / on the stream . . ."

Many great poems, many good poems have been written, for centuries, in the poem-in-a-setting mode, but perhaps this has become a bit too comfortable a way to proceed. O'Driscoll's poems tend to come at you from out of nowhere, often seemingly prompted by an idea—the idea behind "Someone," for example, being the unpredictability of death. Here is how it begins:

> someone is dressing up for death today, a change of skirt or
>   tie
> eating a final feast of buttered sliced pan, tea
> scarcely having noticed the erection that was his last
> shaving his face to marble for the icy laying out
> spraying with deodorant her coarse armpit grass
> someone today is leaving home on business
> saluting, terminally, the neighbours who will join in the
>   cortege

Perhaps the first thing one notices about this poem, beyond its boldness of presentation, is its impersonality, its evocation of all these different someones, each saved from abstraction by precise details: "someone's waist will not be marked with elastic in the future / someone is putting out milkbottles for a day that will not come." O'Driscoll's poems are at home with unrealized potentiality—"Spoiled Child," for instance, which begins

> my child recedes inside me
> and need never puzzle where it came from
> or lose a football in the dusty laurel bushes
> or sneak change from my jacket to buy sweets

my child will not engage in active military service
or make excuses about its school report
or look up from a picture book, dribbling a pink smile
or qualify for free glasses or school lunch

Another quality that makes his poetry distinctive is that while many poets project a personality that is strikingly exceptional, O'Driscoll likes to write impersonally about the typical, the ordinary. Perhaps he has absorbed some of the impersonality of his role as a civil servant. "Misunderstanding and Muzak" presents a typical modern couple who might be residents of any city in the world, no doubt coming from their separate jobs at the end of the working day:

You are in the Super Valu supermarket
expecting to meet me at 6.15.

I am in the Extra Valu supermarket
Expecting to meet you at 6.15.

Danny Boy is calling you down special-offer aisles.
Johann Strauss is waltzing me down special-offer aisles.

There may be early poems by O'Driscoll that show the influence of Irish exemplars, but I've no evidence of it, if it exists. The raptures and high rhetoric of Yeats would not suit his temperament, while the rootedness of Kavanagh and Heaney might have seemed a bit too familiar to a young man growing up in the town of Thurles, County Tipperary. I catch a note of Larkin's hard-bittenness from time to time in O'Driscoll's lines; but on the whole it seems to me that he has gone to school to the Eastern Europeans and the Americans. He has learned impersonality and simplicity from translations of poets like Miroslav Holub, Czesław Milosz, and Wisława Szymborska, and he may have acquired "the common touch" from his reading of American poetry. "Them and You" deftly summarizes the class divide in an Ireland where the beneficiaries of the Celtic Tiger live uneasily side by side with those for whom the new Ireland is no different from the old, only everything is more expensive. Here are the first four couplets (an estate is a down-market subdivision or subsidized housing unit):

They wait for the bus.
You spray them with puddles.

They queue for curry and chips.
You phone an order for delivery.

They place themselves under the protection
of the Marian Grotto at the front of their estate.

You put your trust in gilts, managed funds,
income continuation plans.

Through his job with the Customs department of the Irish government, O'Driscoll has acquired a familiarity with the world of business, a familiarity he uses to advantage in the long sequence, *The Bottom Line*. In the following stanza he constructs a chilling metaphor for death from that world. You can see here how clearly he has subverted the familiar emblems of death:

Death, once brushed against,
does not seem in the least
like a stubbly ghost with scythe
reaping dry grass in the graveyard,
but shows up as a brash executive
cutting recklessly across your lane,
lights making eye-contact with yours,
ready to meet head-on as though

by previous appointment; ram home
your car horn like a panic button:
his cellphone's bell will toll for you.

If literature's two great themes are death and love, you won't
find much of the latter here. Love poetry is, in fact, a territory
that Irish writers have approached only with hesitation and reti-
cence. It is not really surprising that one of Heaney's most forthright attempts in this genre is called "The Skunk"! Tenderness
enters the world of O'Driscoll's poetry in a most indirect and
qualified way, in the rather horrifying "In Memory of Alois
Alzheimer," a graphic description of the gruesome effects of the
disease. The last section, distanced from any personal construance by being printed in italics, goes as following:

Lie closer to me in the dry sheets
while I can still tell who you are.

Let me declare how much I love you
before our bed is sorely tested.

Love me with drooling toxins, with carbon monoxide,
with rope, with arrows through my heart.

I would credit his readings of American poetry for O'Driscoll's way of using the "you" to mean "one," suggesting a stand-
in for the first-person singular when he ventures onto personal
ground. Perhaps I am wrong, but "Vigil" certainly sounds like
the closest thing to a personal credo we are likely to get from this
quintessentially circumspect poet. Here is part of it, from the
middle of the poem:

You are alone in the bone-weary tower
of your bleary-eyed, blinking lighthouse,
watching the spillage of tide on the shingle inlet.

You are the single-minded one who hears
time shaking from the clock's fingertips
like drops, who watches its hands
chop years into diced seconds, . . .

Dennis O'Driscoll has produced an extraordinary body of work by going to work patiently and quietly on what would appear to be most ordinary. In the Dublin literary world he is regarded in the way Samuel Johnson was thought of in eighteenth-century London. Some of his poems have already achieved the status of classics.

To include in a single book five poets, two in their fifties, three in their thirties, does not make for an ideal collection. The reader of the Wake Forest anthology implicitly makes comparisons that are not really fair to the younger poets. Unlike philosophers and mathematicians, few poets have found themselves before the age of forty. David Wheatley has high visibility on the Irish and British literary scenes as a prolific book reviewer and co-editor of the excellent magazine *Metre*, which has bases in Dublin, Prague, and the University of Hull in the UK. The magazine is astonishingly inclusive and eclectic. Seamus Heaney is listed as a patron. Contributors include poets from three major centers of writing in English: Britain, Ireland, and the United States.

As an example, I have before me an issue from 2004, which I found remaindered in a Dublin bookstore. This issue includes contributions from four of the poets featured in the Wake Forest anthology—Clifton, O'Driscoll, Wheatley, and Caitríona O'Reilly—as well as poems by Michael Longley, Robert Pinsky, Anne Stevenson, Ben Sonnenberg, a symposium on Robert Lowell's *Collected Poems*, an essay on Polish poetry by the American poet Charles Altieri, and on and on. What I would have least expected to find is a gathering of essays on the Objectivist poet

Carl Rakosi. It would seem that *Metre* is more informed about American poetry than most readers in America. *Metre*'s scope is encyclopedic.

Poetry has always had its entrepreneurs. Wheatley reminds me of the young Ezra Pound plotting the various enterprises, the fly-by-night little magazines, that constituted early Modernism first in South Kensington and then on the Left Bank; of the young Robert Bly, a Harvard graduate holed up at his farm on the plains of Minnesota, rallying the forces of the Midwestern "deep image" school of James Wright, Galway Kinnell, Donald Hall. The trick for the poetry entrepreneur is to keep focused on his own writing without getting carried away by peripheral activities. Pound, whose early poetry is still his lasting achievement in my view, had seriously lost focus during his last years in London and Paris, and only gained it again when he moved to Italy and poured his awe-inspiring energies into the composition of the *Cantos*. Many readers of Bly would feel that his poetry has, over the years, taken second place to his work in the "new man" movement and to his activities as a performer of his own work.

David Wheatley is still in the process of finding his way. There is a brittleness, a tentative and emotionally veiled quality to his poems that reminds me both of the English poet Michael Hofmann and of the early Paul Muldoon. Like Muldoon he is an accomplished rhymer, an extraordinarily rare quality in this day and age. Wheatley's skill shows itself to advantage in "Autumn, the Nightwalk, the City, the River." Dublin, like London and Paris, is drenched in literary associations, and it is good to see an update that avoids the obvious. Here are a few lines from the middle of the poem with its crisp, satisfying couplets:

Anywhere would do: I remember suburbs
plush with hatchbacks parked on tidy kerbs,
privets, cherry blossoms, *nouveau riches'*
houses named for saints, complete with cable dishes;

and then the streets where every window was
an iron grid across its pane of glass,
the garden weeds in cracks, a noise ahead—
a bird, a cat—enough to make me cross the road.

Another Dublin poem, "Misery Hill," seizes on the evocative
street-name, captures the atmosphere of urban decay that is not
hard to find in the city, but fails to rise above undifferenti-
ated irony:

> ... a post-office van
> passes silently by with letters
> for anywhere but this grim street
> with its rubble and wire-topped walls,
> featureless and empty besides.

More daring and kinetic is Wheatley's *jeu d'esprit* "St John and
the Eagle," based on illuminations executed for the Gospel of
John from the medieval Lindisfarne Gospels. The saint's emblematic eagle lifts right off the illuminated page in this brilliantly self-consuming poem, and onto the page of the poem:

> ... the eagle will swoop,
> scattering doves as he goes.
> Evangelist's bird, tired
> of the easy kill, the flocculent hare
>
> and deckchair legs of the deer
> folding under a ton's worth of rapt
> persuasion in its claw; from a thousand
> yards up the eagle has spied
>
> and will snatch from your hands
> your book, leaving you only
> a feather with which to scatter
> and sow the Word in his

fugitive image, *imago aquilae:*
no sooner will you have finished
this page than talons will
puncture and carry it off.

Above, I made a comparison between Wheatley and Paul
Muldoon. Like the young Muldoon, Wheatley is curious and
ranges widely in search of poetic models. I enjoy seeing his
poetic experiments that have been appearing in literary magazines since the 2005 anthology was published. For example, two
poems in the autumn 2005 *Poetry Ireland Review,* "An Errancy"
and "Drift," play off traditional models from Irish folklore and
Gaelic poetry with a welcome playfulness and emotional acces-
sibility often lacking in the selections in the Wake Forest anthology. I have the feeling that David Wheatley's poetry is still a
work in progress.

Parenthetically, the efforts of Yeats, MacNeice, Heaney,
and—in his idiosyncratic and oblique way—Kavanagh
to define the Irish nation in its early years must seem largely the
work of the past to the poets in the Wake Forest anthology. But
this is not to say that they would agree with Margaret Thatcher
that "there is no such thing as society." Clifton's short poem
"Military Presence, Cobh 1899" obliquely addresses British colonialism in Ireland; the poem's terse ending—"all you lack /
Is consciousness, judgement, the twentieth century"—suggests
that Irish independence is less a matter of heroism than of historical inevitability. This would ruffle a few feathers among Republican patriots. O'Driscoll's "Them and You" points to the
presence of a class structure in Ireland, even though economic
disparities exist everywhere in the world.

Wheatley's social awareness would seem to attach, at least in
these poems, more to the city of Dublin than to the country of
Ireland. Derek Mahon in *The Yellow Book* has chronicled the

metamorphosis of the city into "a Georgian theme-park for the tourist," "aliens, space invaders clicking at the front door, / goofy in baseball caps and nylon leisurewear," in a Dublin where "foreign investment conspires against old decency, / computer talks to computer, machine to answering machine." In a sonnet sequence addressed to the nineteenth-century poet James Clarence Mangan, Wheatley writes even more caustically:

> Let the city sleep on undisturbed,
> new hotels and apartment blocks replace
> the Dublin that we brick by brick erase;
> let your city die without a word
> of pity, indignation, grief or blame,
> the vampire crime lords fatten on its flesh
> and planners zone the corpse for laundered cash.

Sinéad Morrissey, who was born in Armagh and grew up in Belfast, bears witness to urban destruction brought on not by prosperity, corruption, and "progress" but by bombs. In a startling little poem she personifies the Europa Hotel, a landmark in downtown Belfast, which used regularly to be targeted by IRA bombers:

> It's a hard truth to have to take in the face—
> You wake up one morning with your windows
> Round your ankles and your forehead billowing smoke;
> Your view impaired for another fortnight
> Of the green hills they shatter you for.

The last line briskly anatomizes the ironies of destroying in the name of building a new society.

The first fifteen pages of the thirty-odd pages devoted to Morrissey make it blindingly clear that we are in the presence of a new talent whose "new angels," as she puts it, "are howling, hard," sandpapery, open-hearted. Work of this order renews one's faith in the art of poetry. "Sea Stones" is a poem one is unlikely to forget. This brilliant study of the experience of receiving violence, of the complications of jealousy, of the unfathomable labyrinths of love and passion, begins,

> It is exactly a year today since you slapped me in public.
> I took it standing up. You claimed I just ignored it,
> that I pretended to be hooked on the dumb-show of a sunset,
> splashing, a mile off. Too hooked to register
> the sting of your ring finger
> as it caught on my mouth and brought my skin with it.

I'll pass over an intermediate stanza and quote the ending of this poem that almost in itself is worth the price of the anthology. It is both deeply romantic and at the same time informed by a sense of human deviousness:

> He gave me roses. The surprise of butterflies caged in the
>   palms.
> And sea stones with tracings of juvenile kisses, scented with
>   risk.
> I wrapped them in black at the back of a bottom drawer,
> hidden in underwear. The truth—that you never were so
>   vivid
> or so huge as the second the street turned towards us
> in shock—got dropped between us like a fallen match.
>
> You turned away as the sun disappeared like a ship. And I,
> Suddenly wanting to be struck again, to keep the fire of
>   your anger lit,
> I bit my lip.

The companion piece to this is "& Forgive Us Our Trespasses," which begins, "Of which the first is love." I leave this one to the reader to discover. Morrissey is an astute student of the human heart.

It is always interesting to see what a writer from another country makes of America. Harry Clifton's "Absinthe at New Orleans" combines vivid sketches of American cityscapes with some trenchant criticism of social inequalities in the United States; at the same time, the poem is informed by bizarre Kafkaesque fantasies of the State Department agency that is paying for his tour of the country as a sinister, all-seeing Big Brother pulling strings behind the scenes. One can only wonder what this otherwise seemingly sensible poet had been smoking. Sinéad Morrissey takes a less wild-eyed view of our country. I like her American landscapes, as in "Jo Gravis in His Metal Garden":

> From the window of the midnight-bound Vegas plane
> Tucson flares in the desert—a cactus pricked by rain;
> lit houses, lit highways and floodlit swimming pools—
> a stunned bird in a basin, spreading its wings to cool.

Her extraordinary poem "An Anatomy of Smell" contains a portrait of a couple, one American from the Southwest, one Irish, rendered in terms of smell:

> From you, the smell of the Tucson desert:
> copper deposits, animal skulls, the chalk trajectory
> of stars no cloud covers or stains, ochre and chilli.
> From me, bog cotton, coal fires, wild garlic, river dirt.
> And from the two of us, salt. When we move house
> such genealogies as these will follow us.

Caitríona O'Reilly, just a year younger than Sinéad Morrissey, is an accomplished young poet who—before she can write the poetry she is capable of—is struggling, I feel, to emerge from the complications of the many things she can do well. Look how well, in "Fragment," she does the Plath-influenced ominous landscape:

> This night-breathing deceives, it is so calm,
> The headland glitters with beached faces, lunar stares,
> a tidal moon-haul of wrecks and drownings.
> Their gazes are blank and lasting,
> outfacing constellations even, crystalline.

Jefferson Holdridge closes his thirty-page introduction to the anthology with a couple of sentences that chilled me: "Poetry is ridding itself of everything that is not concerned with poetic perception, impersonal and self-mortifying. Caitríona O'Reilly's efforts to look at the changing world with new eyes are ambitious, even historic, at this pivotal period in Ireland." My own view is that poetry commits suicide when it rids itself of everything that is not concerned with poetic perception. Two adjectives float at the end of the first sentence, so that one cannot be dead sure what they modify, but presumably he is praising a poetic vision that is impersonal and mortifying. "Impersonal" is all right with me if applied to, say, Dennis O'Driscoll's poems, which bypass the self in order to be what Matthew Arnold called "a criticism of life." But "mortifying"? Does one read poetry in order to be mortified? I don't.

The first of O'Reilly's "Two Night Time Pieces," called "Pisces," is a place—Holdridge would probably say a *locus*, where something vital and not at all impersonal or self-mortifying tries and succeeds in making itself felt through a scaffolding of perceptions that are perhaps so precise and "poetic" that they actually get in the way. This very sexy poem, given the reservations I have expressed, made me gasp with pleasure and interrupt the person who was reading beside me in bed, to insist she hear it read aloud:

Thirteen Februaries slept through
before I learned what going under meant.

Pale and thin as sheets,
the near fields burst free of mooring.

Then the turn of the tide,
the sea stack,

the pier-light's onyx eye.
Those teenage dreams

were cuttle-ink tattoos
describing blue-rinse mermen,

each muscular wave awash
with sex and phosphor.

I was awash and rocked,
rocked hard to wake

and woke, drenched to the roots,
my flannelette pyjamas stiff with sand.

Just to concentrate on diction here for a moment, "blue-rinse
mermen" is overly fussy, and I even have my doubts about
"cuttle-ink tattoos," which is *recherché* in a manner reminiscent
of Marianne Moore. But the assonance, the repetitions, the
wood-block tones of "awash and rocked, / rocked hard to wake //
and woke, drenched to the roots" are thrilling. And the domesti-
cally diminutive, adolescent note introduced by "flannelette pyjamas" reminds me, in its rightness, of Leonard Cohen's line in
"Back on Boogie Street" from *Ten New Songs*: "I've tidied up
the kitchenette, / I've tuned the old banjo."

A beautiful example of transformation is O'Reilly's suite of poems, "A Quartet for the Falcon," based, I should think, on her readings in falconry and alchemy. Perhaps she has just made it all up and made it sound plausible. Here is a peregrine falcon hunting a heron:

> They go ringing up the air,
> each in its separate spiral stair
> to the indigo rim of the skies,
>   then descend
>   swift as a murderer's hand
> with a knife. Death's gesture liquefies
>
> in bringing the priestly heron down.
> Her prize, the marrow from a wing-bone
> in which she delights, her spurred
>   fleur-de-lys tongue
>   stained *gold-vermilion*—
> little angel in her hangman's hood.

I believe that Caitríona O'Reilly is on her way to becoming a stunning lyric poet. She is not the first poet to have earned a Ph.D., nor will she be the last. But a way must be found to transmute all the learning into lore.

Wake Forest, founded by Dillon Johnston, has always been a pioneer—almost *the* pioneer—in introducing new Irish poetry to American readers. It will be interesting to see which poets the press decides to present next. Ireland's standing army of poets is as numerous as ever, so there will be no lack of choices.

4

Mount Stewart: Its Gardens, House, and Family

W. B. Yeats: The Labyrinth of Another's Being

Looking for Yeats in Yeats Country

Mount Stewart:
Its Gardens, House,
and Family

Midsummer's Day I was up early, walking in the
Italian Garden at Mount Stewart, County Down.
I was staying for a week or so at a B&B just outside the demesne
wall, in an eighteenth-century farmhouse that had once been
part of the estate, and was spending my days in the gardens. The
rolled and clipped turf felt reassuringly cushy under my feet—
part of the sense of well-being that emanates from a perfectly
tended lawn. Then a soft drizzle descended, and I sheltered in
the tiled pavilion at the foot of the Spanish Garden, one terraced
level lower, the long oval of its pool flanked by bamboo and low-
growing bush wisteria from Japan. Leyland cypresses, severely
clipped into two parallel arcades, wall this small garden in on the
east and west with dark-green living arches. The pavilion faces
north, up a flight of steps, across the central lawn of the Italian
Garden, toward the south front of Mount Stewart House.

From the vantage point of the Spanish Garden, that ordered symmetry which is the essence of classicism asserts itself.
A hundred yards long, fifty yards deep, the Italian Garden,

paralleling the south elevation of the house, is formed around a central lawn flanked by two parterres, in the centers of which circular lily ponds have been sunk. Ringing the lily ponds, purple irises are encircled by beds of yellow roses, lupines in their several colors, dahlias and voluptuous peonies, tall purple delphiniums, and the blinding magenta of Abbotswood Rose. The garden's formal polarity is emphasized by two massive Irish yews, part of the older garden that was here before the seventh Marchioness of Londonderry took the place in hand in 1921 and substantially created the garden as it exists today. The brooding green density of the yews is relieved by the more cheerful green of two large sweet-bay trees from Belgium, 120 years old, neatly clipped and growing in pots on the terrace, flanking the neoclassical south portico.

The garden at Mount Stewart is a living assemblage of pure delight, an eighty-acre ecosystem, a consortium where all the senses are brought into play. The presiding genius here for years was Nigel Marshall, a blue-eyed, plainspoken Englishman with the gnarled fingers and weathered look that go with his occupation. Since 1970 Nigel, with a staff of about eight and temporary help varying by season, was head gardener at Mount Stewart, which many consider the greatest garden in Ireland. Mr. Marshall has since retired and is living in a gate lodge at Mt. Stewart. He has been replaced by Phil Rollinson.

Five miles from the Irish Sea, where the Gulf Stream flows, the place enjoys a subtropical climate with annual rainfall of thirty-five inches, and lime-free soil. The house faces south over the Italian Garden and shelters from the north winds behind a wooded hill. There are heavy dews at night. All of this combines to produce remarkable growth rates and a hospitable environment for plants like the blue and claret-colored Himalayan poppies that grow in the Lily Wood, Kniphofia from Uganda, with its clumps of delicate salmon and pale yellow flowers, and the New Zealand Sophora tetraptera—a small tree with butter-yellow, mimosa-like flowers.

The closer to the house, the more formal and domesticated the style of the gardens. On the outlying paths and hills, things start to look wilder and less planned. The Italian Garden is flanked on the east by the Mairi Garden, designed on the cozy scale of a cottage garden. On the west the ground slopes down into the Lily Wood, an informal, meandering glade planted with fifty-year-old New Zealand tree ferns, cedars, palm trees, beeches, and several delicate rhododendrons including the Victorianum, Edgeworthii, and formosum. These tender plants, along with many varieties of lilies including a Cardiocrinum giganteum from Asia, are sheltered to the north by the high walls of the Sunk Garden, by huge trees like one hundred-foot Caucasian fir, and four varieties of tall eucalyptus that intercept the wintry winds.

The Sunk Garden adjoins the west wing, the oldest part of the house, which was built of grey local stone by George Dance for the first Marquess of Londonderry in 1804–5. Farther beyond it to the west is the Shamrock Garden, well-known for its topiary, and beyond that the Drive, the original main entrance to the house, vibrant with many varieties of rhododendrons, which grow as tall as trees. Around the five-acre artificial lake and in the hills to the north of the house, the gardens take on a woodland look.

Even here, though, the gardener's hand has been at work. The walks are lined with huge old rhododendrons, acacias, myrtles, azaleas, and exotic trees, with a little Japanese garden tucked in where you least expect it. In the open parkland that stretches from the north facade of the house to the lake, several North American conifers planted as exotics in the middle of the nineteenth century have grown magnificently. These are forest trees one has seen in their natural setting in the American West—the Giant Sequoia and the Coast Redwood, and most beautiful of all, the Pinus radiata, or Monterey Pine. Seen here, planted with plenty of growing space around them, pruned to advantage, these huge trees are as exquisite as bonzai.

A good approach to the gardens is to walk through the former stables at the southeast corner of the house and slip through an inconspicuous wooden gate there into the Mairi Garden. When the youngest daughter of the Mount Stewart family, Lady Mairi Vane-Tempest-Stewart (later Viscountess Bury), was a baby, she would be put in her perambulator every day to sleep in a corner of the garden. This corner has become the Mairi Garden, with a pool and fountain containing in its center a statue of Lady Mairi as a little girl. Flowers have been planted to the theme of the nursery rhyme, "Mary, Mary, quite contrary, how does your garden grow?" There are cockle shells around the pool, "silver bells" in the form of various campanulas, and "pretty maids" (Saxifraga granulata), so called because of their bonnet-like blossoms. Also flourishing here, in keeping with the blue-and-white color scheme, are Buddleia fallowiana "Alba," the old white Bourbon Rose called "Boule de Neige," and white fuchsia.

The transition from the whimsy and informality of the Mairi Garden to the classicism of the Italian Garden is accomplished by walking across the Dodo Terrace, whose formal lines are undercut humorously by fantastic statuary—dodos on pillars, red griffins on the roof of a loggia. Here the blues and whites of the Mairi Garden give way to the reds of low-growing rhododendrons, camellias, and fuchsia, whose vigorous growth in the Irish climate excites the envy of an American gardener. To the south of the terrace lies the wild seclusion of the Peace Garden, where pets—dogs, birds and cats, tame macaws, even some of the children's favorite ponies—were buried. This garden is hedged with sweet-smelling Drimys aromatica bearing copper-tinted leaves and tiny white flowers. It is planted with unusual broad-leafed Chilean Lantern Trees, whose blossoms resemble fuchsias, only larger—and the spicy Mountain Pepper from Tasmania.

Crossing the Italian Garden and circling around to the west front of the house, you enter the Sunk Garden, a low lawn and four beds surrounded by a stone pergola covered in roses and clematis, which is the first area Lady Londonderry developed, working from a design by Gertrude Jekyll. Below the steps that issue from this side of the house—occupied by the music room and Lady Londonderry's library—the white flowers of Portuguese heather fill the garden with heady perfume in the spring. Planted on the terrace and growing over the pergola are rare old roses including "Climbing Lady Hillingdon," raised in 1910; "Madame Georges Bruant," 1887; "Alister Stella Gray," 1894. Visiting gardeners from Britain and from other parts of Ireland happily wander the garden, observing and jotting down notes on such curiosities as the climber Billardiera longifolia, which flowers in the summer and then is covered with shiny little purple fruits in the fall.

To the west side of the Sunk Garden you come to the Shamrock Garden, formed in the shape of Ireland's national emblem, with several examples of topiary, including a yew with a table-like top on which stands an Irish harp—strings and all. If you know how slowly yew grows, you can appreciate the patience required of the topiarist. Metal frames are constructed in the estate's workshops, the plant grows up into them, and then the foliage is clipped around the shape of the frame. While I was there, topiary crowns were being shaped atop the yew hedge surrounding the Shamrock Garden.

Lady Mairi still lives in the house at Mount Stewart, a two-story mansion with wings that extend to east and west from the house's main entrance—a pedimented Ionic porte cochère, on whose massive columns the marks made by iron carriage-wheels can still be seen. The somewhat sprawling look of the house—longer than it is high—reflects its history: The original structure designed by George Dance, which is now the west wing, was enlarged as the family's fortunes grew. The Irish architect William Vitruvius Morrison added the main block, including the entrance portico and the central hall, in the late 1830s. Lady Mairi's presence makes the place feel more like a residence than a museum. Her coats are laid out on a table in the entrance hall, and three split-bamboo fly rods belonging to her lean in a corner. Every day while I was visiting she would drive up to the lake in her dark-blue Toyota to minister to an injured swan that limped along the shore.

During Ascot week the staff had strict instructions that Lady Mairi was not to be disturbed. After all, hadn't her horse, Fighting Charlie (named after the third Marquess, a famous duelist), twice won the Gold Cup at Epsom? Horses run, as it were, through the history of Mount Stewart. In the gallery of the hall, with its *faux marbre* columns, black-and-white checkerboard floor, and salmon-and-white walls, hangs a painting of Hermit, winner of the "Snowstorm" Derby in 1867, who belonged to the seventh Marchioness's father, Harry Chaplin. In a pre-Derby trial run, blood gushed from the horse's nostrils and he stumbled. Everyone figured Hermit was a write-off. His trainer divined, however, that the horse was not seriously injured, but had simply burst a vein in his nose. He worked the horse quietly, and on Derby Day, when a freak snowstorm struck, odds against Hermit rose to 1,000/15. Viscount Chaplin bet heavily on his horse and made a killing.

The most valuable painting in the house is George Stubbs's Hambletonian, another legendary racehorse. It hangs on a landing where stairs go up to a gallery. The cast-iron balustrade, designed by George Dance, is lighter than iron has any right to be, and the mahogany handrail is delicately inlaid with ebony. The marquetry floor of oak, mahogany, and bog-fir in the music room, which dates from the 1780s, matches the plasterwork ceiling.

Each of the twenty-two Empire chairs in the dining room, from the Congress of Vienna in 1815, is embroidered in petit point with the arms of the participants in the Congress—including the Duke of Wellington, Talleyrand, and Lord Castlereagh, who was the second Marquess of Londonderry. In the "Rome" bedroom upstairs (the bedrooms are named after European cities) you can see a screen painted with tropical birds by Edward Lear, who stayed here in 1833. Two eighteenth-century gilt Italian pier glasses hanging at either end of the drawing room came from Londonderry House in Park Lane, London. Loveliest of all to my eye is the Venetian glass chandelier in the shape of a ship, a gift from Nancy Cunard, which hangs in Lady Londonderry's sitting room. It was hung so that at night it appeared to float on the waters of Strangford Lough, which was visible out the windows before the garden hedges grew to their present height.

One afternoon I made my way uphill through a copse of ancient beech trees to the Temple of the Winds, built in 1785 by James "Athenian" Stuart. The Temple is a small banqueting house with an elegant spiral staircase, where the Stewarts and their guests would repair on a summer's day. From its hilltop the Temple of the Winds commands a view of the Lough, a saltwater fjord off the Irish Sea. The beech trees below the Temple of the Winds, their smooth, fleshy grey trunks wavy like vegetation under water, looked like illustrations from some exotic children's book. Like many scenes in the remoter parts of the Mount Stewart demesne, it was hard to tell whether they had been planted, or whether they grew there naturally.

It is precisely the point where the gardener's skill encounters the irreducible raw material of nature that the art of gardening becomes most fully itself. So much knowledge, lore, and personal experience go into the choice of plants—not only in terms of their color, height, blooming season, and so forth, but of their capabilities for growing well in a particular location with its own unique climate and weather. Beyond this, gardening is itself a kind of architecture—with materials that grow and move and breathe.

The element of scale is as important in a garden as it is in a house. One's eye focuses at one moment on something very small and exquisitely detailed—like the Iris Douglasiana Watsonii that grows in the Mairi Garden. Then, high up, a breeze

blows, and the eye is drawn to the topmost branches of a Eucalyptus globulus planted in the 1890s, which rustles dryly. At
mid-height between the lawn and the eucalyptuses are flaming
rhododendrons the size of small trees. Birdsong is everywhere,
from the tiny Blue Tit—whose song is described by the Scottish
poet Norman MacCaig as "the sound / of a grain of sawdust
being sawn / by the minutest of saws"—to the song thrush.
When he sings, the whole garden holds its breath and listens.

I like to know the names of things. But the profusion of
aromas here defeated my attempts to identify the source of
every strand of scent. Though it was easy enough to sniff out
the tang of eucalyptus or the musk from cinnamon-barked myrtles in the Lily Wood, it was harder to define the source of other
exotic perfumes. The Lily Wood has fragrant tender rhododendrons that were brought from Burma, Yunnan, Assam. On the
walks around the Sunk Garden and the Italian Garden, old roses
stop you in your tracks with their fragrances, which seem to en-
capsulate some essence of the era when they were first culti-
vated—when life was, by all accounts, sweeter.

To know the gardens is, to an extent, to know the
woman whose inspiration and labor they sprang from:
Edith, the seventh Marchioness of Londonderry, who died in
1959 at the age of 80. "When my husband and I first came here
on a visit," she wrote, "I thought the house and surroundings
were the dampest, darkest, and saddest place I had ever stayed
in." She cut back the large ilexes that were pressing against the
house, and started to plan her garden.

Surely a more remarkable woman never wore a diamond
tiara, sailed a yacht, or rode to hounds. In London, Lady Edith
was the most brilliant political hostess of her day. "When, at her
Eve-of-Parliament reception in 1934," writes Anne de Courcy
in *Circe*, her 1992 biography of Lady Edith, "she stood at the
head of the Londonderry House staircase . . . , she wore a black

and silver sequined sheath dress like a dazzling coat of mail, against which flashed tiara, pendant earrings and a wristful of diamond bracelets." She was not ordinary. As hemlines rose in the 1920s a sensation was created when the newspapers noticed Lady Londonderry's tattoo: a coiling snake on her left leg, which she acquired on a trip she and her husband Charley made to the Orient in 1903. It might be added that she had a splendid figure. Her bosom—*beaucoup du monde au balcon*, as one admirer nicely put it—seemed, as it were, designed by nature to display the dazzling Londonderry family diamonds.

The life that Lord and Lady Londonderry led at Mount Stewart in the 1920s and '30s seems, today, the stuff of fantasy. The fragrance of cut flowers and Lady Edith's potpourris filled the house. There were a dozen or so dogs: Irish wolfhounds, lurchers, "a small pack of Pekineses that followed her everywhere," dachshunds, and her husband Charley's bull mastiff. The house was full of guests such as Harold Nicolson and Vita Sackville-West (great gardeners in their own right), the Sitwells, Yeats, and Seán O'Casey, as well as her children and grandchildren. There was swimming in the saltwater pool, riding, tennis, *thés dansant*, golf, croquet. The family were keen aviators who built an airfield at nearby Newtownards, where they flew their Gypsy One Moths and Avro Cadets, their De Haviland Hornet Moth and six-seater Percival Q6. They raced their sailboats on the Lough. Edith and Charley each had a Rolls. There were four chauffeurs for four cars, too many servants to count. Butler and under-butler, three or four footmen, Groom of the Chambers, piper, night watchman, two housekeepers, cook, many kitchen-maids, schoolroom maid, telephonist, hospital nurse, et al. The world is full of rich people today who spend their money with much less flair.

Today the Rollses have ended up in vintage car collections, and Londonderry House has been demolished and a hotel built on its site. In Northern Ireland the latest phase of the Troubles seems to be over; Sinn Féin and the Democratic Unionist Party have formed a government together. The garden remains. It has grown into more than the sum of its parts, becoming host to a world of wildlife as well as its human visitors. Mallards and wild swans glide on the lake, absurd officious coots paddle and squawk, a cormorant dives and surfaces with an eel in its beak, swallows scissor the air. A brown squirrel scrambles overhead up the side of a giant Monterey Pine in the park, making a sound like silk ribbon being jerked rapidly off a spool. In April massive plantings of daffodils poke up out of the ground on the south shore of the lake as in a poem by Wordsworth. They bloom and then they wither and turn brown. The fiery reds and opulent purples of rhododendrons flare and revert to greenness, followed by roses, china-blue and lavender clematis, powder-blue, pink, and white hydrangeas, and thousands of perennials, each in its season. The gardener and his staff plant and fertilize, mulch and weed, mow and prune.

Mount Stewart

W. B. Yeats: The Labyrinth
of Another's Being

The veils surrounding William Butler Yeats come in such degrees of thickness and coloration that we shall probably never see the man plain. The title of one of the first major critical studies, *Yeats, the Man and the Masks*, by Richard Ellmann, addressed questions of disguise and shifting identities—questions that have continued to engage commentators. Yeats's early work planted so persuasively in readers' minds a picture of the dreamer swathed in the mists of the Celtic Twilight that the conflicting reality of him as a man of the world, a shrewd man of business keenly aware of cash flow and reputation, has come as a surprise and even a betrayal of some readers' images of him. Yeats went to his grave a convinced occultist and believer in the spirit world. Recent biography reveals that this mystic was also skillful at self-promotion, an experienced committee man, a trenchant debater and politician—not to mention a fierce competitor at croquet.

All this is complicated even further by Yeats's reinvention of himself in the early years of Modernism, producing a flowering of mature poetry probably unequalled since the late plays of Shakespeare. In retrospect, because of our high valuation of his later poetry, it is hard to grasp that for Yeats's contemporaries at the outbreak of the first World War, he seemed a man whose best work was already behind him. The tendency among American readers to view all things Irish through a green veil of sentimentality—a tendency Yeats himself played along with—is another obstacle to clear vision. Perhaps no life can be thoroughly understood, but the student of this great poet finds himself especially awed by the complex task of entering into what Yeats called "the labyrinth of another's being." In this essay I intend to concentrate on Yeats's first fifty years.

G. K. Chesterton, who encountered him wearing a top hat and carrying binoculars at the Dublin Horse Show in the early 1920s, was amazed by how much the supposedly otherworldly poet knew about horseflesh and handicapping. But such knowledge would have come naturally to Yeats, who as a young man lived in Sligo with his uncle George Pollexfen,

> In muscular youth well known to Mayo men
> For horsemanship at meets or at racecourses,
> That could have shown how pure-bred horses
> And solid men, for all their passion, live
> But as the outrageous stars incline
> By opposition, square and trine . . .
>   ("In Memory of Major Robert Gregory")

His Uncle George was a convert to Yeats's belief in astrology and, like his nephew, evidently found nothing contradictory about parallel interests in the stars and the turf. Perhaps the ostensible contradiction lies less in Yeats's prismatic self than in our own ideas about what constitutes an integrated personality.

A story often told, usually with an air of mildly scandalized amusement over pints of Guinness in Dublin's literary pubs, involves Yeats's reaction to being informed over the telephone by *Irish Times* editor Bertie Smyllie that he had won the Nobel Prize for Literature in 1923. "Yeats halted the journalist's flow," as

Keith Alldritt recounts the tale in his 1997 biography, *W.B. Yeats: The Man and the Milieu*, "with a short, practical question. 'How much, Smyllie, how much is it?' The answer was 7,000 pounds."

What the Irish call begrudgery is pandemic in the Dublin literary world, and no writer's success has been more grudgingly acknowledged by his compatriots—during his own time and continuing into the present. In the "How much is it?" anecdote Yeats figures as a hypocrite: the air of Parnassus is supposed to be unadulterated by the smell of money. The first volume of R. F. Foster's monumental *W.B. Yeats: A Life*, however, reveals for the first time the poverty of Yeats's youth. As an adult he kept a sharp eye on the pounds, shillings, and pence because life under the rented and frequently shifting roof provided in London or Dublin by his father, the artist John B. Yeats, had been precarious and humiliating. In an age of agents, publishers, and book deals, it is easy to overlook the importance of patronage in the writing lives of the great Modernists: "In literary history Augusta Gregory's enduring support of Yeats compares in importance with that given to James Joyce by Harriet Shaw Weaver. Modernist literature was in considerable part a literature of patronage rather than of the market-place." This useful insight of Foster's may partially explain the willful obscurity often encountered in Modernist works.

Other aspects of fin de siècle and early-twentieth-century life are easy to lose sight of. Shortly before Yeats's arrival in Paris during the 1890s, when he first met Synge and helped steer him toward the Aran Islands, where the young playwright would discover his true subjects, there were large demonstrations led by the Socialists. In 1893 the anarchist Vaillant hurled a bomb into the Chamber of Deputies, and Captain Dreyfus was court-martialed the same year. The ultranationalism and anti-Semitism of the Dreyfus period help us understand the political orientation of Yeats's beloved Maud Gonne, who was carrying on an affair of long standing with the rightwing French politician Lucien Millevoye.

Here is Yeats in Dublin just after winning the Nobel Prize and buying a large Georgian house in Merrion Square, one of Dublin's most impressive addresses: "As a host Yeats dressed the part of the world-famous poet. He wore a black velvet coat and silver buckled shoes, a wide black ribbon attached to his tortoiseshell rimmed glasses. On his little finger he wore a large ring of gold. One of his guests was Seán O'Casey, a gauche, prickly little man wearing a cloth cap and steel-rimmed glasses who had grown up in the poorer neighborhoods in Dublin."

Looking back in his autobiographical book, *Reveries over Childhood and Youth*, Yeats in his late forties drew a veil over his painfully threadbare years as an unsuccessful artist's son in London and Dublin, preferring to dwell on carefree days spent in Sligo with his mother's family, the Pollexfens, wealthy merchants and shipowners. His father's people, the Yeatses, had a distinguished history but, in common with other members of the Protestant establishment or Ascendancy, had come down in the world as a result of the famine, land agitation, and emigration that deprived the *rentier* class of their incomes during the mid-nineteenth century.

Yeats's romantic view of imperiled aristocracy was fed in his youth by sojourns at Sandymount Castle, a turreted and castellated Gothic mansion in the suburbs of Dublin. Here they rode to hounds and drank out of silver cups; Yeats's sister Lily would remember an older relative who "had a most impressive way of dropping his voice and saying sadly, 'so very sad that so and so had to be sold.'" The Yeatses, linen merchants from Yorkshire, had come over to Dublin in the early eighteenth century. In 1773 one Benjamin Yeats married Mary Butler, from the distinguished family of the Dukes of Ormonde, among the most powerful Anglo-Norman families in Ireland. The Yeatses were proud of their Ormonde connection and used Butler as a middle name for the next two centuries.

Yeats's mother's family derived from a less aristocratic lineage and were less caught up in regretting a vanished, partially fictional past. Unlike the Yeatses, they had the advantage of being rich: "The house was so big that there was always a room to hide in, and I had a red pony and a garden where I could wander, and there were two dogs to follow at my heels, one white with some black spots on his head and the other with long black hair all over him." The details of the two dogs are characteristic of Yeats's descriptive writing—always vivid but not necessarily going in any perceptible direction. His writing is wonderfully succinct and concrete, always with an eye to vigorous action.

Of his grandfather William Pollexfen he writes: "He had a violent temper and kept a hatchet at his bedside for burglars and would knock a man down instead of going to law, and I once saw him hunt a party of men with a horsewhip." Mr. Pollexfen may have been "in trade" and thus excluded from houses like Lissadell and Coole where Yeats would later be welcomed; but in his grandson's eyes he had all the virtues of the landed gentry. Thus a strong poet like Yeats not only reinvented himself but even went back and reinvented his past.

Decisive, cleanly defined action is the meat and drink of Yeats's poetry. He associated it with a tradition growing out of the Middle Ages, a way of life whose mainstays were the aristocracy and the peasantry. A vigorous set of values centered around personal courage, sound workmanship, and pride has been his legacy not only to the Irish poets he addressed a month or two before his death in "Under Ben Bulben," but to a century of English-speaking poets who have apprenticed themselves to him:

> Irish poets, learn your trade,
> Sing whatever is well made,
> Scorn the sort now growing up
> All out of shape from toe to top,
> Their unremembering hearts and heads
> Base-born products of base beds.
> Sing the peasantry, and then
> Hard-riding country gentlemen . . .

Yeats's pride in ancestry, his scorn of anything common, made him anathema to critics on the left who have dominated the intellectual life of the twentieth century.

John B. Yeats, a Trinity College graduate and barrister who gave up the law just two years after the birth of his eldest son in order to study art, was, as Foster puts it, "an un-Victorian father" who wrote his wife during one of their frequent separations, "Working and caring for children makes me anxious and careful of them, but amusing them makes me fond of them." As inept as he was at supporting his children, and lacking the means to send them to good schools, he nevertheless provided them with an incomparable education for leading the artistic lives they were to lead: W. B. Yeats in poetry, Jack B. Yeats as a painter, whose canvases fetch higher and higher prices every year, and the sisters "Lily" and "Lolly" as printers, book designers, weavers, and craftswomen.

When Yeats was in his mid-teens the family moved back to Ireland from London, to live near Dublin in Howth, then a picturesque fishing village. At the age of fifteen or sixteen he began to compose verses. In *Reveries over Childhood and Youth*, creating atmosphere with broad descriptive strokes, he writes, "My father's influence upon my thoughts was at its height. We went to Dublin by train every morning, breakfasting at his studio. He had taken a large room with a beautiful eighteenth-century mantelpiece in a York Street tenement-house, and at breakfast he read passages from the poets, and always from the play or poem at its most passionate moment." It is typical of Yeats's approach that the "beautiful eighteenth-century mantelpiece" somehow dominates the mood of the passage. What is striking is that the aesthetic of the obscure and unsuccessful portrait painter John B. Yeats would become such an important part of the prevailing aesthetic of Modernist poetry: "He never read me a passage because of its speculative interest, and indeed did not care at all for poetry where there was generalization or abstraction however impassioned." Think of the Victorian poetry that was then in vogue and you will see how radical these ideas were at the time.

He fostered in his son a conviction that the best poetry is always personal and dramatic: "He did not care even for a fine lyric passage unless he felt some actual man behind its elaboration of beauty . . . He thought Keats a greater poet than Shelley, because less abstract, but did not read him, caring little, I think, for any of that most beautiful poetry which has come in modern times from the influence of painting. All must be an idealization of speech, and at some moment of passionate action or somnambulistic reverie."

John B. Yeats's fitful to-ing and fro-ing between Dublin and London continued until 1907, when he moved to New York, where he lived in exile until his death. He could not be persuaded to return. "To leave New York is to leave a huge fair where at any moment I might meet with some huge bit of luck," this Micawber-like prodigal father wrote. "Why do birds migrate? Looking for food—that's why I'm here." Eventually his son worked out an agreement with the wealthy Irish American lawyer and collector John Quinn whereby the poet sent him manuscripts and first editions and, in return, Quinn helped support the elder Yeats.

Alldritt memorably evokes one of the houses, 58 Eardsley Crescent in Earl's Court, where the Yeatses lived when the children were still under their parents' roof. In doing so he brings out a strange bit of interaction between nineteenth-century England and America, with the twenty-two-year-old poet stuck in one of the dreariest corners of industrial England pondering a mythic Ireland in his own as-yet unformed imagination:

> An end house in a stuccoed row in the debased classical style typical of mid-Victorian developments, their new home seemed to them even more squalid than the one at Terenure [a suburb of Dublin]. John Yeats himself described it as "old and dirty and dank and noisy," while Lily wrote that the

house was "horrible" and the garden just a bit of sooty ground dirtied by cats. Like Terenure, this western edge of Kensington was a lower-middle-class suburb and clearly up-setting to the family of one who had once contemplated practicing at the Dublin Bar. For the large Earl's Court Exhibition ground, which was very close to the house, gave to the area a funfair atmosphere and a noisy vulgarity. Steam organs blared out the music-hall songs of the day and at the time the Yeats family unenthusiastically moved in, Buffalo Bill and his Cowboy and Indian troupe were putting on shows that entailed whooping war cries and rattling gunfire. As the slender, bespectacled Willie went down into the underground station pondering his new project, a poem about Oisin, one of the noble heroes of ancient Ireland, he was met by crowds of working-class cockneys surging up from the steam-hauled trains, eager to cross the street to the Wild West Show.

The precariousness of his upbringing had profound implications for the values he arrived at in maturity. "[I]f I had not been an unsuccessful & struggling man Willie & Jack would not have been so strenuous," John B. Yeats later mused in a letter to a friend. "—& Lily & Lollie? Perhaps they'd have been married like your daughter—a successful father is good for the daughters. For the sons it is another matter."

Yeats's mother comes across as a shadowy non-presence. She seems never to have quite recovered from the shock of marrying a man who proved himself incapable of supporting her in the style to which she was accustomed. In accounts of the Yeats household, she sits silent and resentful in the corner while her husband and her children argue passionately about the Pre-Raphaelites and Irish nationalism. After years of ill health and a series of strokes, she died in 1900, when Yeats was thirty-five. "She was prim and austere, suffered all in silence," Lily Yeats would later remark. "She asked no sympathy and gave none."

It is not difficult to imagine Yeats in this dreary London, dreaming of the country around Sligo he knew as a boy. In "The Trembling of the Veil" from his *Autobiographies* he describes the inception of what remains his best-known poem, "The Lake Isle of Innisfree":

> I had still the ambition, formed in Sligo in my teens, of living in imitation of Thoreau on Innisfree, a little island in Lough Gill, and when walking through Fleet Street very homesick I heard a little tinkle of water and saw a fountain in a shop-window which balanced a little ball upon its jet, and began to remember lake water. From the sudden remembrance came my poem Innisfree, my first lyric with anything in its rhythm of my own music. I had begun to loosen rhythm as an escape from rhetoric and from that emotion of the crowd that rhetoric brings, but I only understood vaguely and occasionally that I must for my special purpose use nothing but the common syntax. A couple of years later I would not have written that first line with its conventional archaism—"Arise and go"—nor the inversion in the last stanza.

Since Yeats speaks of discovering the rhythm of his own music—and unfortunately for the student of meter, he never writes in technical terms about prosody—it might be instructive to scan the last stanza of that much-loved and over-quoted poem (I will use the *accent grave* to indicate secondary stress, partway between the accented and the unaccented syllable):

```
\ x  x /  x   /  \  x / x    /  x  /
```
I will arise and go now, for always night and day

```
x  /  /  / x  / x   x   /   /   x x   /
```
I hear lake water lapping with low sounds by the shore;

```
x   x   /   x x    /   \ x \ x   /    x      /
```
While I stand on the roadway, or on the pavements grey,

```
x  /  x x  x    /      /      /
```
I hear it in the deep heart's core.

This is brilliant versification. Yeats usually adapted his verse forms from his reading, and he may have gleaned this stanza from one of the nineteenth-century Irish poets writing in English, like Mangan or Ferguson; its exact source is unknown to me. The stanza is made up of three six-beat (hexameter) lines, each divided by a medial caesura. The pause is signaled in lines one and three by a comma following a secondary stress (\); in line two the caesura is effected by the unstressed syllables of the second syllable of "lapping" and the unstressed preposition "with." The fourth line is tetrameter, in accordance with the common principle of rounding off a stanza by moving from a longer to a shorter line, as in the ballad or the Sapphic stanza. It is all comfortably iambic, counterpointed against contrasting rhythms. The lulling, watery feeling is reflected in several anapestic (x x /) phrases: "will arise," "by the shore," "while I stand," "in the deep." The poet's yearning is hammered home with emphatic spondaic phrases: "low sounds," "deep heart's core."

The metrical approach of other popular lyrics by Yeats in his Celtic Twilight mode is more conventional but no less beautiful. "Down by the Salley Gardens" contains fewer metrical surprises: an inverted trochaic (/ x) foot at the beginning of the first line, where an iamb would be expected; and the occasional anapest throughout. A salley is a kind of willow. Here is the well-known eight-line poem in its entirety:

Down by the salley gardens my love and I did meet;
She passed the salley gardens with little snow-white feet.
She bid me take love easy, as the leaves grow on the tree;
But I, being young and foolish, with her would not agree.

W. B. Yeats

In a field by the river my love and I did stand,
And on my leaning shoulder she laid her snow-white hand.
She bid me take life easy, as the grass grows on the weirs;
But I was young and foolish, and now am full of tears.

Though the long lines, as printed, contain six beats apiece, each divides naturally into two units of three beats each. The poem reads aloud like a ballad in four stanzas rhyming abcb, differing from the usual ballad stanza only by virtue of having three beats in the first and third lines of each stanza rather than the usual four. It is utterly lovely and utterly conventional.

As an artist Yeats was restless; he was also proud, and it annoyed him that lesser poets imitated his early work, turning it into an Edwardian period style. Later, well into the new century, he published the following quatrain, titled "To a Poet, Who Would Have Me Praise Certain Bad Poets, Imitators of His and Mine":

You say, as I have often given tongue
In praise of what another's said or sung,
'Twere politic to do the like by these;
But was there ever dog that praised his fleas?

As early as 1904, fifteen years after "Down by the Salley Gardens" and eleven years later than "Innisfree," as part of the collection *In the Seven Woods* (a reference to the seven woods at Coole, Lady Gregory's estate), Yeats in "Adam's Curse" hit on the plain-spoken and forceful but still intensely musical form of expression that would evolve into his mature style. Here he abandons the shorter lines and four-line stanzas that typify his early, ballad-like poems for pentameter couplets that owe something to eighteenth-century masters like Swift and Pope. He also—not surprisingly in a man on the verge of turning forty—abandons the languor of his early lyrics for the solid virtues of hard work:

We sat together at one summer's end,
That beautiful mild woman, your close friend,
And you and I, and talked of poetry.
I said, 'A line will take us hours maybe;
Yet if it does not seem a moment's thought,
Our stitching and unstitching has been naught.
Better go down upon your marrow-bones
And scrub a kitchen pavement, or break stones
Like an old pauper, in all kinds of weather;
For to articulate sweet sounds together
Is to work harder than all these, and yet
Be thought an idler by the noisy set
Of bankers, schoolmasters, and clergymen
The martyrs call the world.'

Fortunate in many things, Yeats was perhaps most fortunate in the friends he made. Published the year before his death, "The Municipal Gallery Revisited" memorializes several friends, chief among them Augusta Gregory, who was for fifty years the poet's patron, confidante, and fellow soldier in the struggle for an Irish theatre, which in itself embodied the struggle to define the emerging nation. In the forceful rhetoric he learned to appreciate from his vacillating father, Yeats—in a rare self-congratulatory mood—celebrates his friendship with Lady Gregory and the third leg of the Abbey Theatre triumvirate, John Millington Synge:

John Synge, I and Augusta Gregory, thought
All that we did, all that we said or sang
Must come from contact with the soil, from that
Contact everything Antaeus-like grew strong.
We three alone in modern times had brought
Everything down to that sole test again,
Dream of the noble and the beggar-man.

W. B. Yeats

The poem continues:

> You that would judge me, do not judge alone
> This book or that, come to this hallowed place
> Where my friends' portraits hang and look thereon;
> Ireland's history in their lineaments trace;
> Think where man's glory most begins and ends,
> And say my glory was I had such friends.

What would have become of the penniless young poet without Lady Gregory, one hates to speculate. From their meeting in 1896 on, she was an ally whose background was reassuringly familiar, in that she was an Irish Protestant, but exotic and exciting in that while Yeats had always been on the outside looking in, Lady Gregory was able to provide him with the aristocratic culture to which he was spiritually attuned. Coole was a haven where the malnourished young bohemian could be restored to health, with time to write, freed from the pressures of literary journalism. She became the mother he had never really had. He reciprocated by turning Coole Park into a symbol for the ordered, traditional life that represented for him an ideal organization of culture and society.

Yeats was undeniably an elitist and a snob. The first of these qualities seems to me, as it informed his views on art and society, a positive value. As to the latter, admirers of his poetry might be more inclined to regard it as a peccadillo than to recoil from it in horror. Yeats was prophetic in the alarm with which he viewed the Roman Catholic nativism that came to dominate the nationalist movement, culminating in the Puritanism and censorship of Eamon de Valera's Ireland. Yeats had been among the earliest advocates of Home Rule, but as events moved inexorably toward independence he became, like his ally Synge, more and more an opponent of the merchants and priests who typified the Catholic Establishment. Only in the early twenty-first century has Irish society freed itself from the Church's unquestioned position of authority.

In "September 1913" Yeats stirringly elegizes the Fenian John O'Leary, whom the British sentenced to six years of hard labor in the stone quarries of the Portland Prison on the south coast of England, then exiled from Ireland for fourteen years more. The poem contrasts the idealism of O'Leary, who died in 1907, to the venality of the emerging Catholic mercantile class that was coming to dominate Ireland:

> What need you, being come to sense,
> But fumble in a greasy till
> And add the halfpence to the pence
> And prayer to shivering prayer, until
> You have dried the marrow from the bone?
> For men were born to pray and save:
> Romantic Ireland's dead and gone,
> It's with O'Leary in the grave.

R. F. Foster sees Yeats's position as consistent with his spiritual and aesthetic leanings: "He was clear in his mind that [Catholic middle class] institutions represented the faith and assumptions of the majority of the country, and therefore enjoyed a legitimacy not possessed by their predecessors, but he was equally convinced that—for all the rhetoric of nationalist rectitude—they shared many values founded on the debased intellectual currency of Victorian materialism, and its denial of ancient tradition." As for Yeats's increasing love of country-house weekends and dinner parties in fashionable London houses as his fame grew, Foster takes an understanding approach: "snobbery is never simple, being founded on an insecurity that can be psychological as much as social; and preoccupation with family is a natural response to entering one's late forties childless, with the landmark figures of the last generation crumbling away."

Yeats's elitism was later to elevate eighteenth-century Anglo-Irish culture as an ideal and to focus on the great houses of the aristocracy as symbols not only of beauty but of a distinguished and fully integrated way of life. In making such claims for a class that, beginning with the land agitation of the late nineteenth century and increasingly during the Irish War of Independence and the subsequent Civil War, came to be roundly despised and rejected, with many of their houses put to the torch, Yeats praised a living culture that embodied not what today would be called privilege, but responsibility, wisdom, and dedication. In two great companion poems, "Coole Park, 1929" and "Coole Park and Ballylee, 1931," composed in eight-line stanzas as monolithic and awe-inspiring as marble slabs, Yeats memorializes the life to which he had been introduced by Lady Gregory:

> Sound of a stick upon the floor, a sound
> From somebody that toils from chair to chair;
> Beloved books that famous hands have bound,
> Old marble heads, old pictures everywhere;
> Great rooms where travelled men and children found
> Content or joy; a last inheritor
> Where none has reigned that lacked a name and fame
> Or out of folly into folly came.
>
> ("Coole Park and Ballylee, 1931")

Distinguished by an inimitable tone Yeats would call, in "The Fisherman," "as cold and passionate as the dawn," these monumental poems derive some of their power from being prophetic elegies. Yeats knew that the tradition he loved was coming to its end. He bade it, and his friend Augusta Gregory, who in his eyes embodied a tradition of patronage and noblesse oblige, farewell in some of the noblest lines ever written:

> Here, traveller, scholar, poet, take your stand
> When all those rooms and passages are gone,

When nettles wave upon a shapeless mound
And saplings root among the broken stone,
And dedicate—eyes bent upon the ground,
Back turned upon the brightness of the sun
And all the sensuality of the shade—
A moment's memory to that laurelled head.
                              ("Coole Park, 1929")

His prophecy has proved accurate. The house at Coole was pulled down in 1941 and sold to a local farmer for the value of its stones and the lead from its roof. The lines quoted above are displayed behind plexiglass for the visitor to Coole Park to contemplate.

W. B. Yeats

Looking for Yeats
in Yeats Country

January 28, 2009, marks the seventieth anniversary of
the death of William Butler Yeats. As time is reckoned
in this country, seventy years are not many, and most of the
places associated with Yeats are easily found and conveniently
visited. Yeats spent most of his boyhood in Dublin and London,
where as we have seen, his father pursued a not very successful
career as a portrait painter. But to find places that carry the true
flavor of his poetry we must leave these cities behind.

The young Yeats spent summers and holidays in Sligo, his
mother's home. Later he would return there often in his imagination. In his early verse, it was the natural beauty of the place
that Yeats celebrated. The twin mountains that overlook Sligo—
Knocknarea, the legendary burial place of Queen Maeve, and
Ben Bulben, in whose shadow the poet is buried, brood over his
writing like ancestral presences. In his first book Yeats made
Glencar waterfall—nine miles north of town—the setting of
his lovely early poem "The Stolen Child," quoted in an earlier
chapter.

Fifteen miles south of Sligo Town is Lough Gill, site of the
Lake Isle of Innisfree. In the previous chapter I recount the

story of how Yeats says he came to write the poem in London, where the family was living at the time. But Sligo's natural beauty was not the only thing that endeared the place to Yeats. A lifelong admirer of aristocratic values and a bit of a snob, he loved the big houses of the gentry. One such place, Lissadell, which the poet visited at least once as a house guest, stands nine miles northwest of the town. Built in 1830, it was until recently the home of the Gore-Booths, a distinguished Anglo-Irish family. Sir David Gore-Booth resigned as recently as a few decades ago from his post as British High Commissioner to India, a position his father also held. Yeats immortalized the place in his poem "In Memory of Eva Gore-Booth and Con Markiewicz," which begins:

> The light of evening, Lissadell,
> Great windows open to the south,
> Two girls in silk kimonos, both
> Beautiful, one a gazelle.

In the 1930s Yeats took a dim view of what had become of Countess Markiewicz, who fought in the Easter Rising and was captured by the British—

> The older is condemned to death,
> Pardoned, drags out lonely years
> Conspiring among the ignorant

—but he loved the style of her ancestral home.

The house has been sold out of the family, but on occasion you can tour this massive, fortress-like mansion. Take in the view from its expansive south-facing windows, and see in the dining room the famous mural portraits of family members, the butler, the gamekeeper, and a beloved family dog. Count Markiewicz painted these. Also on the dining-room walls hang family portraits by Sarah Purser.

Below-stairs is just as fascinating as above-stairs at Lissadell. Here you can see the massive kitchen that provided for the household. Twenty-eight hefty mugs are arranged on a big pine table, as if waiting for the staff to come in for their tea. The old-fashioned range stands in one corner, the dumbwaiter, a marvelous contraption for sending dishes up to the dining room, in another. And in an alcove, great hooks to hang smoked bacon and fish. Twenty-four tons of coal were burned each year to heat this establishment, as well as three trees.

I was lucky enough to see the house in the last years of the Gore-Booth tenancy, before the place was tidied up. The billiard room was home to an exotic hodgepodge of stuff: a collection of mounted butterflies, arrowheads, harpoons, and other curios from an ancestor's voyages of exploration to foreign parts. The warren of offices and maids' rooms downstairs was like someone's old attic, a treasure-trove of Anglo-Irish history. I remember an old-fashioned post-bag with the initials G-B stenciled on it, a helmet from the Boer War, molding piles of bills and Church of Ireland circulars. I pocketed a nineteenth-century bill for boot blacking from a London shop with the idea of framing it as a memento.

Traveling back in the direction of Sligo Town on the main highway, you come to Drumcliff Churchyard, where Yeats is buried. In keeping with the poet's ideal of beauty, the church itself is austere, its tall steeple rising from among the graves. Yeats's marker, a plain rectangle of local limestone, is equally simple but impressive. Unlike many traditional gravestones, which ask the passerby to stop and say a prayer, Yeats's advises stoicism and disinterestedness:

Cast a cold Eye
On life, on Death.
Horseman, pass by.

If Sligo gives us scenes from Yeats's childhood and youth, as well as being his burial place, in his middle years the poet came to County Galway, where he met Lady Gregory, the woman who would be his friend, collaborator, patron, and surrogate mother from the time they met in 1896 until her death in 1932. He wrote many of his greatest poems just north of Gort in her house at Coole, which sadly has been demolished. The former national school at Kiltartan crossroads, built of red brick and stone in 1892, has been turned into a Gregory museum. At Coole Park itself, you can see where the house once stood, and wander through the famous Seven Woods of Coole.

A short drive north of Coole you come to Thoor Ballylee, which Yeats bought in 1916 for £35 and restored. Because of his busy life and poor health, he used the tower mainly as a summer home and abandoned it altogether in 1928. But it remains the poet's lasting monument and symbol. The titles of two of his greatest books, *The Tower* and *The Winding Stair*, evoke the place, which he describes in "Meditations in Time of Civil War."

As I have pointed out in the previous chapter, Yeats the dreamer inherited from his mother's mercantile family a brisk approach to practical affairs. He took pride in getting the tower restored economically and well. "We are surrounded with plans," he wrote to the New York lawyer and patron of the arts, John Quinn. "The war is improving the work, for, being unable to import anything, we have bought the whole contents of an old mill—great beams and three-inch planks, and old paving stones; and the local carpenter and mason and blacksmith are at work for us."

Moving out in the countryside from Gort, you can still find some of the places Yeats mentions in his elegy "In Memory of Major Robert Gregory":

When with the Galway foxhounds he would ride
From Castle Taylor to the Roxborough side
Or Esserkelly plain, few kept his pace . . .

Castle Taylor, north of Ardrahan, is in ruins now, but more picturesque ruins you will not see. The mansion incorporated a tower house not unlike Thoor Ballylee. A rusty door from an old Morris was leaning against the tower wall when I was last there. Climbing among the broken stones you can contemplate the passing from the scene of both the medieval Anglo-Normans and the more recent Anglo-Irish. Roxborough House, near the Fishpond crossroads off the road to Loughrea, was the seat of the Persses, a family of distillers. Lady Gregory, née Persse, grew up here, though her family also owned the big stone house in Lower Dominick Street in Galway that now houses the Arts Centre. What remains of Roxborough is not impressive, but walk through the former stable yards to the Gothic battlements and gate built on the banks of the little river that runs downstream toward Ballylee and Coole. With no company here but the jackdaws and swallows, you'll feel you have strayed back into a romantic dream of the Middle Ages.

5

From Venice to Tipperary

From Venice to Tipperary

1.

It is November now, the wind roars across this hillside acre as if it wanted to wrench the garden shed where I write off its foundations and scatter its pine boards across the face of Sliabh na mBan. I live on the side of the mountain at the end of an unmarked lane in a remote corner of Tipperary, three miles from the nearest stop sign. Even when the wind is still, there is no traffic noise—no sirens, no horns. If we hear a motor, it probably means our neighbor is driving his tractor up the lane, bringing hay to the cattle. When a solitary airplane flies over, its silent passing is a singular enough event to make one look up and follow its progress across the sky.

The wind is relentless. It whispers, whistles, swoops and swerves, rattles the gutters and windowpanes. The rain-saturated meadows I see out the window glow emerald green, and there is a velvety denseness in the foliage of pines that grow along the demarcations between fields. Here and there the ghostly grey trunk of a beech tree shows through, and the black and white of Friesian cattle decorate a field. The only color other than natural tones is our red car parked in front of the house.

Part of me is in Tipperary, part of me is still in Venice. We have just returned. While we were gone a gale blew the hinges off the henhouse door, then blew the door off, and the fox killed one of our chickens. This morning when I got up I saw him out there, looking for another opening. He pranced away when he saw me, looking for all the world like a Renaissance dandy in a russet-colored tunic, his gorgeous tail pluming behind him. He was light on his feet and carried himself with the style of a young courtier in a painting by Vittore Carpaccio in the Accademia Gallery.

We go to Venice for the intoxication of spending a few days in a place that is utterly beautiful. By comparison with many parts of the world, we already live in such a place, even though Ireland is changing every day, and not necessarily for the better. Despite our remoteness, we ourselves are impatient for broadband Internet service to arrive where we live. No one escapes the modern world, and most of us don't care to completely. Even antimodernists like ourselves are selective in our refusals.

Both Venice and the Irish hinterland still carry some flavor of life in Europe during the Middle Ages. Both are ancient cultures the contemplation of which allows one to travel back in human history and entertain ways of thinking that can raise us for a few moments above the day's trivia. In the eighth century, when Venice was first establishing herself as a city-state with a more or less secure foundation in its lagoon, trading for salt and grain between the mainland of Lombardy and the Byzantine Empire to the east (much of my information about Venetian history comes from Jan Morris's *Venice*), Ireland had already achieved a rich monastic culture, which produced illuminated manuscripts like the Book of Kells and sent missionaries to nearby Scotland and England, and to Germany and Switzerland on the continent. The first Viking incursions lay a century or so in the future, when predators would sail their fast ships down from the northern fjords to ravage their more settled neighbors.

(A good source for the broad outlines of this story is Maire and Conor Cruise O'Brien, *A Concise History of Ireland*.)

After the breakup of the Roman Empire the problem for cultures all over Europe was how to sustain commerce, trade, prayer, the making of art and artefacts, as all this had been carried on under the Romans, and at the same time to keep themselves safe from marauders like the Vikings in northern Europe, the Goths, Visigoths, and Huns in Central Europe and Italy, and the Turks and Arabs at the borders of the Byzantine Empire. Ireland, protected from outside interference by its remoteness, had never had the Romans either as conquerors, or as overlords who could provide a garrison of centurions to keep watch over the sea while a monk shaped the capital letter at the beginning of the book of John into an eagle, or applied gold leaf to the façade of a mansion in paradise.

Julius Caesar conquered Britain but must never have thought it worth his while to cross the Irish Sea—perhaps he thought there was nothing here worth having. A recently excavated Roman camp north of Dublin tells us that the imperial army must at least have sent a party over to reconnoitre, but there is little other than a few coins and a rusty belt-buckle or two to show they came here. Unaccountably, a Roman doctor's kit has been discovered at the Rock of Cashel in County Tipperary; no one knows how it got there.

To the Romans, Ireland was Hibernia, the land of winter. According to the annals of Irish piety, Christianity reached this island in the person of a British slave, who became St. Patrick. The monasteries with their scriptoria where manuscripts were copied out and illuminated, their round towers where bells and chalices wrought in bronze, silver, and gold by local artisans were put for safekeeping and a ladder pulled up when the local warlords or invading Vikings threatened, had somehow to survive on their own remoteness and ingenuity. Even before the Vikings got wind of the treasures to be plundered, however, the monasteries were not safe: the local Irish lords and petty kings themselves plundered the monasteries whenever they took the notion.

Consider a few of the terms John Ruskin, in *The Stones of Venice*, uses to invoke a vision of the city in its magnificence: its *brightness*, its *walls* and *towers*, its *princes*, *palaces*, and *pride*. One may apply any of these six nouns to Ireland, but when one does, they immediately begin to suggest sadness and irony, if not bitterness—the sorrow, the irony, the bitterness of history. Outside the windows of my studio there is no blue sky, no shimmering sunlight, no sherbety tones of sun-faded plaster. No bezants of lapis lazuli and porphyry have been set into the walls of our shed; the Renaissance never reached the misty hills of Tipperary. The Mediterranean is far away. Our cottage and outbuildings are designed with the traditional angles and dignified beauty of vernacular farmhouse architecture.

Looking from the buff-colored sandstone of the house and shed to the steely sky and the rain lashing through the fields outside, I see muted gradations of brown, grey, and green. When one ventures forth to look at architecture in the Irish countryside, its very limitations, its imperfections, are what one has to contemplate. Ireland's history has, until recently, been ruinous and troubled, and one sees this history in its ruined abbeys and churches, its crumbling tower houses, the bastions of what little security could be achieved amid the chaos of medieval life. Venetian sunlight fades to Northern European darkness. Glory gives way to embattlement.

It takes an act of imagination to see the old structures as they must have been in their prime, because just about every building of note in Ireland from before the eighteenth century has been at least partially destroyed by fire, war, neglect, or a combination of all three. While Venice has been preserved as a world treasure, premodern Ireland is a landscape of ruins. Architectural pilgrims who take the trouble to drive or cycle around Ireland are rewarded with discoveries of a very different nature from what is to be experienced in a place like Venice, where crowds often get in the way—not to mention the humbling realization that as far as other visitors are concerned, you yourself may be in the way, blocking their view of the mosaics in San Marco or the Carpaccios in the Scuola di San Giorgio.

In the Irish countryside it is a pleasure to pull on your Wellingtons and muck through a cow pasture to look at a well-carved flamboyant sedilia in a roofless church or the fragments of cloisters in what was once a thriving abbey or priory. Most often, few others are in the hunt, and on the rare occasions one encounters them, their presence is more a pleasure than an annoyance.

The Rock of Cashel juts up from the Tipperary plain, a massive outcropping of limestone as grey as the winter sky. In Irish a cashel or *caiseal* is a stone fort, and there must have been one here originally, now eradicated by the passage of time. A great moment occurs on the road to Cashel when, just as one is coming up on the village of Rosegreen, the Rock appears above the horizon like a Gothic fantasy, like a toy castle in a child's model railroad set. One can imagine how imposing it would have been when approached on foot or horseback. As a defensive position it must have been impregnable.

There is perhaps no way to see Venice as it ideally should be seen, no season of the year to see the city as it must have looked before the advent of tourism. As for Cashel, it is possible to see it and not be bothered by crowds in winter, when the tour buses go into mothballs for the season. To me it is at its best on a December afternoon just at dusk, when the smoke from coal and turf fires gives the air a bitter perfume and there is feeling of the town recovering from the tourists and becoming itself again.

The Rock takes one back to the days of the kings of Munster, who ruled most of southern Ireland beginning roughly in the fourth century. The history of changing religions in Ireland is suggested by the Rock's early name, the "Fairy Ridge." When St. Patrick arrived at Cashel to baptise Aongus, a king of Munster, the story goes that Patrick was leaning on his crozier while baptising the king, unconsciously driving the sharp point of it into the king's foot. Aongus "neither winced nor cried aloud," according to Mairtín Ó Corrbui's book *Tipperary*, "deeming the pain suffered part of the ceremony, and little enough to endure when compared with Christ's agony on the cross." In 1101 King Murtagh Ó Brien handed Cashel over to the Church, and the king-bishop Cormaic Mac Carthach built that jewel of Irish Romanesque, the Teampuill Chormaic, called Cormac's Chapel in English, in the early twelfth century.

Cormac's Chapel stands toward one edge of the Rock, and today it looks cramped, as if jockeying for position, angled into a tiny corner of space beside and underneath the cathedral, which, before most of it was destroyed, would have stood much taller than the chapel. While Venice was a city of rich merchants, with a fleet at their command, an empire to draw materials to build with, Ireland had none of that. The chapel was built from buff-colored sandstone that stands out curiously both here and among other buildings one sees in Ireland, though it is familiar to me because our cottage and shed are made of the same material.

Given sandstone's susceptibility to the ravages of time and weather, it seems a curious choice as a building material. Maybe sandstone was all that could be found. According to Harold G. Leask's *Irish Churches and Monastic Buildings*, the sandstone is "axed," meaning, I suppose, that it was literally shaped with axes. I know sandstone is a soft material, but I also know how hard it is to drill into because I have taken the power drill to our own sandstone in order to attach a trellis to the walls of the cottage. There is a tradition that the stone used at Cashel was quarried at Drumbane twelve miles away and the blocks were passed from hand to hand all the way to the Rock.

That the chapel should bear such close resemblance to churches being built in Germany during this same period is surprising until one realizes that Ireland had close ties to the Continent throughout the Middle Ages. Like the Turkish carpets that Venetian artists placed in their paintings beneath the throne of the Virgin, and like the Chinese porcelains that appear in Persian art under the Safavids, influences detected in architectural styles give us insights into the flow of ideas and goods in periods, such as the Irish Middle Ages, that are hard for us to visualize. Irish monks did missionary work on the continent as early as the sixth century, and ties were closely maintained.

From the tenth century on, there were Irish-run monasteries at Cologne, Metz, Erfurt, Ratisbon, and in other Germanic lands. A German abbot with the name of Dionysius sent a delegation of Irishmen home to collect money for the new monastery he was building. So it is not surprising that, along with churchmen and craftsmen, ideas about architecture traveled between these two countries, which would seem to us rather distant from each other geographically. The twin Germanic squared-off towers, the blank wall-arcading, and the style of much of the carving are unique in Ireland.

Blank arcading in a church makes sense in Venice because of the beauty of the marble available for construction, the presumed desire to isolate the church from the houses that surround it so closely, and because the windows at the top of the church brighten it sufficiently in its sunny climate. At Cashel were windows eliminated because of the strong winds and rain? For whatever reason, Cormac's Chapel is very dark. Interestingly, the architect designed a showy entrance on its north side, and originally there were three windows open on the west façade. There is some speculation that Cormaic Mac Carthach was buried in the chapel, which would make it plausible that the chapel was darkened deliberately. Other historians say that it was yet another Cormac, with the surname of MacArt, who was laid to rest in the great sarcophagus in the nave; but it is also said that the sarcophagus itself was moved to the chapel from the south nave of the cathedral.

Why so many Cormacs within such a short period of time? If one looks at the lineage of the kings of Desmond, Shakespeare's line, "Uneasy lies the head that wears a crown" applies only too well to the kings of medieval Ireland. From the look of it, about half their reigns ended in violent death. Cormaic Mac Carthach had two reigns. The first of these came to an abrupt end when he was deposed by the nobles of Munster. When he fought his way back into power, he banished his erstwhile successor to Connacht—which tells us that Oliver Cromwell must have learned his famous stratagem of dispatching his enemies "to Hell or Connacht!" from his Irish predecessors. As for Cormaic, he himself was "treacherously murdered" in 1138, four years after the consecration of his chapel. One of his successors was struck by lightning "through vengeance of God for his misdeeds."

When the cathedral was built, overshadowing Cormac's Chapel, the new Gothic style must have been stunning. The three archbishops responsible for the church, Marianus O'Brien, David MacKelly, and David MacCarwill, were all Irishmen vying for power with the Normans, who, with their new military technology of the armored knight on horseback, were in the process of conquering the country. Peace seems the rarest of commodities at Cashel. Gerald Mór, known as the Great Earl of Kildare, burned the cathedral in 1494 in at attempt to smoke out his enemy, one of the archbishops. By this time the English were rulers of Ireland, or at least they attempted to rule this fractious country. Henry VII was not pleased by the burning of the cathedral, and remonstrated with Gerald. "By Jesus," the Earl is said to have replied, "I woulde never have done it, had it not bin tolde me that the Archbishoppe was within."

The cathedral was the scene of even more serious damage and slaughter during the Cromwellian wars of the 1640s. When Murrough O'Brien, Lord Inchiquin, attacked Cashel, the town had three thousand inhabitants. Most of them fled to the cathedral in hopes of being protected by soldiers on the Catholic side of the conflict. Rifle volleys were fired into the church, and ultimately Lord Inchiquin ordered that turf be piled against the walls and set afire. Those inside, including twenty priests, were roasted to death.

A contemporary witness, Father Andrew Sall, wrote, "The large crucifix that towered above the entrance to the choir had its head, hands and feet struck off, the organ was broken, and the bells, whose chimes cheered our soldiers as they fought, were deprived of their clappers and their beautiful tone . . . all the passages, even the altars, chapels, sacristies, bell-tower steps, and seats were so thickly covered with corpses, that one could not walk a step without treading on them." A fire in 1749 accounted for the final ruination of this melancholy church. By this point the Roman Catholic faith had been superseded by the Protestant Church of Ireland, and the archbishop of that faith had the lead and timbers of the ruined cathedral removed to the Church of St. John in the town, which became the Protestant cathedral.

2.

Last week I visited the ruins of Kilcash, another of Ireland's legendary centers of past glory. To get there I drove five miles along the mountain road that skirts the flank of Sliabh na mBan, then dropped down to Kilcash among bleak pastures and mountainy farms to Ballypatrick, which now, like the rest of Ireland, is filling up with housing estates. I wanted to look at the ruins of a little church and castle celebrated in the nineteenth-century song "Cill Cháis" (Kilcash), best known in Frank O'Connor's melodious if slightly archaic translation, which mourns the death of Margaret Butler, née Burke, Viscountess Iveagh, locally known as Lady Veagh. It is thought that there was some sort of monastic site here as early as the sixth century. In the sixteenth century a house was built here, Kilcash Castle, where Lord Castlehaven, noted Confederate Catholic commander in the 1641–52 war, wrote his memoirs. The big house later passed into the hands of a branch of the Butlers, Dukes of Ormonde in Kilkenny.

Though "nominal Protestants," the Butlers were secretly loyal to the old religion, sheltering Catholic clergy, whose very presence in Ireland was a capital crime under the Penal Laws. These people were part of the old aristocracy, Jacobites who backed James II, loser to the Protestant William of Orange at the Battle of the Boyne. Thomas Butler, Lady Veagh's second husband, fought on the losing side at Aughrim, another of the great battles the Stuarts lost to the house of Orange.

The old Irish aristocracy, with their traditional position in the country, the respect of the people, and their family connections to English power, managed to some extent to ride out the storm of changing political fortunes in the two islands, even though they would eventually lose out to the new English settlers. Thomas Butler's cousin was the Duke of Ormonde. Though the new legal system carried strict penalties against Catholics, Colonel Butler received a special license to retain in his possession his gun, his sword, and a case of pistols. Even then, during a troubled period in 1714 he was forced to hand over his weapons to the Protestant mayor of nearby Clonmel.

At the same time, families like the lords of Kilcash made their compromises with the new Protestant Anglo-Irish regime. Thomas Butler's daughter Honoria married Valentine Brown of Kenmare, occasioning a poem from the Gaelic bard Aogán O'Rahilly, who was at that time in favor with the Kenmares. I mentioned the Browns and O'Rahilly in my chapter on Elizabeth Bowen. Irish bards earned their bread and board by writing two kinds of poems: the encomium and the curse. They were valued for the former and feared for the latter. Here is a translation from Irish of "The Good Omen," a sycophantic poem O'Rahilly wrote to celebrate the match between Honoria Butler and Valentine Brown:

Druids and prophets have unraveled
From the prophecies of Patrick, and Brigid,
And of holy Colm the truly saintly, sayings
Which were full of the grace of the Holy Spirit;
Since a prince of Kilcash has bestowed
On the King of Killarney his daughter,
That their sons might inherit the place
Till the destruction and consummation of the world.

Lady Veagh is one of those rare characters who step fully-fleshed from the pages of history. Under her tenure, Kilcash was a center of aristocratic culture and patronage. Bards, singers, and harpers entertained the gentry and in turn were given food, shelter, and gifts. A surviving portrait in Kilkenny Castle suggests that she was not a beautiful woman, but she looks kind and sensible—a pleasure to know, condescending in the old-fashioned sense of someone of high rank who is gracious and generous to people at all levels of society. A contemporary priest, Father Hogan, wrote, "Her House was open to all Ranks, Degrees, and Stations of People, none excluded. . . . *Killcash* was the known Refuge of poor Gentry of both sexes." Her hospitality would have been severely put to the test during the famine of 1740–41, known in Irish as *bliadbain an air* (the year of the slaughter), when seven years of bad weather, famine, and disease were said to have killed between 250,000 and 400,000 people.

Aogán O'Rahilly is one of the great elegists of the old, bardic Ireland. Not too many years after he welcomed the alliance of the old Butlers of Kilcash with the newly established English Kenmares in the person of Valentine Brown, it became clear to O'Rahilly that he could not expect from the new dispensation the kind of patronage he had enjoyed from the dispossessed Gaelic lords he praised in many of his poems, including the McCarthys, kings of Munster, descendants of the builders of Cormac's Chapel. In his bitter lament "A Grey Eye Weeping," which I invoked in my earlier chapter on Elizabeth Bowen, it's as if O'Rahilly can hardly bring himself to say the name of the *arriviste* Valentine Brown without spitting out the words. Here is his poem in Frank O'Connor's memorable translation:

> That my old bitter heart was pierced in this black doom,
> That foreign devils have made our land a tomb,
> That the sun that was Munster's glory has gone down
> Has made me a beggar before you, Valentine Brown.
>
> That royal Cashel is bare of house and guest,
> That Brian's turreted home is the otter's nest,
> That the kings of the land have neither land nor crown
> Has made me a beggar before you, Valentine Brown.
>
> Garnish away in the west with its master banned,
> Hamburg the refuge of him who has lost his land,
> An old grey eye, weeping for lost renown,
> Have made me a beggar before you, Valentine Brown.

What remains of the formerly great house at Kilcash is a tower whose ruined walls are overgrown with ivy, visible from the road that passes from Clonmel to Kilkenny through Nine Mile House near where I live. You'd be hard pressed to find Lady Veagh's grave among the old tombs in the churchyard, their lettering eroded by time and weather. Even though, according to Maírtín Ó Corrbuí in his little book on Tipperary, the house escaped bombardment by Cromwell's cannon, stones from its walls and those of the chapel were taken away and used for building and road work. Local legend has it that the metal figures on the tombs of the Butler bishops were removed by the insurgents in 1848 and melted down to make bullets.

"Cill Cháis," the lament written after the final dissolution of the estate in the first half of the nineteenth century, is best known, as I have already mentioned, in the English translation made of it by Frank O'Connor. Thomas Kinsella's version is perhaps more accurate, if less musical. I like Eiléan Ní Chuilleanáin's version and give it here:

Lament for Kilcash

What will we do now for timber
With the last of the woods laid low—
No word of Kilcash nor its household,
Their bell is silenced now.
Where the lady lived with such honour,
No woman so heaped with praise,
Earls came across oceans to see her
And heard the sweet words of Mass.

It's the cause of my long affliction
To see your neat gates knocked down.
The long walks affording no shade now
And the avenue overgrown,
The fine house that kept out the weather,
Its people depressed and tamed,
And their names with the faithful departed,
The Bishop and Lady Iveagh!

The geese and the ducks' commotion,
The eagle's shout are no more,
The roar of the bees gone silent,
Their wax and their honey store

Deserted. Now at evening
The musical birds are stilled
And the cuckoo is dumb in the treetops
That sung lullaby to the world.

Even the deer and the hunters
That follow the mountain way
Look down upon us with pity,
The house that was famed in its day;
The smooth wide lawn is all broken,
No shelter from wind and rain;
The paddock has turned to a dairy
Where the fine creatures grazed.

Mist hangs low on the branches
No sunlight can sweep aside,
Darkness falls among daylight.
And the streams are all run dry;
No hazel, no holly or berry,
Bare naked rocks and cold;
The forest park is leafless
And all the game gone wild.

And now the worst of our troubles,
She has followed the prince of the Gaels—
He has borne off the gentle maiden,
Summoned to France and to Spain.
Her company laments her
That she fed with silver and gold;
One who never preyed on the people:
But was the poor souls' friend.

My prayer to Mary and Jesus
She may come safe home to us here

From Venice to Tipperary

To dancing and rejoicing
To fiddling and bonfire
That our ancestors' house will rise up,
Kilcash built up anew
And from now to the end of the story
May it never again be laid low.

(Interestingly, in the Gaelic original, the words *paddock*, *dairy*, *game*, and *Lady Iveagh* all appear in English, the equivalents apparently not existing in Irish.) Traditionally in Ireland, life centered around big houses like Kilcash; towns were negligible. The poem paints a picture not only of the remarkable woman who was the source of largesse and graciousness, but of the life that was lived there.

Significantly the poem begins as a lament for the loss of timber. One of Ireland's tragedies is the loss of its trees. The tradition here is to blame everything on the British, and much of the blame is deserved, because in its earliest days Ireland was covered in dense hardwood forests. But the erosion down to bare limestone that gives the Burren over in County Clare its characteristically bare landscape, for example, was caused by poor farming methods in the Stone Age. The British can hardly be blamed for that. Still, the "adventurers"—those who fought the Irish wars under Essex and Cromwell and King William—who were granted huge acreage in this country in the sixteenth and seventeenth centuries, commonly made profits by leveling the forests and selling the timber. John and Phil Flood record in their little *Kilcash: A History, 1190–1801* that "The famous trees of Kilcash were sold in two lots in 1797 and in 1801; in 1797 the timber on the avenue that went to the Carrick road 'together with the trees in the Church-grove and Deerpark, consisting of fine oak, ash, beech and elm' were offered for sale, while in 1801 the remaining timber on the estate was advertised."

Popular ballads and songs often offer little of the imagery modern poetry has taught us to expect in poetry; "Lament for Kilcash," however, is filled with sensory images, particularly with images of sound. What is more mournful than the line, "Their bell is silenced now"? Who could tell us what happened to that bell? Does it hang in some church now, or on one of the surrounding farms, or was it melted down for the bronze or silver in it? While Frank O'Connor gives us "No sound of duck or geese there, / Hawk's cry or eagle's call, / No humming of the bees there," Eiléan Ní Chuilleanáin's rendering of the same lines is more emphatic, and louder: "The geese and the ducks' commotion, / The eagle's shout are no more, / The roar of the bees gone silent." If you've ever been close enough to an eagle to hear its call, you know that it is loud. The close-up sound of bees is not a hum; it is deafening.

The day I went to Kilcash, there was nothing to lift the sense of bitterness and desolation from the scene. Like many places in Ireland, Kilcash is haunted by the past. I ignored the Danger Keep Out signs, scaled a wall, and had a look round. Clearly the tower had been well fortified at one time: the rounded machicolation that was constructed at one corner of the tower's roof would have given defenders a protected defensive position from which to fire down on attackers; likewise the smaller rectangular machicolation above the door would have allowed those inside to fire or drop things down on anyone trying to force entrance. You could see from the gable mark on the side of the tower where the bulk of the house had been that this wing was once substantial. It looks massive from the highway, less impressive close-up. Time, weather, and decay have had their way with the ruins, and Kilcash has not been immune to other forces. During the Civil War, Republican soldiers sheltered here, and General Prout of the Free State Army shelled the castle, causing even more damage to an already battered and dilapidated structure. History has laid a destructive hand on the glory of Kilcash and the memory of Lady Veagh.

3.

Wandering through the Doge's Palace in Venice one day, I came across a room whose walls are painted with old murals of maps, very detailed maps of the world. There Damascus was, and Aleppo and Jaffa, Beirut and Jerusalem—all the cities, ports, and towns of the ancient Ottoman provinces of Palestine and Mesopotamia, ports of call all the way down the shores of the Persian Gulf to India and then to China and beyond. The same detailed coverage was there for Europe. On our part of the continent, I would have expected London—it was a regular port of call for Venetian galleys. What surprised me was the detail with which Ireland was represented. Not just Dublin but Galway, Cork, and Waterford—even Kilkenny, just half an hour's drive up the road from where I am sitting. Ireland was on the map for Venice. When Cormac's Chapel was being built, when Lady Veagh was holding court at Kilcash, was Venice on the map for Ireland? Probably not, except as a legend of fabulous wealth. Yet Venice's lifeblood was trade and commerce, and the Venetians made it their business to learn about the world.

The very different stories of Venice and Ireland are stories of rise and fall, wealth and poverty, perfection and imperfection. There are lessons in these two histories about what fosters a sense of beauty, what destroys and degrades it. History is a structure of irony, and irony is born from a sense of difference. In terms of how this country is placed in relation to empire, the famous luck of the Irish has meant mostly bad luck. The course of Irish history has been determined by the country's position as an island off the far northwestern edge of Europe, next door to the seat of one of the greatest empires the world has seen.

Because of its location, Ireland had from the sixteenth century forward one main trading partner, its larger neighbor to the east. It was unable to gain political independence until the twentieth century, when the British no longer deemed Ireland crucial to their own security. The Irish finally only achieved prosperity and fully emerged from the shadow of the British Empire when it joined another kind of empire, the European Union—a level of prosperity enhanced by its role as an offshore subsidiary of the American economic empire in the late twentieth century, when Ireland was able to put its well-educated, English-speaking work force into jobs connected with the burgeoning computer industry.

The Normans came to Ireland because Dermot Mac Murrough, King of Leinster, obtained permission from King Henry II of England to invite some of the Norman knights over to Ireland to fight on his side in a feud. Once the knights, under the Earl of Pembroke, who bore the colorful name of Strongbow, arrived and joined in the fight, they chose to stay, carving out kingdoms of their own. But Britain would inevitably have wanted, even needed, to control this island. No sensible ruler of an island kingdom with powerful enemies on the continent of Europe was going to leave his western flank undefended. After the Reformation, when England emerged as a Protestant power at war with the Catholic Spaniards, this gave them one more reason to distrust the Irish. And with reason, because Irish history from the sixteenth to the twentieth centuries consists of an impressive list of wars, risings, and rebellions.

With a unity of purpose motivated by the need for self-defense, the desire to make money, and subsequently the business of running a successful empire, the Venetians faced the world with a solid front. For the Irish it was a different story. Until the twentieth century Ireland continued to be a country but not a nation, adhering to the old religion while its powerful neighbor fought under the standard of the reformed faith, where tribal rivalries kept this country in a state of chaos and insecurity too easily exploited by foreigners—first the Vikings, then the Normans, and finally the English. Though the slaughter I have described at Cashel Cathedral nominally resulted from a religious conflict, it can just as well be seen as a battle between rival factions in a civil war.

While England colonized Ireland, controlled it militarily and economically, imposed English as a language, and dominated the smaller island in every respect, this relationship was not without benefits. The English and their allies among the Irish middle and upper classes made Dublin into one of the great cities of the Empire, second in importance only to London. When trade with the New World reached its peak in the eighteenth century, the Irish economy flourished. Whatever the Irish lost by having their native tongue replaced by English, if they still spoke only Irish today, they would not be qualified to benefit from the computer boom, largely coming from another former English colony, the United States. And so while Venice has become a theme park for tourists, more museum than city, Ireland now has become one of the greatest economic success stories in Europe.

4.

History is exhausting. Civilization is a great fuss and flurry, an exhausting expenditure of substance and energy, a heavy weight of deeds and accomplishments our species has imposed upon the earth through our ambition and restlessness, our desire for wealth, fame, and power. The noble buildings, the thousands of ducats spent on marble and gold leaf in Venice, the blocks of Drumbane sandstone passed from hand to hand on their way to the Rock of Cashel; the mind of the architect, the hand of the craftsman; the brief and embattled life of King Cormaic Mac Carthach, the largesse of Lady Veagh—all of it seems far distant today as I sit in this garden shed and look out at the placid countryside of South Tipperary.

An ancient lane runs through our acre of ground. No one knows how long it has been here. Too small to appear on the

1777 map that shows the Butler house at Kilcash and the few other widely scattered big houses in the neighborhood, this is a humble thoroughfare of no concern to the great world. For the local people it was a turf road, running along the brow of the hill and up the side of the mountain to the bog where peat was dug for fuel. The land lies on a slope. On the high side of the lane, the road-builders dug into the ground and reinforced one margin of their path with a stone wall inserted into the slope. On the downhill side they erected a dry-stone wall. In the 1930s the forestry department cut off the lane, put up a fence, and planted a forest of pine trees on the mountainside. Through the imposition of those non-indigenous trees and that barbed wire fence, they interrupted the course of a road that had been here for centuries. I look down on it from the windows of the shed. Sometimes on full-moon nights I fancy that the spirits of the old people walk down this lane and are puzzled when their way is blocked at the forestry plantation.

When those anonymous builders constructed their stone walls to delineate this boreen and divide it from the surrounding pasture land, they used no mortar, artfully positioning the pieces together, occasionally inserting a huge stone as the jewel in the crown of the wall. I often wonder how they managed to lift such pieces into place. Perhaps a group of men all struggled with the big stones, perhaps a donkey was pressed into service to drag them into place. Were they aware what a beautiful thing they were building, or were they simply building a road because they needed to get up the mountain to dig turf and cart it back down to their farms? The answer is, I think, yes and yes.

I think they knew what a lovely piece of work these walls were, perhaps even had a sense of what it would grow into as hedges grew up above the stones, fragrant and colorful with wild roses, foxgloves, stonecrop, primroses, and buttercups, and musical with birdsong. A road is, in addition, a social space, particularly in the country. Conversations between neighbors would be carried along the lane, news exchanged, games played. Lovers would meet on the lane away from the supervision at home. Even now it is not just a means of getting from one place to another.

The men who found, transported, lifted, and set into place these stones, the women in those days before gender equality who sewed their clothes, bore their sons and daughters, cooked their meals, and brought tea to them where they worked, were not the great ones of this world, but the plain people of Ireland, unlettered subjects of the kings of Munster and the dukes of Ormonde, "small people" who in the words of Seamus Heaney's poem, "The Haw Lantern," desire only to "keep / the wick of self-respect from dying out," to put bread on the table, and hope the calf won't be still-born, the newborn lamb won't have its eyes pecked out by the hooded crow or magpie, the chickens won't be killed by the fox. Yet like those who were responsible for Cormac's Chapel and the castle at Kilcash, they were builders. And what they built is a form of architecture.

If it has never occurred to us to think of walls as architecture, it is interesting to note that John Ruskin devotes three entire chapters in *The Stones of Venice* to the subject. It is comforting, in this world of exaltation and cataclysm, glory and decline, to walk along the modest lane those anonymous Irish farmers constructed. The walls bordering our lane represent one of the humblest but not the most unworthy use to which stone can be put. The cathedral on the Rock of Cashel was burned three and a half centuries ago. The big house at Kilcash has been an empty shell since the beginning of the nineteenth century. But the walls of this ancient turf road endure. They never rose very high, but here they are.

INDEX

Mac Murrough, Dermot, King of Leinster, 272

MacNeice, Louis, 180, 182, 185, 194, 197, 202; "Autumn Journal," 194, 211; "Cushenden" from *The Closing Album*, 196; "Train to Dublin," 198

Mahon, Derek, 14, 22, 179–93, 198–99; "Afterlives," 181; "At the Shelbourne," 191; "The Attic," 185; "Auden on St. Mark's Place," 189; "Day Trip to Donegal," 182–84; "Ford Manor," 187–88; "Glengormley," 186; "Global Village," 190; *High Times*, 180; *The Hudson Letter*, 179–80, 188–90; "The Idiocy of Human Aspiration," 192; "Imbolc: JBY," 189–90; "In Carrowdore Churchyard," 185; "Knut Hamsun in Old Age," 182; "A Lighthouse in Maine," 180; "Lives," 184–85; "Night Thoughts," 37; "Rathlin," 186–87; *Selected Poems*, 179–80; "'shiver in your tenement,'" 38; *The Yaddo Letter*, 180; *The Yellow Book*, 37–38, 179, 190–91, 211

Manet, Edouard, 54, 90–91, 102; *Portrait of George Moore*, 91, 92

Mangan, James Clarence, 212, 240

Markiewicz, Countess (Constance), 22, 248

Marshall, Nigel, 222

Martyn, Edward, 93–95, 100–102; *The Heather Field*, 94

Marxism, 119

Mason, James, 160

McCann, Donal, 21, 161

McGahern, John, 5

McGuckian, Mebdh, 193

McGuinness, Martin, 19

McPherson, Connor, 4; *The Weir*, 43

McQuaid, John Charles, Archbishop of Dublin, 13, 43

McSorley, Gerard, 159

Merton, Thomas, 201

Metre, 208–9

Mhac an tSaoi (O'Brien), Máire, 172; *A Concise History of Ireland*, 257

Millevoye, Lucien, 233

Milosz, Czesław, 205

Milton, John: *Il Penseroso*, 35

Monaghan, County, 195–96

Moore, George, 14, 20, 22, 53–54, 89–103; *A Drama in Muslin*, 22, 96–98, 100, 103; *Esther Waters*, 92, 98; *Hail and Farewell*, 20, 89–90, 99–102; *Modern Painting*, 91; *A Mummer's Wife*, 92; *Parnell and His Island*, 92; *Reminiscences of the Impressionist Painters*, 91

Moore, Marianne, 216

Morgan, Lady (Sydney Owenson): *The Wild Irish Girl*, 40

Morrison, Conall, 44, 49

Morrison, William Vitruvius, 225

Morrissey, Sinéad, 194, 212–14; "An Anatomy of Smell," 214; "& Forgive Us Our Trespasses," 213; "Europa Hotel," 212; "Jo Gravis in His Metal Garden," 214; "Sea Stones," 213

Mount Stewart, County Down, 25, 221–30

Moynahan, Julian: *Anglo-Irish: The Literary Imagination in a Hyphenated Culture*, 61–66, 80

Muldoon, Paul, 5, 186, 193, 203, 209, 211

RICHARD TILLINGHAST's most recent poetry and essay
collections are *Six Mile Mountain* and *Poetry and What Is Real*,
respectively. He lives in County Tipperary.